'In both the Old and New Testaments, the promise and presence of God's Spirit is closely associated with his people being prophetic. By sharing her own adventure and diving deeply into the Scriptures, Tania has produced a book that is clear and compelling. We pray that it will help many people discover a more intimate and fruitful relationship with the God who speaks, as well as helping churches handle a gift that is both precious and necessary, but is not without its challenges.'

Paul Harcourt, Leader, New Wine, England; and Becky Harcourt

'Tania Harris awakens the church to a marvellous fact that is so easily overlooked: *the Lord of the universe speaks to us*! She weaves together a compelling narrative of scriptural commentary and personal story that is sure to help her readers rediscover the grand adventure of following Christ. This book was a truly delightful read for me.'

Frank D. Macchia, professor of Systematic Theology,
Vanguard University of Southern California

'Tania Harris has provided us with a readable, scholarly and insightful study of the ways in which God speaks to us and through us in the church. The work is thoroughly and carefully grounded in the Scriptures, a broad-based understanding of Christian theology, and the wisdom of the various Christian traditions, including my own Catholic perspective. Stories of people's encounters with God give flesh-and-blood context to Tania's reflections, and spell out in practical terms the ways in which we may respond to our engagements with the sacred. The breadth of Tania's research and her gift of storytelling make this a valuable resource for scholars and casual readers alike. The undoubted faith which underscores the whole work serves as an inspiration and encouragement to anyone who cares to engage with it. I am sure that people from all traditions will find nourishment here, as well as a fresh understanding of their own community's story. I commend Tania's book to you with glad enthusiasm.'

Father Kevin Bates SM, OAM, parish priest,
Holy Name of Mary parish, Australia

'"What is God saying to me? Where is God leading me? How do I know for sure it's God and not me?" I would be surprised if most, if not all, Christians have not asked one of these questions at one time or another. I know I have. In her book, Revd Dr Tania Harris helps us to find the answers within the community of the local church. Rather than an individual adventure, we live as Christians in community – and it's in this context we hear God speaking to us. This book is a much-needed, balanced approach to hearing God's voice. Applying its teaching will help us to move closer to God, and in so doing, discern God's direction and purpose in our lives.'

Dr Freddy Boswell, Bible translator and former CEO,
SIL International

'Tania's book is genuinely the most comprehensive, satisfying and challenging book I have read on the relationship between prophetic revelations and the Bible.'

Pastor Mike Breen, leader, 3D Discipleship Movement

'Revd Dr Tania Harris's newest release couldn't be more timely. In a postmodern world where disenchantment has led to the quest for reconnection with transcendence, Tania has reminded us that the triune God, who is communion in his very being, seeks communion with his creatures. As the late Francis Schaeffer noted, "He is there and is not silent." Tania takes a careful and compelling look at the manner in which the Spirit of God interacts with those whom he has made in his image, so that we might walk in his paths. He speaks! The real challenge is whether we are listening. Tania builds a bridge between the world of theology and the world of the average Christian by making hearing God's voice accessible. Take your time as you read this monumental work and start listening. Indeed, God is there, and he is not silent.'

Dr Mark J. Chironna, pastor, theo-semiotician
and prophetic mentor, US

'As a Baptist pastor seeking to help our church discover how to hear from God for themselves, *The Church Who Hears God's Voice* is just what we needed! There is so much in the book to resource and inspire the local church pastor, as well as plenty of insights that shine a light on problems that have been previously untouched. The book is compelling in its argument that churches flourish when they hear the voice of God. Well written and heartily recommended!'

Mark Edwards, senior pastor,
Inglewood Community Church, Australia

'Communication is the cornerstone of our relationship with God. Revd Dr Tania Harris offers a solid theological background and lots of practical insights for why and how we all should listen to God. I highly recommend this book!'

Pastor Jürgen Galonska, senior pastor,
City Church, Aarhus, Denmark

'Tania Harris, in her brilliant new book, builds a safe bridge between pastors and prophets . . . as well as for the sceptic to cross over into a well-founded prophetic lifestyle. The same God who inspired the Bible writers and the apostles in Acts continues to speak to and lead his disciples of today.'

Pastor Pernille Liland, founder,
Nordic Prophetic Network

'Tania Harris's excellent book helps us to reflect both theologically and practically, weaving together biblical truth with lived experience for an empowering and inspiring read. This will surely become a go-to book for all of us seeking to equip ourselves and others to discern God's voice in this noisy and distracting world. Highly recommended.'

Cathy Madavan, writer, speaker, broadcaster, UK

'Revd Dr Tania Harris has done an excellent job setting out a programme for recovering the often "lost art" of hearing God's voice in the twenty-first-century church. Building on substantial theological discussion as well as both positive and negative testimonies, she explores the practical issues for the individual Christian and the local church that seeks to hear direct from God. This book will open new vistas for everyone who reads it!'

Revd Dr Jon Newton, associate professor,
Alphacrucis College, Australia

'This thoroughly researched and determinedly biblical book grabbed my attention and held it throughout – the topic of hearing God's voice is so important! If we are called to follow Jesus, what can be more important? Revd Dr Harris's book gives the answer . . . recognising his voice and responding to it! *The Church Who Hears God's Voice* reintroduces the mystical experience of the Spirit without weirdness or sensationalism. This book will stimulate your spirit and refresh your soul.'

Dr Peter Read, vice-principal,
Regents Theological College, UK

'Tania Harris has done her homework! Her book helps us to nail the questions people are asking, particularly from those streams of Christianity that are wary of the idea. Through historical context and biblical knowledge, Revd Dr Harris helps to overcome our objections and fears about hearing God's voice and challenges us to consider that hearing from the Spirit is normal for all Christians. She has struck the right balance between academic research, personal story, biblical knowledge and digestible, practical, how-to steps to make this book an easy and enjoyable read for every church leader and parishioner.'

Revd Dr Jackie Roese, founder and president of
The Marcella Project, US

'This book is holy ground. *The Church Who Hears God's Voice* outlines a clear roadmap to maturity in one of the key areas of controversy in the contemporary church: does God speak today? While Tania has many years' experience as a pastor, teacher, theologian and leader, in this book she becomes our friend, carefully walking us through this challenging subject with love, grace and truth. For those of us from a Pentecostal–Charismatic background, Tania offers wisdom, insight, balance and safety. For those from a more traditional or Reformed background, Tania sets forth a clear biblical narrative that will give us courage to embrace this gift from above. *The Church Who Hears God's Voice* is an important book, beautifully written, approachable and compelling, offering us both the theory and practice as to how we can all hear, discern and follow the voice of the Lord.'

Fergus Scarfe, regional director, God TV UK and Ireland

'This book is a feast. I spent my weekends devouring its richness and depth! As a pastor in Asia who is responsible for training leaders, I've witnessed first-hand the struggle even mature believers have in "hearing" the voice of the Spirit. In *The Church Who Hears God's Voice*, Revd Dr Harris dives deeply into the common traps believers face, spelling out both the diagnosis and the remedy in ways that any on-the-ground pastor will benefit from, while satisfying the questions of Bible scholars and theologians. If you're a church leader seeking a fresh and engaging theological examination on the topic of God's voice, coupled with real-life do's and don'ts, this is the book for you. There is no book like this out there!'

Pastor Lindy Heung Shea, assistant director of Cells &
Empowerment Ministry, International Church Assembly,
Hong Kong

'The church is in the midst of a Spirit reformation and Tania's book is a voice in the centre of it.'

Pastor Vicki Simpson, prophet and speaker, Australia

'I see *The Church Who Hears God's Voice* becoming a classic. The book blends personal testimonies, a firm understanding of Scripture and scholarly research to examine the topic of hearing the Spirit. As a pastor, I love that the book gives plenty of advice on how to guide the church through the process of hearing the Spirit. One of the ground-breaking aspects of Tania's work is the recognition of the potential for damage Spirit experiences can bring when handled badly. Tania does not shy away from this, including stories of how improper discernment has led to, at best, disillusionment and disappointment, and at worst, loss of faith. But she does not stop there, showing how to facilitate discernment within the context of the local church community. Revd Dr Harris consistently brings the reader back to the heart of the New Covenant, which is that every person in the church is able to hear directly from the Spirit. Every pastor needs to read this excellent book!'

Revd Dr John Snelgrove, lead pastor, Kong Fok Church International and pastor-at-large, Hong Kong

'*The Church Who Hears God's Voice* is a gift to the church. Tania does not shy away from the problems associated with hearing the Spirit, but creates frameworks for how to address them pastorally. Wonderfully warm stories and case studies are woven throughout the book, making it readable and practical. Her strategic approach to building the church who hears God's voice is a game-changer! I loved this book.'

Pastor Sarah Whittleston, national prayer leader, Elim Pentecostal churches, UK and Ireland

The Church Who Hears God's Voice

Equipping everyone to recognise and respond to the Spirit

Tania Harris PhD

To Melinda,
who listened and followed,
and who continues to listen and follow

Contents

Foreword

Some time in the year AD 386, a young man sat in a garden in Milan. Although familiar with Christian teaching, and blessed with a praying mother, he had spent much of the past decade running from God and throwing himself into his career and a dissolute lifestyle, which he was unwilling to leave. Much of his summer reading was in preparation for his academic teaching, but one book – a collection of the letters of St Paul – was there simply because he could not dismiss the way in which it spoke to his troubled soul. As a familiar wave of shame regarding his manner of life overcame him, he found himself weeping. At that point, he heard a child's voice from over the wall, perhaps in a game, repeatedly chanting the words, 'Take up and read!' As he later said, 'I rose up, interpreting it no other way than as a command to me from heaven to open the book, and to read the first chapter I should light upon.'[1] Finding the book opened at Romans 13, he read, 'Clothe yourselves with the Lord Jesus Christ, and do not think about how to gratify the desires of the flesh' (Rom. 13:14). In that moment, Augustine of Hippo was fully and finally converted, and the history of western Christianity much changed.

Augustine was clear that God had spoken through a child's song, which then led him to the authoritative Scripture. Such stories are common in Christian history, yet the idea of God speaking outside of the Bible remains controversial and challenging for many.

I would argue that a relationship with God the Father through Jesus must necessarily be one of intimate two-way communication, involving the Spirit. As Paul says, 'Those who are led by the Spirit of God are the children of God' (Rom. 8:14). Adam and Eve enjoyed face to face communication with God in Eden; after the fall, God continued to speak to his people through the prophets; and Moses looked forward to a day when all of God's people would enjoy the privilege (Num. 11:29). Throughout the Old Testament, there is a connection between the Spirit of God falling on a person and them exercising prophetic gifts. The prophet Joel draws this growing hope together, so that the future he envisages, when the Spirit is poured out on all flesh, is marked above all else by dreams, visions and prophecy (Joel 2:28–29). This is the birthright of all the born again: as Jesus says, 'My sheep listen to my voice' (John 10:27).

But this raises a host of practical and theological questions. What level of authority do these subjective experiences have? How are various revelations of the Spirit submitted to others in the church? When abuse or misuse have occurred, how should we respond? Tania systematically and bravely steps into all these areas, bringing us back to the Scripture and challenging us not to live with less than God has promised to his people.

There is a great danger of throwing the baby out with the bathwater when considering the prophetic. Our evangelical forebears were comfortable with words and concepts such as 'being led', 'feeling a burden', 'having something put on my heart' – none of which were heard to imply any challenge to the Scriptures' controlling authority. Great preachers like Spurgeon were familiar with God's divine interruptions, giving them specific revelation of the lives of those to whom they ministered.[2] How much more can the Church today not afford to neglect what God has given!

Perhaps the most telling word of Scripture is 1 Thessalonians 5:20–22: 'Do not treat prophecies with contempt but test them all; hold on to what is good, reject every kind of evil.' From the earliest days of the church, prophetic experiences were clearly difficult to handle, but what God has given, he has given for our good! I pray this book will encourage us all to faithfully and fearlessly explore and embrace all that God has made available to us through the Spirit.

Paul Harcourt
National Leader, New Wine England
Vicar, All Saints' Woodford Wells

Preface

I still remember the sense of wonder I felt when I first learned that God could speak. After hearing throughout my childhood that God's voice was for ever frozen on the biblical page, the news came as a delightful surprise. As a 21-year-old university graduate, life stretched out like an open field and I wondered what difference hearing from God would make. I was insatiably curious and ready to try anything, but I also had plenty of questions. So I prayed a simple prayer: 'God, speak to me; teach me what you sound like, and whatever you say, I will do.'

In some ways, my ministry, God Conversations, started that day. Though officially launched two decades later, it began with all those questions at the age of 21. Back then, I was steeped in the Scriptures and had plenty of resources to draw from, but the answers still weren't clear. Why had I been taught that God had stopped talking? Why did people say we can't hear God's voice in the same way the biblical characters did? And if you do hear a voice, can you really know if it's God? I continued asking those questions even as I began having my own Spirit-experiences, and I reflected on them by studying Scripture, reading books on the topic and having discussions with pastors. Then, when I started my ministry, I continued listening for answers in the testimonies of those I met in churches around the world. Finally, twenty years later, I investigated my questions formally in conversation with academics, culminating in a PhD in practical theology.

After years of seeking answers, my findings all converged in the same place. This book is the presentation of those findings. It shows that even though hearing the voice of the Spirit lies at the core of the New Covenant promises, we haven't always seen it. Our fears, doubts and mistakes have created a confusing subterfuge that has obscured our understanding of this key feature of the biblical narrative and the central thrust of the New Covenant – to hear the direct voice of God for ourselves. The lack of theological coherence has meant that we've inadvertently relegated the revelatory experience to the sidelines and, in doing so, lost the full thrust of its power.

Of course, even through the confusion, God has still been speaking and people have still been hearing. The Holy Spirit's revelatory work can hardly be contained. During my PhD research, there was a moment that still stands out in my mind. My project was a qualitative study that involved gathering data from up to 100 interviews. It was a lengthy process of listening, recording and transcribing, and then doing it all over again. This stage of research is not usually the fun part, but for me, it turned out to be the highlight. Even as I laboured through recording after recording, checking muffled words and going over rewinds, I listened in awe as people shared their 'hearing God' experiences. Story after story told of how the Spirit spoke to transform their lives. People were being challenged to forgive and show generosity. Deep wounds were being healed and addictions were being broken. People were being called to step out in their giftings and participate in mission.

As a pastor, I know just how challenging it can be to lead people into Christlikeness. I know all the effort it takes to make discipleship happen in our churches – the service organisation, midweek programmes and sermon preparation week after week after week. We work tirelessly with singular effort and dedication – our time and gifts a powerful offering to the One who called us. And yet, here it was: the Spirit was doing the work! One genuine Spirit-inspired experience provided the motivation, resource and grace to fulfil God's purposes. Better still, it was tailored to the individual and perfectly timed to set them free. Of course, people didn't always respond. But it was far harder to resist the word of a sovereign God than the humble admonitions of a pastor. One conversation with God had the potential to change everything.

That truth makes it much easier for us as church leaders. It sharpens our focus, simplifies our strategy and clarifies our priorities. When we realise the transformation that comes when people hear God's voice for themselves, we gain a whole new understanding of our role – to *facilitate* the hearing God experience. Our job as disciplers is to teach people about Jesus and then help them recognise and respond to the Spirit as Jesus' continuing voice. This is what it means to *make* disciples (Matt. 28:19–20). As we do this, people will grow, our world will be reached and God's kingdom will come.

Since my prayer at 21, I've seen first-hand the difference that hearing God's voice for yourself can make. I've been privileged to discover the answers I sought for so long. The reason I wrote this book is to share them with you. I have no doubt the Spirit is already speaking to members of your congregation and that, in our efforts to build God's church,[1] our ideas and actions may be more God-breathed than we realise. But when we see our experiences more clearly in the light of the biblical testimony, we are in a far better position to release them into the fullness of their power. We can better pass them on to others so that they too can realise the potential of hearing from the Spirit. This is where this book finds its place. It articulates a theology for hearing God's voice and provides the strategies to facilitate the experience in the life of your church. This book will equip you to build the church who hears God's voice. It is based on the premise that the local church is the place where God intended us to recognise and respond to the Spirit. The goal is that every member of your congregation will be able to recognise and respond to God's voice for themselves.

Of course, we also have our individual journeys with the Spirit to navigate. This book is not only for church leaders but also for Christian thinkers who have questions about hearing God's voice in their own lives. The process of hearing, recognising and responding to God's voice is not always clear-cut, and the diversity of our circumstances only adds to the complexity. My prayer is that you will find resolution and clarity in these pages.

The book is divided into three parts. The first part describes the *power* of hearing from the Spirit as well as the *problems* wrought by the experience. The second (and most important) part provides a theological framework for hearing God's voice. The third part outlines the practical strategies needed to build the church where everyone can hear God's voice for themselves, as well as some guidance for the pastoral issues that inevitably arise.

I'm excited to share this book with you. My prayer and that of the God Conversations team is that you will be able to build a church where every person will recognise God's voice for themselves and, in doing so, find the courage to follow.

Tania Harris PhD
Founding Director, God Conversations

Thank You

This book is the product of a thirty-year journey, full of exhilarating 'aha' moments, bouts of confusion, startling Spirit-experiences and long conversations. The heroes are those who have stayed alongside me all the way. In academia, we call them 'dialogue partners'. In my life, I call them *family*. To Anita, Pete and Claire, thank you for digging deep, for always listening and for persevering, even through the shadows.

To my PhD supervisors, Jon, Angelo and Darren, thank you for sharing in the joy of discovery, the fruit of hard conversations and your diligent attention to detail.

To the God Conversations leadership team, Pete, Dave and Vicki, and team members, Jenny, Ali, Aaron 'Ruffy', Emma, Erica and Steph, for your encouragement, hard work and faith in a vision that goes beyond yourselves, thank you.

To the pastors all over the world who have hosted me, shared their stories and generously supported the ministry of God Conversations, thank you.

To my beta-readers, for giving your time, thought and perspective, thank you.

To my publishers, Paternoster and Authentic, for believing in my ministry from the beginning, thank you.

And to the Holy Spirit, the ultimate teacher, who has not only worked in my life to reveal the knowledge of God in creative and personal ways but has also taught me how to lead others along the same path with sensitivity and ingenuity, thank you.

Author's Note

Throughout the book, I frequently use the male pronouns 'he', 'his' and 'him' to refer to God. This is a not due to a conviction that God is male, but rather a reflection of the limitations of the English language and the absence of a gender-neutral personal pronoun (i.e. God should not be called 'it'). The Scriptures are clear that the Creator God is Spirit, and as such is neither male nor female. In God, both males and females find their identity (Gen. 1:26–27; John 4:24).

Prologue

The words God spoke were gentle and affirming, but I had no idea how they could come to pass.

It was a warm Melbourne afternoon in late 1995 when I first heard the Spirit speak to me about my position in church: 'You'll be raised up in leadership, mentored by the senior pastor and work here one day a week.' At the time, I had only been in my church for a few weeks, having moved there because God had told me to. This was the place, God said, where my life's purpose would be fulfilled. It was a radical directive and one I didn't particularly like. My former church was my home – a loving community who supported me through young adulthood and taught me the ways of the Spirit. I had grown used to the same seat in the third row, I knew all the latest worship songs, and I liked the pastor, whose voice was gentle and made you feel loved even when he was telling you off. Now here I was, thrust into a new community, where I knew virtually no one and the pastor was a distant figure on the platform.

Each week I would wonder how God's words would be fulfilled. How could I get the pastor to mentor me? We had talked once or twice and she seemed friendly enough, but there were plenty of others she could choose from. Perhaps I could sit on the front row so she would notice me? Maybe I could offer to babysit her daughter?

The whole idea of hearing from God was still relatively new, but I was hooked. Ever since my friend at university had told me about the possibility of hearing the Spirit, I had been eager to experience it for myself. It had happened several times already, but now in my mid-twenties, contemplating a change in career from schoolteaching to ministry, the experience carried a lot more weight. I felt privileged and expectant, but a bit lost too, like someone out at sea who has cast all her bearings aside.

My new church was starting to feel more like home when, one Sunday evening, the pastor invited people to the front for prayer. I tentatively made my way forward, eager to receive all that God had for me. It wasn't a large church – about eighty people or so – but at least half of them had responded. Worship music played in the background as people knelt or stood, waiting to receive ministry from the prayer team. A few minutes passed before the pastor moved over to face me. My heart picked up a beat as she laid her hands on my shoulders and smiled.

'The Lord has spoken to me,' she said. 'He's asked me to mentor you. I'm going to raise you up in leadership and you will work here one day a week.'

It's an odd phenomenon watching the word of the Lord coming to pass. Like a rocket breaking through the stratosphere, in a single moment, reality shifts. Where once I had read about the God who had good plans for us, now I knew it. Where once I had heard about the One who had power to bring them to pass, now I had seen it.

Part I

Introduction: The Spirit at Work

'The capacity for everyone to hear from God through the Spirit is one of the most groundbreaking and world-changing initiatives that has ever occurred.'

1

The Power of Hearing God's Voice

The vision that saved a drought-stricken farm

Jarrod was an Australian farmer facing the worst drought of his life. A sun-bronzed man with a broad smile and buffed muscles from working long hours in the field, he was more resilient than most. But this drought had been wearing him down. With each turning of the seasons, he and his wife waited for the rains to come, but they never did. Now the creek-beds had become ditches of dust and the green fields a barren brown. Without water, the land laboured to produce a fraction of its normal yield. How could Jarrod provide for his lively brood of six children?

For months, Jarrod had tried to steward the family's waning resources to eke out a living, carefully tracking supplies and stretching out their savings, but the bills continued to mount. Like many, he had reached the end of his ability to cope. All across Australia, farmers had resorted to suicide as their farms dried out, cattle died of starvation, and hope withered with every sunrise. The fight to stave off depression was a daily one.

Then Jarrod had a dream. In the dream, he saw the paddock in the north-east corner of his property. But it wasn't the usual scene. In place of the dusty plot was a crop of leafy canola, the stalks all rising to a height of 15 to 20 centimetres. Somehow, he knew that the canola had been sown in dry soil, but for some reason the plants were flourishing. He woke up thinking, *Wouldn't it be good if it was real?*

The next day, Jarrod shared his dream with his wife, Emma. Could it be from God? They had never sown canola before, but they knew it to be a high-risk crop. What's more, the seed alone would cost over $35,000 – and there was still no sign of rain.

Jarrod turned to his agronomist for advice. Tom was a trusted voice in the region and had a wealth of expertise on his side. His advice was emphatic but not unexpected: no, Jarrod should not plant canola – the risk was too high.

And yet it seemed like the dream had come from God . . .

After wrestling over it together, Jarrod and Emma made a decision. They defied the agronomist's counsel, purchased 1,100 kilograms of seed and began planting in the north-east paddock. It took them nearly three days, sowing through the night to cover as much of the 1,000 acres as they could.

The paddock was 80% sown when the rain came. Jarrod and Emma marvelled as the seed took root and grew. Over the coming weeks, the plants rose to the same height as Jarrod had seen in the dream. His canola field soon became the talk of the town. It produced the finest crop of the year and raised 80% of their income at market. That income was the difference between bankruptcy and keeping the farm.

It's a simple story, but a profound one. Hearing God's voice saved Jarrod and Emma's farm. Obeying the Spirit led to a life-saving miracle and the knowledge of a God who is greater than the Australian drought. Yet the pattern of hearing and following God's voice and seeing it manifest is not unusual in biblical terms. The whole narrative of Scripture is a demonstration of the same process. Time after time, God speaks, people respond and miracles unfold.

In this chapter, we look at the *power* of hearing God's voice. We learn that hearing God's voice has always precipitated the miraculous, both within the Bible and outside it. Then we define what it means to 'hear God's voice' and see that the meaning will vary according to your church tradition. Finally, we discuss how hearing God's voice was understood in Scripture and how the Spirit's outpouring at Pentecost means that we can all hear from God in the same way as the biblical characters.

The most powerful experience on earth

How was the earth created? Think about it. It began with God speaking (Gen. 1). How are people healed? It is the word 'sent forth' that overcomes disease and death (Ps. 107:20; Mark 7:34; 9:25; John 11:43). How are people saved? It is made possible through the living Word, Jesus, who became flesh to atone for our sin (John 1:1). This is the pattern throughout the Scriptures. It all starts with God speaking. According to the prophet Amos, God does *nothing* without first revealing it (Amos 3:7). Every act of God in biblical history was preceded by an act of communication. Even Jesus did nothing without first hearing it (John 5:19).

It is the words themselves that carry the power. God's words are the vehicle of his authority and the expression of his intent. God's ability to align a downpour of rain with the planting of canola at Jarrod's farm was contained in his voice. Words from God transmit creative force and have the potential to bring themselves to pass (Gen. 1:3). They are like a fire and a hammer that breaks rock into pieces (Jer. 23:29). Once spoken, they are diligently watched over so that they perform the task for which they were sent (Jer. 1:12). They transcend time, reverse the circumstances and overtake the generations (Zech. 1:6). Their purpose will always be fulfilled (Isa. 55:11), for to fail is to defy the nature of the One who spoke them (Num. 23:19; Isa. 45:23).

The efficacy of divine communiqués lies not only in their metaphysical ability. What makes hearing from God even more potent is the disclosure of divine information. As God said to the prophet Jeremiah: 'Call to me and I will answer you and tell you great and *unsearchable things you do not know*' (Jer. 33:3). The prophetic experience takes us into the boardroom of the heavenly Council where God's plans are divulged (Jer. 23:18–22). Hearing God's voice gives us insight into what is going on behind the scenes of the natural world. It opens the door to the spiritual realm where we experience the knowledge of God first hand.

Thus, Daniel saw why his prayer was delayed when the angel appeared (Dan. 10:3), and Samuel was able to anoint the next king of

Israel when God revealed it to him (1 Sam. 16:12). Joshua the high priest saw the reason for the attack on the construction of the Second Temple and the strategy for getting it going again (Zech. 3 – 4), and Paul saw the reason for his pain and how to respond to it (2 Cor. 12:7–10). John saw the forces behind the threat of oppression from the Roman Empire and was able to tell the seven churches how to endure it (Rev. 5:6–8), and Jarrod saw what seed to plant and when to sow it, in line with the coming rains.

Divine revelation is necessary for God's purposes to be known on earth. But God doesn't do it alone. Instead, he chooses to involve creation in his plan. God's words become the means through which humanity can partner with him in bringing his plans to earth. Since God is an invisible deity, they become his outreached arm and the manifest touch of his presence. They are the link from the spiritual realm to the natural, from the non-physical world to the material. When we respond to them, we are empowered to do God's will so that God's presence is experienced first hand. Like a rocket bursting through the stratosphere, we see intangible truths break into tangible realities. Not only do we witness God's miraculous power but we get to know the One who bears it (Isa. 45:21). We *know* that God is truly among us (1 Cor. 14:25).

Hearing from God not only enlists our participation in the divine plan; it allows God to work *in us*. God's words have the power to change us from the inside out. They are sent to save, sustain and heal us. As a light to our path and a lamp to our feet, they guide and direct our lives (Ps. 119:105). Sharper than any two-edged sword, they expose our thoughts and divide our spirits (Heb. 4:12). Like bread to our bodies and food to our souls, they feed, nourish and sustain us (John 6:63). It's not difficult to conclude, as the psalmist does, that God's words are 'sweeter than honey' and more 'precious than gold' (Ps. 19:10). As the very source of life, we can't live without them (Matt. 4:4).

The impact of 'love energy'

The power of hearing from God is not limited to the pages of the Bible. Today, stories akin to those of Daniel, Samuel, Peter and Paul are seen in churches around the world. Testimony after testimony recalls the power of hearing from the Spirit in the same way as the biblical characters.

So potent is the hearing God experience in the contemporary church that it has attracted the attention of sociologists. Of course, as neutral observers, these academics are not making assessments about *if* God is speaking, since that is empirically impossible. Rather, they are interested in the *impact* of revelatory experience on people. Their work gives us insight into the power of God's voice in individual lives and the local church community.

American scholar Margaret Poloma is well known for her work in this area. A charismatic Catholic, Poloma became interested in spiritual phenomena such as prayer, revival and divine healing early on in her career. Since then, she has completed an impressive raft of studies in the USA and Canada. Her first study in 1989 was with the American Assemblies of God (AG) and drew on the revelatory experiences of pastors and congregation members in over sixty churches from eleven different states.[1] These findings were followed up twenty years later in a second study involving twenty-one congregations with fellow sociologist John Green.[2]

The findings of both studies are telling. Poloma and Green found that the 'hearing God' experience made a significant difference to individual lives and was strongly linked to 'acts of service', such as prayer for healing, giving and evangelism. That is, people were more likely to offer prayer when someone was ill, forgive people when wronged, give to the poor and get involved in the community *after they had heard from God*. This benevolence extended beyond the church into the public arena and avenues of social welfare. An overall increase in church growth was the result.

Poloma and Green went on to analyse their findings using a sociological theory developed by American-Russian scholar Pitirim

Sorokin. They proposed that having a revelatory encounter produces a form of 'love energy'. This energising power (which they termed 'godly love') came from direct interaction with God. When people experienced this divine love, it energised and expanded their benevolence. As the scholars describe it, 'interactions in the divine–human (vertical) relationship provided a "love energy" that empowered benevolent action in human–human (horizontal) relationships'.[3] In short, the 'love energy' arising from Spirit experience motivated people to love and serve others.

The links between hearing God and serving others are not limited to North America. Similar outcomes have been found in studies around the world including Pentecostal congregations in the UK,[4] Singapore and Hong Kong.[5] Poloma herself found consistent results in North American Episcopalian churches.[6]

My own research revealed similar findings, albeit with a far smaller sample.[7] Individuals reported significant change as a result of their Spirit encounters. When people heard from God, they were saved, healed and released from addictions. They received hope for the future, insight for day-to-day challenges and new strategies for relationships. They started businesses and ministries. They relocated to different countries and discovered new giftings. The experience often led them to do things they wouldn't normally do. Like farmer Jarrod, they saw miracles when they did. After hearing from God, they were never the same.

These sorts of findings should not be surprising for Bible-believing Christians. What we see in the sociological studies of the contemporary church was the norm for the church of the New Testament. The book of Acts recounts how the Spirit's revelatory activity directed all the main players and became the impetus for the church's expansion.[8] In fact, hearing God experiences were the kick-starter for every major event! They provided the 'love energy' to do God's work, often in radical ways. Consider the salvation of Paul after receiving God's message in a vision on the Damascus road (Acts 9:3–19); the conversion of the Ethiopian eunuch after Philip received a Spirit directive (Acts 8:26–40); Peter's call to the Gentiles after his vision on the rooftop

(Acts 10); and the outreach of the Jerusalem church after a famine was prophesied by Agabus (Acts 11:27–30). Then there was the commissioning of Saul and Barnabas as prompted by Spirit-leading (Acts 13:2–4), the launch of the mission to the West after a dream (Acts 16:9), and the perseverance of Paul following the Spirit's encouragement in Corinth (Acts 18:9–11), Rome and Jerusalem (Acts 23:11). Time and time again, the Spirit spoke and the works of God followed. As American missiologist Craig Van Gelder observed, the Spirit was *doing the work* of 'changing lives and transforming communities'; new types of communities were being created, leaders were being appointed, lives were being sanctified, and people were being led into active gift-based ministry to confront principalities and powers in the world.[9] In each case, the Spirit was initiating and guiding the process. Growth came when people heard from God.

The biblical meaning of hearing God's voice

We've seen something of the power of hearing God's voice, but before we go further, it is important to define what we actually mean by the experience. Even though the claim to hearing God's voice is common in Christianity (as a 'revelatory religion', Christianity is predicated on the concept of a *communicating* deity), it doesn't always carry the same meaning. While all Christian denominations believe that God 'speaks' in some way today, there are widely different beliefs about *how* God speaks, *what* God says and what our *response* should be.

For many in the Protestant tradition, hearing God's voice is most commonly associated with Scripture-reading and preaching. The Spirit speaks largely to illuminate and apply *past* revelation – that is, the truths laid out in the Bible – rather than introduce new information. So, in these settings, you're most likely to hear that the Spirit speaks through Scripture, sermons, nature, Christian books and the 'wisdom of counsel'.

In other traditions – specifically the Pentecostal and Charismatic streams of Protestantism and the Catholic Church – hearing God's voice includes these modes of receiving revelation but also allows for encounters that do not require the involvement of other people, liturgies, sermons or books. Here, people believe that they can hear God's voice in the same way as the biblical characters – that is, through dreams, visions, voices and the like.[10] These experiences are 'immediate' and 'spontaneous', meaning they do not arise from our own cognition or thinking. They are also *revelatory* in that they include the possibility of information that was previously unknown or points to the future.

A helpful way of conceiving the difference between the traditions is to consider Jesus' instructions about the Spirit's revelatory work to his disciples. Jesus said that the Spirit would speak about *two areas* after he left. First, the Spirit would *remind* his followers of all the teachings he had established while on earth (John 14:26). Thus, the Spirit would speak about the truths of salvation, kingdom life and the ways of God – teachings that are now recorded for us as Scripture. Hence, the Spirit speaks today as we read and hear from the Bible. For conservative Protestants, this is the only way God speaks today.

However, Jesus also spoke of a second area. Not only would the Spirit reiterate the core foundations of Christian faith; he would also speak about *things to come* (John 16:13). This referred to the issues the disciples would face after Jesus left the earth (John 16:12). Since they couldn't handle all the information at once, the Spirit would be given to *continue* speaking after Jesus had gone. In other words, the Spirit would speak about contemporary questions and concerns, applying the message of the gospel to particular situations. It is this second type of God-speech that Pentecostals, Charismatics and Catholics also embrace. These sectors of the church believe that we can hear from God apart from Scripture. That is, the Spirit's voice is heard in the same way as the biblical characters heard it – through direct revelatory encounters.

As we'll later see (in Chapter 9), it is this type of *direct* hearing God experience that was the most common mode of revelation under the Old and New Covenants. However, there is one significant difference between the two epochs. While God's words have always been the source of his power and presence, not everyone has been able to access them as easily.

The democratisation of the Spirit

As we've seen, God has always been speaking in order to reveal his nature. However, not everyone has been able to hear it. Under the Old Covenant, direct revelation by the Spirit was largely only available to the *prophets*. The prophets were a select group of individuals who were specifically called to hear God's voice on behalf of others. They would hear from God (mostly in dreams and visions) and then pass his messages on (prophesy them) to God's people (Num. 12:6). When the people acted on what they heard, they were able to partner with God and witness his manifest presence. This pattern continued into the incarnation when, as the living Word, Jesus came to reveal God's life-giving power and the fullness of God's nature. Jesus was known as a prophet, and indeed the greatest of *all* prophets.[11] In his death and resurrection, Jesus fulfilled all the words that had been spoken by the prophets, culminating in the display of God's supreme power over sin and death.

After Jesus' ascension came the seismic shift. On the Day of Pentecost, the Spirit was poured out on the *entire church*. Many signs and wonders occurred that day, but notice the first point of Peter's sermon. Quoting from the prophet Joel, he declared that the Spirit's outpouring meant that *everyone* – young and old, male and female – could now receive revelatory messages in the same way as the Old Covenant prophets. They could all hear God's voice in dreams and visions and speak them forth as prophecy (Acts 2:16–17). Every person who chose to follow Jesus could now hear directly from God *without* the mediation of a prophet.

This gift was not only given to the people assembled in Jerusalem that day. As Peter proclaimed, the promise was for those who lived in Jerusalem and beyond – Judea and Samaria and all those who were 'far off' (Acts 2:39). Now everyone could receive the power and knowledge of God through hearing the Spirit's voice. Everyone could access the divine wisdom and revelation of God for themselves. That makes the act of receiving the Spirit with the capacity to hear from God – often termed the 'democratisation' of the Spirit – one of the most ground-breaking and world-changing initiatives that has ever occurred.

***

Looking back on Jarrod's story, we may ask: what would have happened if Jarrod hadn't listened to his dream? What if he had merely passed it off as a figment of his imagination? He wouldn't have bought the canola seed and he wouldn't have sown it through the night. He certainly wouldn't have seen a miracle. He might even have had to sell his farm.

This is the power and privilege of hearing from God. When we hear from the Spirit, we receive access to God's power. We receive the knowledge of God's plans and the ability to partner with him to see them manifest on the earth. The 'love energy' we experience motivates us to serve, love and forgive. This was the testimony of the early church after Jesus, and it remains the reality of many in the church today.

As we've seen, not everyone will be convinced of the validity of Jarrod's dream, preferring to confine God's voice to Scripture-reading and preaching. Later in the book, we explore the reasons for this and take time to address them. But here we start with the understanding that the gift of the revelatory Spirit at Pentecost was for all – sons and daughters, young and old. The promise of the New Covenant remains. As Christians following in the tradition of our predecessors, our privilege is to hear the Spirit's voice and follow it. There is no other way.

2

History's Pendulum Swing

The bronze ladder

Perpetua was still breastfeeding her son when she was imprisoned by the Romans in AD 203. An aristocratic woman of only 22 years, she had recently become a Christian and was taking classes with her church in Carthage to prepare for baptism. It was a difficult time to be a Christian in Roman-ruled North Africa. Perpetua, her slave girl Felicity and their teacher Saturus had all been charged with refusing to worship the emperor. If found guilty, the penalty was death.

While in prison, Perpetua prayed about the outcome of her upcoming trial: would she be released or would she be executed? Her answer came in a vision. She saw a great bronze ladder extending to the heavens with an enormous serpent lying at its foot. Strung along both sides of the ladder was a collection of deadly weapons, including swords, spears, hooks and knives. Perpetua realised that if she were to climb the ladder, she would need to tread carefully and keep her gaze upwards or have her limbs torn apart.

In the dream, Saturus was the first to climb. Then it was Perpetua's turn. She tentatively placed her foot on the serpent's head and was surprised to see the frightening creature submit to her. Then, step by step, she began to ascend. On reaching the top, a beautiful garden opened up before her and a white-haired man in shepherd's robes welcomed her with open arms. Behind him, Perpetua saw a crowd dressed in white and heard them cheer a joyous 'Amen'. Then she woke up.

It wasn't long before Perpetua was summoned to her trial. There, she was presented with two options by the Roman governor: either offer sacrifices to the emperor or be executed. Perpetua stood firm, refusing to worship the emperor over her Saviour. Even when her father pleaded with her for the sake of her son, she remained steadfast.

On the day of execution, Perpetua, Felicity and three other prisoners were dressed in belted tunics and taken to the Roman amphitheatre under guard. First, they were whipped. Then they were set upon by a line of gladiators and a group of wild animals, including a leopard, boar and wild cow. It didn't take long for the prisoners' tunics to be saturated with blood. Finally, Perpetua and her friends were put to death by the sword.

Perpetua's story is a testament to the sustaining power of God's words. The vision provided her with the strength to endure Roman brutality and remain faithful to the end. When tempted to recant, Perpetua was able to stand on the head of the serpent. When faced with the gladiators' knives and the wild boar's teeth, she was able to fix her eyes on the Shepherd at the top of the ladder. Because she recognised the true source of her suffering, she was also able to show grace to her persecutors. We know her story today because her diary survived and became a source of encouragement for Christians all across the Roman Empire.[1]

Church history is littered with stories like Perpetua's. In every age, there are testimonies of those who heard God's voice and followed it. As in Bible times, the voice of the Spirit continued to guide, encourage and sustain the people of God. Yet, even while we laud Perpetua's testimony and others like it, it doesn't take long to uncover an equal number of stories that testify to the dangers of seeking to hear directly from the Spirit. Anything that has potential for good also has potential for evil when handled poorly. Indeed, problems with the 'hearing God' experience have plagued the church throughout its history.[2]

The outcome has been that the revelatory experience has fallen into a continuous cycle of embrace and rejection. At times, it has been enthusiastically welcomed as the norm, and at other times it has been condemned as heresy. The pendulum has swung back and forth, sometimes wildly so. In this chapter, we trace the path of the hearing God experience in history and, in doing so, highlight the challenges it brings along the way. If we are to be faithful to our New Covenant inheritance in the present, we must learn the lessons of the past.

The second generation

You can only imagine the excitement of the early church when they first received the ability to hear God's voice for themselves. Every person, no matter their age, gender or status, could enjoy the coveted experience of the old-time prophets! For those first disciples, the absence of Jesus was compensated for by the abiding presence of the Spirit. They could continue to draw on the wisdom of God through hearing the Spirit.

We know that in the early days after Christ, the hearing God experience was warmly and openly embraced. The Scriptures show that Spirit-talking experiences played a central role in directing mission and providing impetus for the church as it grew beyond Jerusalem. Although the experience was not without its problems – the Corinthian church is a case in point – it was readily welcomed as central to New Covenant living.

Receptivity to the Spirit's voice continued into the next generation and the time of the second- and third-century church fathers. Early apologists such as Justin Martyr and Irenaeus, along with later theologians like Tertullian, Origen and Cyprian, all anticipated direct revelation from the Spirit.[3] In fact many of the popular Christian writings of the day featured detailed accounts of their God-conversations. One of the best known was *The Shepherd of Hermas*. Echoing the style of the book of Revelation, this second-century letter to the Roman church opens and ends with dream sequences and tells of five visions of its author Hermas, a former slave. The book was so popular that it was translated into several languages and continued to be read into the next three centuries.[4]

Other popular writings of the time included the account of Polycarp, a student of the apostle John.[5] Like Perpetua, Polycarp found the courage to face his impending martyrdom in a dream. His vision of the pillow beneath his head bursting into flames was fulfilled when he was executed by burning. Both Perpetua's and Polycarp's testimonies were circulated widely in the church and held up as examples for others to follow.

However, it wasn't all smooth sailing. Serious problems with the revelatory experience began to emerge when a man named Montanus began a movement in the mid-second century dubbed the 'New Prophecy'. Starting in North Africa, it spread quickly throughout the Roman Empire. It appears that Montanus and his followers were well meaning. They were zealous to bring the prophetic voice of God back to the church at a time of growing apathy and institutionalisation, and it's likely there were some legitimate experiences among them. Even the famed theologian Tertullian (AD 155–240), known as the 'father' of Latin Christianity and the founder of Western theology, embraced Montanism early on.[6]

But as time wore on, the Montanists began to pose a serious threat to church authorities. Eventually, they were declared heretics. While it's difficult to know the rationale behind the church's decision (Montanist writings no longer exist and we only have their opponents' works),[7] the issues seem to boil down to a clash between the revelatory experience and the two key sources of authority in the church: ecclesial leadership and the teachings of the gospel (which by then had been written down and were on their way to becoming canonical Scripture). It may have started well, but when Montanus declared himself the 'new prophet' and claimed to *fulfil* the revelation given by the apostles, he had clearly overstepped the mark.

The voices of the Montanists had been silenced, but as is often the way, the pendulum swung too far in the opposite direction. Instead of addressing the excesses *within* Montanism, the church reacted by rejecting the movement altogether. This response dealt the church a near-fatal blow for the Spirit, as the 'baby was thrown out with the bathwater' and the voice of God was pushed out of the institutional church.[8]

Out to the fringes

Of course, the life-giving power of God never stopped flowing as the Spirit continued to speak and people continued to listen. Even while revelatory experiences were officially rejected in the church, they did not die out altogether. As we enter the medieval period, we see that Spirit-speech moved out to the fringes, into the monasteries and convents. Catholic scholar Niels Hvidt wrote that while

> prophecy as it had been known at Corinth, was no longer considered proper for the sanctuary . . . it did not, however, wholly die. It went instead to the arena with the martyrs, to the desert with the fathers, to the monasteries with Benedict, to the streets with Francis, to the cloisters with Teresa of Avila and John of the Cross, to the heathen with Frances Xavier.[9]

Hvidt goes on to tell of the numerous saints of the period who pioneered ministries and missions *because of* visions and heavenly directives.

St Benedict was one such person. His response to the Spirit's call in the late fifth century issued a radical charge to holy living that was outworked through the establishment of monasteries.[10] These became centres of prayer and renewal that went on to impact the civilisation of Western Europe far beyond Benedict's lifetime.

St Patrick was another prominent leader of the time who heard the Spirit's voice. His vision of an Irish church lit by the glory of God was the impetus for a powerful ministry that brought Christianity to Ireland and saw the conversion of the Picts and Anglo-Saxons.[11] Patrick devoted his entire life to seeing his vision fulfilled, baptising thousands of new converts, training priests and evangelising the sons of kings, as well as becoming the first major figure in history to reject slavery.

Four centuries after Patrick, another Spirit-inspired vision spurred St Ansgar, the 'Apostle to the North', to pioneer mission to Scandinavia.[12] This was a time when the Northmen were known for their brutal raids against Christian communities. Ansgar's visionary experience enabled him to defy their terrifying reputation, resist the arguments of detractors and persevere through a myriad of setbacks in his ministry.

Moving into the thirteenth century, St Francis of Assisi was another figure whose ministry was initiated by a revelatory experience.[13] As a young man, Francis longed for the glory of battle, and a privileged background meant he was well placed to see it come to pass. But then he heard the Spirit speak, calling him to 'repair the church'. At first Francis thought that God was asking him to repair the dilapidated building he was praying in, but he later realised the call was to the wider church, which had fallen into scandal and avarice. As a result of the vision, Francis relinquished his wealth and redirected his efforts into reform. Today his legacy lives on through his teachings, his example and the famed 'Prayer of Peace'.

The stories of Benedict, Patrick, Ansgar and Francis all reveal the power of God's voice to further the ministry of Jesus in medieval times. As in the biblical accounts, the Spirit spoke wherever his voice could be heard, and whenever the people of God responded, the mission of God came to pass.

Downside to the Reformation

From the medieval period, we move into one of the most pivotal seasons in church history – the sixteenth-century Reformation. The changes in this period were revolutionary, bringing reform to a church that was in dire need of it. Politicking, greed and immorality were all confronted as the church was challenged to live out its true call to grace and faith. However, it wasn't all good news. Openness to the Spirit's voice took a tragic turn during the Reformation and has left a devastating legacy in its wake.

It all began in the small town of Wittenberg in Germany, with one of the church's most loyal adherents, monk and teacher Martin Luther. The endemic corruption of the church prompted Luther to embark on his own spiritual search for peace and salvation. Back in the church of the sixteenth century, the only way to achieve this was to perform plenty of good works, surrender your coins and visit the bones of apostles on long pilgrimages. Once the list was complete, you could receive absolution, but only through the official channels of the church. For Luther, this answer led to torment, for the questions remained: How many works should be done? How many prayers should be prayed? How many pilgrimages should be made before you were saved?

Luther devoted all his time and energy to his quest, eventually finding answers in careful study of the Scriptures and, in particular, the book of Romans. There he discovered that salvation was found only in receiving God's gift of grace. It could be neither earned by good works and penances, nor pronounced by the church. Rather, it came through a personal act of faith. This revelation changed Luther's life. In his own words, he was 'altogether born again' and 'entered paradise itself through open gates'.[14] Afterwards, he published his famous 'ninety-five theses' on the local university noticeboard. These 'protesting' ideas were picked up by the newly invented printing press and quickly began to take hold across Germany and beyond. The Protestant Reformation had begun.

The issues raised by Luther were enormously important. The truths of justification by faith not only released him from his burden but also opened the door of freedom to all those who came after him. The problem was that his teachings explicitly defied the established church. The battle lines were drawn and the debates began, with the underlying question: who was right? Luther had the Scriptures, but the church had centuries of teaching and tradition linked by papal succession to the original apostles. They also had a collection of miraculous experiences to strengthen their position. This was a major coup. Who could compete with a marble statue of Mary weeping real tears?

Thus, while arguments raged over justification, grace and faith, the underlying issue was the *source* of divine authority and where it lay. Did it belong with the Scriptures or did it belong with the church? In order to argue their case, Luther and his fellow Reformers discredited the Catholic position by maintaining that miracles were limited to the age of the apostles and that the voice of the Spirit had ceased with the closing of the canon. John Calvin argued that prophecy was 'simply the right understanding of Scripture and the particular gift of expounding it'.[15] Luther criticised the 'Heavenly Prophets' who heard a 'living voice from heaven' and acted in response to the 'fanatic' Spirit.[16] As a result, hearing from the Spirit became equated solely with reading the Bible. It is easy to see, then, why Luther began to argue for the book of Revelation to be ousted from the canon and why he favoured the epistles over the gospels and Acts. Even though Luther himself had known Spirit experiences (including a visionary confrontation with the devil[17]), he effectively dismissed them for the sake of the Reformed cause.[18]

The outcome of the Protestant tactic was that the experience of hearing directly from the Spirit was rendered illegitimate. The doctrine we know as *Sola Scriptura* ('only Scripture') meant that revelation was only possible when the Bible was read or preached about. Because of the polemic underlying the Protestant–Catholic debates and ultimately the Catholic Church's *misuse* of revelatory experience, Spirit-activity was effectively conflated with the biblical text. Now you could only 'hear' God through the Bible. The ability to experience the Spirit's voice directly, which had been freely given to 'sons and daughters' and 'young and old', was now limited to those who were wealthy and literate enough to access a physical book.

Since then, the Reformers' position, known as *cessationism*, became the Protestant norm. The tradition was sealed by the Westminster Confession a century later. This document, which was drawn up in 1646 for the Church of England (and has since become the standard for several other Protestant denominations), discounts revelatory experience in its opening paragraph: 'Therefore it pleased the Lord, at sundry times, and in divers manners, to reveal Himself, and to declare that His will unto His Church (Heb. 1:1); and . . . to commit the same wholly unto writing; which maketh the Holy Scripture to be most necessary; those former ways of God's revealing his will unto his people being now ceased.'[19] This statement, born of debate and error, is a tragic one, setting a trajectory that has hampered the Protestant tradition ever since. The power of direct Spirit-speech that was given to further the ministry of Jesus in contemporary contexts was essentially cut off.

Spirit movement in the Catholic Church

Of course, it wasn't all bad news. As in medieval times, the Spirit's voice was still being heard in some branches of the church during the Reformation. Several Catholic movements were inspired by the Spirit to rise up and further Christ's mission during the time known as the Counter-Reformation.

One of those movements was led by Ignatius of Loyola, a Spanish priest and theologian. In response to a Spirit-inspired vision, he set up the Jesuit community – a group of priests who became known for their charity, education and missionary work. Ignatius went on to send out a thousand missionaries to Europe to pioneer schools, colleges and seminaries.[20] Today his ministry continues across the world through the 'Ignatian exercises', a set of Christian meditations, contemplations and prayers that help people experience the Spirit in prayer.

Another prominent figure of the time was St Teresa of Avila. Like Ignatius, Teresa lived a life that emphasised the importance of hearing from God. As the official 'Doctor of Prayer' for the Catholic Church today, her teachings on revelatory experience have set the example for many to follow.[21]

But as with the Protestants, revelatory activity in the Catholic Church was not without its problems. The potential for clashes with the church hierarchy that first arose with the second-century Montanists was ever present. Mystics such as Ignatius and Teresa were constantly in danger of being hauled before the authorities over their practice of revelatory experiences.[22] Pastoral issues were also a problem. A peer and contemporary of Teresa, St John of the Cross, was so concerned about the fallout from Spirit experiences that he adamantly warned *against* them. His concern was that some people hankered after supernatural experiences merely to satiate their curiosity and desire for sensationalism. For John, the result of their obsession was 'ravages wreaked in souls'.[23] St John's writings were so influential that the pendulum again swung back in the opposite direction. Tragically, his advice went on to become the norm in the Catholic Church until the Second Vatican Council (1962) when the older tradition began to be embraced once more.

Enlightened?

As we move into the late 1600s to the 1700s, the experience of hearing God's voice was dealt a further blow. This time, the problem arose from outside the church rather than from within it. This period – known as the Enlightenment – saw a radical change in Western thinking and culture. Scientific rationalism and humanism took centre stage and brought with them the rejection of any phenomenon that could not be proven empirically. Belief in supernatural resurrections, miracles and hearing from God became laughable under the scrutiny of the Enlightenment lens.

It's not difficult to see how this philosophy impacted the church. Instead of responding from a position of faith in a supernatural God, the church countered with human argument. As a result, the idea of revelation became less about inspired experience and more about intellectual reflection. Protestant theology was now driven by academic thinking and the skills of historical-critical exegesis.[24] This meant that the primary way to know God was through educational tools and intellectual know-how, rather than by the direct revelation of the Spirit. In the words of the apostle Paul, the church began to favour 'human wisdom' over the divine revelation that comes from 'Spirit-taught words' (1 Cor. 2:10–14). It was a further turn against Spirit-speech.

Breakouts and revivals

Even as the philosophies of the Reformation and Enlightenment threatened to shut down revelatory experiences in the Protestant Church, there were some distinct exceptions. In Luther's time, the 'radical Reformers' (such as the Anabaptists) embraced hearing from the Spirit,[25] as did one of the key Reformers, Ulrich Zwingli of Switzerland. In the seventeenth, eighteenth and nineteenth centuries, Spirit-speech was also welcomed by revivalists John Wesley, George Whitefield, the Moravians, Edward Irving, the Pietists in Germany and the Quaker movement pioneered by George Fox. Over in the

New World, Jonathan Edwards regularly saw Spirit manifestations in his church, and Methodist Charles Finney's ministry was founded on a visionary experience during the Second Great Awakening.[26]

Then, as the twentieth century dawned, the experience of hearing God's voice was again brought to the fore with the advent of Pentecostalism. Visions, dreams and prophecies became the impetus for new churches and outreaches, churches were planted, missionaries were sent out and ministries were birthed as people heard from the Spirit and determined to follow.

Today, there are still some streams in the Protestant Church which oppose the direct Spirit-experience. In the early decades of the twentieth century, Benjamin Warfield and the Princeton School led the cessationist charge, followed by J.I. Packer, Carl Henry and John MacArthur in more recent times. For these leaders, 'prophecy' in Scripture is equivalent to 'inspired' preaching, and hearing God's voice only occurs through reading the Bible. While this perspective is not as popular nowadays, with the rise of Pentecostalism and the Charismatic movement, its thinking still permeates our churches, colleges and Bible translations.[27] Even the popular Bible version *The Message* translates 'prophecy' in 1 Corinthians as 'preaching'.[28]

***

Whichever way you look at it, hearing from God is a risky business. History shows us that inviting the voice of the Spirit into our lives and communities will always threaten the status quo. Whether it's the question of where the boundary lines fall (from the Montanists), who has ultimate authority (from the Reformers), or whether the supernatural exists (from Enlightenment thinkers), the experience of hearing from God will always raise its detractors. The cycle of embrace and rejection of Spirit-speech will continue as long as we fail to address the underlying issues at its core.

At the same time, we also need to recognise that the magnitude of the experience's problems reflects its power. If the revelatory experience is truly from God, then it is worth unleashing. As the grand prize of the New Covenant and the central vehicle by which God works on earth, it is worth discovering how to manage it well. Instead of rejecting it outright, we must understand the questions and concerns and then address them in ways that are theologically sound and pastorally safe. If we don't, we run the risk of denying the core premise of God's *better* covenant and rejecting his plan for the dynamic work of the Spirit on earth. In the next chapter, we take time to look more closely at the problems of hearing God's voice in order to prevent the pendulum swinging too far in the other direction.

3

The Ministry Problems of Hearing God's Voice

Joseph's vision of light

Joseph set his mind to seek God early on in his teens. He had heard about the revival meetings in his home town in western New York state and longed to know more, but he was confused about which church was right for him. Some argued for the Methodists, others for the Presbyterians, still others for the Baptists.

Inspired by the teaching in the book of James that if you lack wisdom you should ask for it, Joseph ventured out into the woods near his home to pray. As he knelt on the ground, he experienced a startling vision. Thick darkness fell around him and he was struck mute by a bolt of power. Then a pillar of light appeared, and in it Joseph saw a vision of Jesus and the Father. As the light descended, he experienced a profound sense of God's forgiveness for his sins.[1]

During his vision, Joseph asked God the question that had been constantly on his mind: 'Which church should I attend?' In response, he heard Jesus say that 'none of them' were part of God's kingdom. The message of God had been corrupted since the time of the early apostles. Joseph would be the one who would restore this truth to the church.

Three years later, Joseph received another revelatory experience. In a dream, an angel named Moroni told him about a set of golden plates buried under a tree. When Joseph later discovered them, he found that they were inscribed with ancient writings which only he was able to translate with the aid of a special 'seer' stone revealed in another revelatory experience. The plates described the religious history of an ancient American civilisation to whom Jesus had appeared. Seven years later, Joseph published an English translation of the plates, calling it the Book of Mormon. This and other works were compiled to address the corruption of the Bible. It was 1830 and the Church of Jesus Christ of Latter-day Saints – the Mormons – was born.

Over the next ten years, the Mormon church expanded across a number of American states. Growth was rapid, but not without its troubles. Persecution arose from both inside and out, with members of the leadership team jostling for position based on competing revelations. Joseph responded with claims of further revelation from Moses and the apostles Peter, James and John. As 'God's self-proclaimed ordained prophet and apostle akin to Elijah and Moses', he maintained that he alone had the ability to provide doctrine and Scripture for the church and was only acting on divine authority. 'Why persecute me for telling the truth?' he wrote. 'I have actually seen a vision; and who am I that I can withstand God, or why does the world think to make me deny what I have actually seen? For I had seen a vision; I knew it, and I knew that God knew it, and I could not deny it'.[2]

The concept of hearing God's voice for yourself bears enormous God-given potential, but it is also fraught with pitfalls. And as in Joseph's case, these are *serious* pitfalls. Today, the Church of Latter-day Saints numbers in the millions and is believed by its followers to be the only true church in a sea of apostasy. Unorthodox teachings such as baptism for the dead, polygamy, distortions of the Trinity and the attainment of godhood all come from the personal revelations of one man, Joseph Smith.

Indeed, the entire scope of history tells of the problems associated with claims to divine revelation. These are more than just theological. Torrid tales of manipulation, deception, and even murder have all been justified by the claim: 'God told me'. The proliferation of a wide range of unorthodox beliefs and abuses of power have been so heinous, it's not surprising that many church leaders throw their hands up in the air and reject any idea of personal communication with God.

The dynamic experience given at Pentecost not only has the power to bring God's kingdom to earth but can also work astoundingly against it. If we are to harness the potential of hearing God in our churches, we need to identify the problems that arise from the experience and the reasons for them. In this chapter, we expose the ugly side of hearing 'God's voice' in order to pave the way for solutions. Specifically, we look at the three most significant problems of revelatory experience: 1) breaches in theological orthodoxy; 2) pastoral fallout; and 3) institutional instability. We also describe various attempts to address these problems and explain why they fail so miserably.

1. Breaches in theological orthodoxy

Joseph Smith's story illustrates the first problem we have in hearing God's voice. Because revelatory experiences act as a claim to divine authority, they can be used to challenge the teachings of traditional Christianity. The advent of Mormonism is not an isolated case. The religion of Islam began in the early seventh century when a man named Muhammad who was disillusioned with his experience of Judaism and Christianity claimed to receive new revelations via the angel Gabriel in a cave. He also asserted that the Scriptures had been corrupted and that his experiences (now transcribed as the Qur'an) offer the correct version of events.

In terms of day-to-day church life, however, the kind of claims made by Muhammad and Joseph Smith are rare. It is unlikely that a member of our churches will stand up and declare an idea that overtly contravenes fundamental Christian teaching. While there have been plenty of theological debates about Christianity in church history (as seen in the proliferation of denominations), the essential core has always been maintained. Yet, since revelatory experience represents a claim to divine authority, it still poses a significant threat. The problem of false teaching has confronted the church since its beginnings, and the possibility of every person hearing from God only compounds the threat.

The most common solution to the problem of breaches in theological orthodoxy is to *reject* the hearing God experience entirely. As we've seen, this was the strategy of the Reformation. The Reformers' answer to the misuse of revelatory experience in the Catholic Church was to completely shut it down. However, this response betrays the teaching of the New Testament. The problem is *not* with the experience itself.

We see this in another testimony from a contemporary of Joseph Smith. A year after Smith's first vision, a second young man retreated to the woods in search of God. Like Joseph, Charles Finney was inspired by the words of Scripture: 'If you seek me, you will find me.' After spending the day in prayer, Charles experienced a vision of Jesus at home in his room. Though it was dark, the room appeared 'as perfectly light'. Finney's experience radically changed his life. He relinquished his law practice and became a full-time minister in the Presbyterian Church. Later he became a prominent revivalist and advocated for a wide range of social reforms, including the abolition of slavery and the promotion of universal education.[3]

It should be no surprise that both Joseph Smith's and Charles Finney's revelations came during the Second Great Awakening. This was a time when the Spirit was moving powerfully in North America. There were revival camp meetings, Wesleyan circuit riders spreading the gospel, and radical conversions in all the Presbyterian, Methodist and Baptist churches. Fifty thousand people made decisions to follow Jesus every week. This was also an era of experiential fervour. Visions, dreams and prophetic revelations were commonplace.[4] The fact that Joseph Smith and Charles Finney had visionary experiences was not so unusual.

It is likely that the experiences of Joseph and Charles were both real to *them*. Both incidents had a profound impact on their lives and those around them. However, their message had very different outcomes for the church. According to orthodox Christianity, one got it right and one got it wrong. God may have been speaking, but so too were other voices. Where did it go wrong for Joseph?

The solution cannot be to reject spiritual experience entirely. If that had been the choice of the nineteenth-century American church, Charles's call would have been invalidated and the Awakening movement might never have happened. Instead, the spotlight must fall on *how* experiences are discerned and *where* the boundaries of orthodoxy stand. The early church points us in this direction. They too had problems with unorthodox teaching (see e.g. Acts 20:28–31; 2 Thess. 3:6; Titus 1:10–16) and, as in nineteenth-century America, some of those claims were due to revelatory experiences (1 Thess. 4:1). The solution then, as it is now, was not to dismiss them but to *discern* them. As John wrote, we are not to believe every spirit but to 'test' them to see whether they are from God (1 John 4:1). The process of discernment is vital for the New Covenant church. This process must be clear and accessible, and must allow the standard theological orthodoxy to be maintained. The issue is so important we devote three chapters to it in this book (Chapters 10–12).

2. Pastoral fallout

The second problem of revelatory experience is the issue of pastoral fallout. Our Spirit-talking experiences may be theologically acceptable, but they can still lead to pastoral headaches. People can intentionally manipulate spiritual experience for their own ends or they can just plain get it wrong. Either way, the potential for harm is devastating. In Nigeria, the leader of the terrorist organisation Boko Haram kidnapped 250 teenage girls, declaring that 'God told him' to do it.[5] In the USA in the early 1990s, an ex-pastor shot dead a doctor outside an abortion clinic under the auspices of a divine directive.[6]

For the average church leader, the pastoral challenges are likely to be on a smaller scale, but they can still have grave consequences. There may be the overzealous person who seems to hear from God every moment of the day and can't make a decision without it; the infertile couple whose promise of a child leads to overwhelming disappointment month after month; the doe-eyed teenager who claims God told her she would marry the youth pastor and loses her faith when he marries someone else. Experiences such as these can be so damaging that people walk away from God for ever.

It's these kinds of situations that typically represent the greatest headache for pastors and leaders. They tend to be seen most frequently in the Pentecostal branches of the church. In his book *Thus Saith the Lord?* American minister John Bevere labels current prophetic ministry as a 'church-wide crisis'. He details a damning list of the effects of counterfeit prophecy: 'broken marriages, dashed hopes, divided congregations, unrealizable promises, terrorized pastors, rebellion, despair, guilt and discouragement'.[7] Of course, these primarily relate to the operation of prophecy where one person hears from God on behalf of another, but the problems remain much the same. The mishandling of revelatory experiences can lead to disappointment and dysfunction, manipulative behaviour and power struggles. Too often they pander to human desires and the idols of the heart. One poorly discerned experience can derail a person's faith, their family and even a church. Indeed, the devastating extent of pastoral damage has been used by some as an argument against the legitimacy of hearing God's voice at all.[8]

In many churches, the solution to this problem has been to *restrict* the revelatory experience. Thus, hearing God becomes relegated to the domain of leaders and experts. The experience becomes limited to the public service, where leaders can closely monitor every prophetic act. Sometimes this means that hearing from God is only encouraged when a guest prophet visits and is trusted to hear from God on behalf of others. In other cases, hearing from God may be encouraged outside the public domain, but parishioners still have to check in with their pastors about every experience they have.

While these strategies are employed with good intentions – ultimately to protect our congregations – restricting the revelatory experience to leaders and the public gathering thwarts the democratic intent of the New Covenant. The universal outpouring of the Spirit at Pentecost means that we do not need a church leader, prophet or public service to hear from God. What's more, pastoral supervision is not possible if the Spirit speaks while we're driving to work or sleeping in our beds. Restricting discernment to leadership also implies that the leader is hearing from God for every individual in their congregation. This approach inadvertently sends us back to the Old Covenant where you had to rely on someone else to hear God's voice.

While opening up to the revelatory experience certainly invites the risk of pastoral fallout in our churches, if the experience is from God it will always be for our good (1 Cor. 14:3). If the Spirit is truly speaking, we will be led into truth (John 16:13). Hence, as in the case of breaches in theological orthodoxy, the solution is not to restrict the Spirit's voice but rather to implement a process of discernment that is accessible to all. This process must allow for experiences outside the public domain. It must also clarify the role of the church leader.

3. Institutional instability

The final problem that revelatory experience poses to the church concerns the stability of the church community. You may have experienced the 'God told me to leave' scenario in your own congregation. Hearing from God can easily become a cover for someone's personal agenda or an excuse to abscond when tensions are rife. This can lead to splits and spin-offs, acts of defiance against the church leadership and even a complete breakdown of the community. Churches have been known to be pulled apart by competing claims to revelation.

However, the problem of institutional instability is not always due to sin, deception or lack of discernment. Sometimes instability arises *because* someone has heard from God.

Loren Cunningham's story is a case in point. Loren was 20 years old when he experienced a powerful vision. He saw a large map of the world, with waves washing over the continents. As the waves receded, they morphed into throngs of young people. Across the map, they spread, taking the gospel message into the nations: from house to house, on street corners and outside bars.[9]

The vision stirred Loren into action and he began to prepare for his call. Four years later, he presented his plans to the leadership of his denomination, the American Assemblies of God (AG). But there was nowhere in the current structure to accommodate such a radical vision and the church leaders offered him an administrative role at the office instead. Loren's choice was to disobey the voice of God or break with his denomination. With a heavy heart, he walked away.

History reveals the fruit of Loren's decision. Sixty years later, Youth With a Mission (YWAM) is one of the world's largest missionary training and sending organisations, with nearly 20,000 workers, and ministries in 180 countries around the world.[10] Loren's obedience to his vision meant that thousands of people around the globe have been transformed by YWAM's ministry.

Loren's story shows that the problem of institutional stability in our churches and denominations is not always due to a lack of proper discernment or a sinful heart. God himself may be the cause. Revelatory experiences create problems in the church when they clash with existing ecclesial structures and goals. The core issue is the power tussle between the 'voice of God' and the 'voice' of institutional leadership. As sociologist James Coleman describes it, the Spirit acts like a 'third person [in] the mix, bringing the constant threat of social cleavage'.[11] Of course, Scripture also tells us that we should submit to the church leaders who watch over us (Heb. 13:17). The question becomes: who do you obey when the 'voice of God' conflicts with the voice of human leadership?

The dynamic seen in Loren's story has been investigated by sociologists across the globe. Poloma examined it in her original study of the American AG via the work of German sociologist and economist Max Weber.[12] Weber's theory, known as the 'routinisation of charisma', says that the charismatic experiences needed to pioneer a new organisation diminish over time as the institution grows and becomes more formalised. Once valued for their life-giving stimulus, new experiences become increasingly dangerous for the institution because they challenge the structures that have been built to maintain organisational needs. No one wants to see a well-run institution come under threat. Stability and security are powerful drivers.

Poloma discovered signs of this routinisation in her studies. As much as the AG leadership valued charismatic experience in theory, in practice it was diminishing. This same process has been found in church movements in Australia and South Africa.[13] It is clear that the tension is difficult to manage. Institutional stability and charismatic experience are mutually opposed: when you welcome one, you risk the loss of the other.

The most common solution to the problem of church instability is to *dilute* the revelatory experience. This is done by steering people towards experiences that contain *known* information – that is, we confine the hearing of God's voice to Scripture. There is no danger, after all, in encouraging people to hear afresh that God loves them, that his Son died for them and that they are called to be kind, generous and gracious. But as soon as you open the door to the possibility that God might want someone to sell their home, start a ministry or move cities, you are in dangerous territory. Sociologists have observed that revelatory experiences that contain *new, previously unknown or future-oriented information* pose the highest threat.

The insights of a North American study help us to understand this dynamic in more detail. Sociologists Charles Glock and Rodney Stark conducted a large study of Protestant and Catholic churches in the San Francisco region of the USA. They drew on interviews with members in order to understand the nature of revelatory experience and its impact on the local church.[14]

Afterwards, Glock and Stark organised their findings into a taxonomy that emphasised the relational dynamic between the 'divine and human actor'. People were seen to move from one stage to the next as their relationship with God grew. The first type of experience (Type 1) was termed *confirming*. At this stage, hearing from God enabled someone to feel a sense of God's presence. Experiences could be compared to an 'acquaintance' relationship and often involved a sudden conviction that one's beliefs were true. The second type of experience

(Type 2) was described as *responsive*. These experiences acted like a closer 'introduction' to God, such that God was perceived as responding to the individual. They included instances of affirmation such as 'You are loved', 'I am with you' and 'I'll take care of you'.

The third type of experience (Type 3) was labelled *ecstatic*. This category moved the person up the relational scale to the level of 'friendship' with God. Instead of merely feeling 'chosen', they felt 'embraced'. The sense of divine presence was replaced with stronger affections of love and belonging. Finally, the fourth category of experience (Type 4) was described as *revelational* and represented partnership – the highest level of relationship. Here, the person was commissioned to partner with God's plans. This type of 'high-level' revelatory experience often included divine directives and the possibility of previously unknown and future-oriented information.

When Glock and Stark reviewed their work, they made a further set of observations. Churches were seen to *actively encourage* the lower experiences on the taxonomy while *discouraging* the higher ones.[15] Hearing from God was acceptable as long as it contained known information, thus maintaining the status quo and minimising any chance of disruption.

As church leaders, Glock and Stark's research is both insightful and confronting. The taxonomy highlights the choice laid before us: we can either dilute revelatory experiences and quell the reforming work of the Spirit, or we can find better ways to respond to them. Either we keep the peace or we allow God to disturb it.

Some churches have chosen to buck the trend highlighted by Glock and Stark. A high incidence of Type 4 experiences was observed in several British churches at the time of the so-called Toronto Blessing,[16] at a Pentecostal church in Canada[17] and in my own research in Australia. If these experiences are an indicator of relational intimacy with God, as Glock and Stark show them to be, there are excellent reasons to find a way to facilitate them without compromising the health of our church communities.

***

The problems of revelatory experience are real. Whenever you invite sinful people to hear from God, you run the risk of fallout, as in the lives of Joseph Smith and the man who killed the abortion doctor. Revelatory experiences may be used for good *or* for ill. As long as sin abounds, the potential for damage will remain.

But just as hearing God brings its problems, so too its power can be seen in the lives of Charles Finney and Loren Cunningham. The options to *reject* it, *dilute* it or *restrict* it to those in a position of church leadership all thwart the intent of the New Covenant and stay the miraculous power of God. We end up settling for less than we were promised.

We must not allow the abuse and misuse of revelatory experience to silence the voice of the New Covenant Spirit. Instead, the problems of breaches in orthodoxy, pastoral fallout and institutional instability must be addressed in theological ways. Answers must draw on Jesus' teaching and the example of the early church. They must provide an adequate process for discernment that is accessible to all in our churches. They must show how to manage the threat to the institutional structures that were designed for the organisation's efficiency and the protection of our people. They must reconcile any conflict between the voice of God and the voice of pastoral leadership.

It *is* possible to deal with the ministry problems of revelatory experiences without compromising their power. Part II of this book provides a theological framework for hearing God's voice within the safety and accountability of the local church. Later, in Chapter 18, we use this framework to address the ministry problems specifically outlined here. But first, we must visit one further problem of revelatory experience and perhaps its most important: the *theological* issue of Spirit versus Scripture.

4

The Theological Problem of Spirit versus Scripture

A radical move

In 2002 I was contemplating an interstate move on the basis of a dream. 'Move to Sydney,' the Spirit had said, 'and you will become the Academic Dean of Hillsong College.' At the time, I had been working two part-time jobs – one at a local Bible college, and the other, pastoring a church in Melbourne. I was thriving in both positions, happily settled in a lovely home and had no plans to move to an unknown city a thousand kilometres away. In Sydney, Hillsong College wasn't advertising a new position externally, nor was it their policy to do so. I was an unknown entity, connected only vaguely through my current networks. Still, the guidance had been spectacularly clear. Dreams and prophecies from six to seven independent sources all pointed in the same direction. The Spirit's leading had checked all the boxes.

At the same time, the idea of leaving my jobs, friends and family with no possibility of employment was a radical one, particularly for a risk-averse single woman. When the time came to move, I was confronted with the ludicrousness of my situation and the all-consuming question: could I trust what God said?

At first, the answer seems obvious. Scripture assures us that God does what he says he will do: the word from God's mouth does not return to him 'empty' but 'achieve[s] the purpose' it was sent for (Isa. 55:11); 'God is not a human, that he should lie . . . Does he speak and then not act?' (Num. 23:19; also 1 Sam. 15:29). But then the question comes: did those verses mean the same for me as they did back then for Samuel? Would God's words 'not return empty' for me just as they wouldn't return empty for Isaiah?

The answer depends on your theology. Some would say 'yes'. Others would say 'no'. Most Protestant theologians would say that my 'hearing God' experience was *not* as authoritative as those in the biblical accounts and could not be trusted in the same way. The experiences of the Bible are seen to be 'special' and unrepeatable, while contemporary encounters are seen to be more subject to human influence. Hence, the only reliable way to hear God today is through studying the Bible, listening to sermons, reading Christian books and obtaining the 'wisdom of counsel'. Conversely, another group of theologians (largely from the Catholic tradition) would say that we *can* hear from God in the same way as the Bible characters did. So, if my Spirit revelation was authentic, I should follow it and believe for it to come to pass. Still another group would say that my experience was illegitimate from the outset: God doesn't speak like that any more, so it was either the product of mental instability or, worse, diabolical influences.

The situation was made more complex when I sought answers in my local Bible college library. There I found two groups of books. One was written by Protestant *theologians*. They applied historical-exegesis skills to make claims about the nature of contemporary experiences such as mine. The other group was written by Pentecostal *practitioners*. They told of amazing hearing God stories that were akin to the biblical accounts but seemed to have little theological depth. I was left with no clear answers. The practitioners had limited theology and the theologians had limited experience.

My questions about moving to Sydney highlighted a theological problem that has existed ever since the Scriptures were canonised in the fourth century. It is the reason why many churches today reject the idea of direct Spirit-revelation. The problem boils down to how we view the relationship of our Spirit-talking experiences to Scripture: how do our Spirit encounters compare with those in the Bible?

As we've seen in Scripture, God's words are both a vessel of his power and a reflection of his character. Therefore, the claim to hearing God's voice represents a claim to divine *authority*. If God has truly spoken, then his words have bearing over our lives and the circumstances to which they refer. At a practical level, that means that when God speaks, we should obey. It also means we should expect God's words to come to pass. So, in this way of thinking, it would be *right* for me to move to Sydney and I *should* believe for my circumstances to come into alignment with God's words. Just as Abraham moved when God told him to go to Canaan, and the apostle Paul moved when God told him to go to Macedonia, so should I move when God tells me to go to Sydney. If their response was to treat God's words as authoritative, so should I.

Can you see our theological conundrum? The practical realities of contemporary revelatory experiences make them as authoritative as the Bible writers. This looks as if we're placing our experience on par with the Bible, something most Protestant Christians would emphatically reject as illegitimate. The question is: how does the *spoken word of the Spirit* relate to the *written word of the Scriptures*?

Four answers to the theological problem

The answer to our theological problem is crucial because it shapes our understandings of how the Spirit speaks today, how we recognise it and how we respond to it. In turn, this frames our ideas about discipleship and ministry, as well as the nature and role of the Scriptures.

Four different frameworks have been proposed to address the problem of 'Spirit versus Scripture'. In this chapter, we examine each of them closely. The first and third approaches assume that our contemporary experiences are *discontinuous* with the biblical experience. The second and fourth anticipate *continuity* with the biblical experience. We will see why the first three options are inadequate and why the fourth provides the only logical basis for a theology of hearing God's voice.

1. God on mute

The first theological framework, 'God on mute', holds that the Spirit no longer speaks in the same way as in Bible times. As we've noted, this position, known as cessationism, holds to the belief that divinely inspired speech ceased with the close of the canon in the early centuries of the church (or when the original apostle died). Hence, the only way God 'speaks' today is via the Scriptures: God's voice is heard through studying the Bible, listening to sermons and reading books that expound the Bible. Direct revelatory encounters are no longer plausible.

This perspective also holds that God can only speak about that which has already been said in the biblical past. The Spirit does not speak specifically on personal matters such as where to live or what job to take. Neither does God speak about his plans for the future or how to deal with ethical issues beyond the Scriptures. Instead, divine insight comes through careful application of the biblical text – we hear God best when we hone our hermeneutical skills. As evangelical theologian James Packer wrote:

> While it is not for us to forbid God to reveal things apart from Scripture, or to do anything else (he is God after all), we may properly insist that the New Testament discourages Christians from expecting to receive God's words to them by any other channel than that of attentive application to themselves of what is given to us twentieth century Christians in holy Scripture.[1]

The cessationist perspective has ebbed and flowed in the church since its inception. Today it is typically found in the Reformed and dispensational segments of the Protestant evangelical tradition,[2] but it is becoming less popular under the influence of Pentecostalism and the Charismatic movement in mainline churches.[3]

The thinking behind contemporary cessationism largely stems from a desire to protect the authority, uniqueness and sufficiency of the Scriptures. This is not an unimportant concern, since history shows us that whenever the Scriptures lose their priority in the church, doctrinal compromise soon follows. For cessationists, then, any claim to extrabiblical revelation is invalid, subversive and even demonic. It is seen to 'add' to the canon and attack the Bible's uniqueness. Any additional voice 'weakens the power of the Word' and results in a 'spiritual free-for-all', giving rise to heretical movements in the church.[4] As one of cessationism's leading proponents, John MacArthur laments: 'New revelation, such as dreams and visions, are considered as binding on the believer's conscience as the book of Romans or the Gospel of John.'[5]

The cessationists have a good point. As we've seen, when we claim to hear God's voice, we are invoking divine authority. The Scriptures themselves tell us that authority derives from the speaker (e.g. Jer. 23:29; Heb. 4:12). If God were truly speaking, we would be expected to obey his words to us as much as the biblical characters were expected to obey his words to them (e.g. Rev. 1:3). Any valid perspective on Spirit versus Scripture must acknowledge that a true word from God is authoritative, whether situated within the Bible or outside it.

However, the great tragedy of the cessationist position is that it silences the voice of the Spirit in the church, the very pinnacle of the New Covenant. It defies the words of the apostle Peter when he proclaimed that Pentecost represented the long-awaited fulfilment of God's promise for the communicating Spirit. Peter made it clear that the ability to hear God's voice in the manner of the Old Covenant prophets (Acts 2:16–17) was *not* just for those gathered in Jerusalem that day but was also for all those who were 'far off' (Acts 2:39) – in Judea, Samaria and the nations beyond. It wasn't just for the first generation, but for their children and all those who followed. As prophesied by Joel, the Spirit would remain *for ever* under the New Covenant.[6]

The promise of the New Covenant remains today. God has spoken and continues to speak by his Spirit. While the preservation of Scripture's role is crucial, there is another way to maintain it.

2. *Christians who don't read the Bible*

There is a tribe of Christians in Zimbabwe who are known as 'Christians who don't read the Bible' – and proudly so. This group, known as the 'Friday Apostolics' (because Friday is their Sabbath), represents a second approach to the relationship of revelatory experience to Scripture.

Unlike the cessationists, the Friday Apostolics believe that contemporary experiences of hearing God are *continuous* with those of the biblical characters. That is, the outpouring of God's Spirit meant that we can all hear from God in ways that are phenomenologically equivalent to the ways the Bible characters heard. Contemporary encounters are analogous to the biblical experience in purpose, manner and kind. At the same time, this capacity to hear from God directly is seen to make Scripture irrelevant. The reason the Friday Apostolics don't read their Bible is because they say it 'gets in the way' of hearing from the Spirit.

To our ears, this perspective is an alarming one, but there is some sound reasoning behind it. The Apostolics recognise that God's presence is always with them and cannot be limited to a material object. Rather than relying on a book, their emphasis is to live 'like the apostles' and have an experience of Christianity that is 'as vibrant and alive as when Jesus walked the earth'. As leader Nzira says: 'Here we don't talk of Bibles. What is the Bible to me? Having it is just trouble. Look, why would you read it? It gets old. After keeping it for some time it falls apart; the pages come out. And then you can take it and use it as toilet paper until it's finished. We don't talk Bible-talk here. We have a true Bible.'[7]

Anthropologist Matthew Engelke, who spent time studying the group, notes that part of the Friday Apostolics' aversion to the Bible is that it is seen as a 'white man's book'. As such, it carries the baggage of colonialism that has plagued the tribe ever since the whites came. Moreover, the Apostolics say that the missionaries often said one thing and the Bible said another. Polygamy is cited as an example.

For one elder, 'We learnt that we could not trust the whites or their book.'[8]

The Friday Apostolics also argue that because the Scriptures are culturally embedded, they are unable to adequately address the needs of modern-day Africa. The ancient Palestinian context of the New Testament means that it has limited relevance in a place that is haunted by AIDS and witchcraft. As they say, it is 'out of date like a newspaper'. Instead, answers are found in hearing from the Holy Spirit *live and direct.*

The Apostolics even go so far as to say that the Bible acts as an *obstacle* to hearing from God. Like all religious artefacts, books are limited by their materialist nature. The very presence of the Bible, they say, threatens to detract from the immediacy of faith. When God's voice is contained in a book, it takes away from the central focus of Christianity.

The position of the Friday Apostolics is not an option for those of us who place high value on Scripture. However, the Apostolics also raise some important questions. It is true that God's presence cannot be contained in a material book. Whether a book, icon or building, God's presence is never limited to a physical object. Solomon observed this in the building of the First Temple (1 Kgs 8:27), as did Paul with the Second Temple (Acts 17:24). People in our churches today can be guilty of this when they use their Bibles like a lucky charm or a magic tool, dipping into it whenever they want their wishes fulfilled. Like any object, the Bible can become an idol that is revered above its maker. Some scholars have even given this tendency a name: 'bibliolatry'[9] – described as worshipping the 'Father, Son and Holy Bible'. As the Apostolics say, when treated in this way, the Bible *can* 'get in the way' of hearing the Spirit.

The Friday Apostolics are also correct in saying that as a first century Greco-Roman text, the Bible does not always speak to contemporary issues. We need to do a lot of hermeneutical back-flipping to make the Bible address the quirks and idiosyncrasies of contemporary ethical concerns. The wisdom insights of the Ancient Near East and the Greco-Roman world cannot always speak to the questions of our day. Indeed, Jesus never said they would. Jesus held to the veracity of the Scriptures (in his case, the Old Testament), but he didn't position them as the one-stop shop for all our questions. This is *why* he sent the Spirit. Jesus knew there was more to say beyond what he could cover in his three-year ministry (John 16:12). The Spirit was given for the very reason of addressing the questions of Samaria, Rome and beyond. This is what makes Christianity such a powerful reality. As 'temples of the Holy Spirit' (1 Cor. 6:19), we can access the wisdom of Jesus wherever we go.

And yet, the Friday Apostolics put themselves in a precarious situation by giving the Bible such a low priority. When you discard the Bible, you risk displacing the church's very foundations. We need the Bible. We need the Spirit. We must not dispense with one at the expense of the other.

3. Good, but not as good

The cessationists dismiss the Spirit; the Friday Apostolics dismiss the Bible. The third approach to our theological problem of 'Spirit versus Scripture' seeks to preserve both. This position says that contemporary revelatory experiences are valid, but they are *phenomenologically inferior* to the experience of the Bible-writing apostles and prophets. In other words, you can hear from God outside the canon, but just not in the same way as the Bible-writing characters did. Our Spirit encounters are 'good, but not *as* good'.

The position is best articulated by Baptist theologian Wayne Grudem in his widely known book *The Gift of Prophecy*. Here, Grudem advocates for two types of revelatory experience. The first is the 'special experience' of the canonical writers, namely the Old Testament prophets and their 'equivalent', the New Testament apostles. The experiences of these characters are held to be flawless; God put his words directly 'into their mouths' and, as such, they are always accurate, infallible and authoritative. The second type is the 'ordinary experience' of New Testament and contemporary church members. For Grudem, these experiences are of lower quality and authority compared with those of biblical figures such as Paul and Peter. Contemporary revelatory messages are described as 'a report in human words which God has brought to mind'. Because they cannot be God's *exact* words, they are neither authoritative nor trustworthy. They can bring 'strength, encouragement and comfort' (see 1 Cor. 14:3) but should be treated in the same way as counselling and pastoral advice. As per the cessationists, Grudem argues that the only reliable way to hear God's voice is via the Scriptures.

This 'two-tier' position is also reflected in the *logos–rhēma* schema so popular in churches today. Like Grudem's framework, this envisages two different types of experience and is based on the idea that there are two meanings for the Greek term 'word' in the New Testament. The first term, *logos* (λόγος), represents the 'written word' of Scripture, which is seen to be objective, infallible and fully authoritative. The second term, *rhēma* (ῥῆμα), represents the 'spoken word' of our contemporary experience, which is seen to be subjective, fallible and of minimal authority.

The goal of the two-tier schema is to preserve the role of the Bible while still allowing for the possibility that the Spirit can speak beyond the canon. As such, Grudem's work was welcomed by Pentecostal–Charismatic Christians around the world. However, there are some real problems with this position. Perhaps the most obvious has to do with what Scripture says about the New Covenant in relation to the Old. While the two-tier position advocates for contemporary experience to be viewed as *inferior* to the Old Covenant experience, Scripture emphasises the opposite. The Old Covenant prophets, Jesus, Paul and the writer of Hebrews all strongly affirm the *superiority* of the New Covenant (see Chapter 6). The church era was long awaited because it was an upgrade of the old regime. This improvement would not just be for the leaders who were responsible for establishing the church, but for *everyone*. It *cannot* be that the New Covenant church has a harder time hearing from God than the Old Covenant prophets.

A second problem points to the biblical evidence used in support of Grudem's position. His work has sustained heavy criticism from cessationist and Pentecostal–Charismatic scholars alike. This has largely been based on exegetical grounds and the grammatically unlikely notion of correlating the role of the Old Testament prophets with that of the New Testament apostles (in Eph. 2:20). It is also clear that Scripture reveals a *spectrum* of quality among the revelatory experiences of biblical characters. Most got it right, but some got it wrong (see Chapter 10). Furthermore, there is simply no textual evidence that God explicitly changed his way of speaking when the original apostles died out.

There are additional complexities with the two-tier position when it comes to its practical outworking. Some of them are seen in my own story as I contemplated relocation from Melbourne to Sydney. The question became: if what I heard was non-authoritative, should I move? And if I did move, should I believe for God to fulfil his word? Unfortunately, Grudem does not address the implications of his position in real-life experience since, as a New Testament scholar, his focus is on the text.

An additional problem lies in the fact that Grudem's work is directed almost entirely towards *prophecy* (where a person hears from God for someone else), rather than the universal experience of hearing the Spirit first-hand. This means that most of his discussion is limited to the specialist gift of prophecy in church meetings, as described in the Corinthian letters (esp. 1 Cor. 12 – 14). While these passages are helpful in providing guidelines for the regulation of prophecy in the public service, they do not give us details about the universal experience in the context of everyday life. For that, we need to look elsewhere.

It is in the books of Acts and Revelation that we find copious examples of the full revelatory experience. We learn how God spoke, how it was discerned and how it was then responded to. It is here that we see that the New Testament characters *all* treated their revelatory experiences as authoritative, irrespective of whether they were apostles or Bible writers (e.g. Philip, Stephen, Barnabas, Agabus, Ananias and

James). Once God's words were received and discerned, they were seen to be reliable enough to act upon in expectation of fulfilment. Their testimonies provide us with clear principles for hearing God in the contemporary church. We cannot ignore them.

And yet oddly we do. In spite of their prevalence in the Bible, these experiences are rarely addressed by academics in the Protestant arena.[10] Grudem's emphasis on the specialist gift of prophecy to the exclusion of everyday revelatory experience is typical of scholars. Part of it has to do with a tradition that values the teaching of the epistles over the New Testament narratives and a mistrust in deriving theology from stories. But if we are to talk about how to hear, recognise and respond to God's voice today, we must take into account how the early Christians heard, recognised and responded to God's voice. After all, it is their revelatory experiences that form the backdrop of the epistles.[11]

In spite of the problems, the idea of an 'inferior quality' for contemporary experience has been adopted by most evangelical Christians in the West, including those in Charismatic and Pentecostal churches. This is a better place to land than cessationism. However, it is still a *modified* form of cessationism. It is good, but not *as* good. We maintain a belief in the ability to hear the Spirit's voice but lose the fullness of its power. It also means that we don't take hearing from the Spirit as seriously as we should. We make it an add-on rather than an essential part of the normal Christian life. It may bring 'strength, comfort and encouragement' (see 1 Cor. 14:3), but it has a low priority in the discipleship process.

As we've seen, the good-but-not-as-good position also leaves us with serious problems when applied to the *practice* of hearing God's voice. Without a framework that assumes consistency with the biblical characters, people end up applying 'discontinuous' thinking to understand their experience and, in doing so, say one thing and practise another.[12] They say their experience isn't 'authoritative', but then they *act as though it is* by obeying it and expecting it to come to pass. The good-but-not-as-good position simply doesn't work. It's as if one of our legs has been broken by cessationism but hasn't been properly reset, and now we walk with a limp. It is time to adjust our thinking. Either we can hear from God in the same way as the biblical characters could, or we can't. If we can, then we must follow the same practices as the biblical characters. Only then can the stories and testimonies of Scripture truly become our model.

4. 'This is that'

The final theological framework in our discussion allows for the fullness of the Spirit's voice to continue today without compromising the uniqueness of the Bible. This approach sees no phenomenological distinction between biblical and contemporary experiences. That is, we can hear from God today in the same way as the New Testament church did. It may be surprising to learn that this fourth perspective is found in the Catholic tradition.

Our reference point here is the Day of Pentecost when the apostle Peter proclaimed his famed words to the crowd: '*this is that* which was spoken by the prophet Joel' (Acts 2:16, KJV). God's promise of the communicating Spirit was for people of all nations and generations. The voice of God that spoke to the Old Covenant prophets and the New Testament church is still the voice that speaks today. The Spirit speaks to continue the mission and ministry of Jesus. This means that the forms and patterns of revelation depicted in the early church continue in today's church. The Bible itself is a collection of God-conversations – the 'journals' of people who heard from God and responded to it. It provides us with the models we need in order to understand and respond to our own experiences.

The 'this is that' position is based on the principle of *consistency*. This consistency applies first to God. It assumes that God's ways of working haven't changed. The God who spoke to the prophets aligns with the God who spoke through the incarnate Jesus and the Spirit in the early church. God continues to speak with love, power and authority. His voice still expresses the divine character, will and plans. Just as God spoke to the early church to apply the message of Jesus to the Greco-Roman setting, God speaks to the contemporary church to apply the message of Jesus to ours.

The notion of consistency also applies at the human end. Humanity has been and always will be flawed, imperfect and sinful. Until Jesus returns, the testing and discernment of our experiences will always be necessary. Regardless of *who* can hear from God – the specialist prophets of the Old Covenant or the sons and daughters of the New – we can all get it wrong. Getting it right comes with learning and development in the context of a two-way relationship. God hasn't changed his ways of working and neither have we. But in spite of our flaws, we can still hear God's plans and act on them. This is the good news of the New Covenant!

Where experience and theology meet

The fourth 'this is that' position was the one I arrived at when contemplating my interstate move back in 2002. It made sense that if God was the 'same yesterday and today and for ever' (Heb. 13:8), the divine principles embedded in the lives of the biblical characters could be applied to *my* life. So, I resigned from my two jobs, farewelled my home and moved to Sydney.

It wasn't easy, but as I acted in obedience and faith, I saw God's hand moving pieces of the puzzle together. One by one, the picture took shape. Watching God's words come to pass was breathtaking. At every step, I witnessed his genius manoeuvres and piercing foresight. Even though my story was vastly different from that of Peter, Paul and other biblical characters, the same patterns remained. God was still faithful, sovereign and deeply personal. Hearing, recognising and responding to God's voice not only helped to build the college in Sydney; it also transformed my life. The kingdom of God moved forward and I began to know God in ways I had never experienced before.

It was experiences like these that also led me to study for a PhD in practical theology. I longed to fill the gap between academia and practice that I had discovered as an undergraduate student in the Bible college library. Driven by a deep conviction that theology must *work*, my goal was to address the problems created by the 'inferior position', as well as to understand why the cessationist church believed as it did. From my vantage point, they have tragically missed out.

The field of practical theology is unique in that it takes Spirit-experience seriously. Practice and theology meet together as scholars bring the voice of everyday people into dialogue with experts. This approach is based on the simple idea that 'everyone's a theologian'.[13] Whether we are aware of it or not, we are all constantly reflecting on how God is working in our lives. This 'ordinary theology' is worked out in the context of everyday circumstances and church traditions, rather than just by theologians, who may be removed from them.[14] It values the insights people have gained from their experience because it assumes that the Spirit operates consistently in us all.

The data from my study was gathered over a nine-month period and involved listening to the 'ordinary theology' of people from three different Pentecostal churches as they reflected on their own 'hearing God' experiences. Each interview lasted up to an hour and involved questions such as: How did you hear God's voice? How did you know it was God? What happened afterwards? After recording, transcribing and collating the findings, I identified notable patterns and themes. Then I examined them closely in the light of the four theological perspectives and the experiences of Scripture.

In the end, my research provided the answers to many of my original questions. Some were surprising; others were not. Many of them challenged the ideas of those I was raised with. Others provided solutions to the problems we face in our churches. The problems of Spirit-revelatory encounters have not gone away. My own experience with the ministry of God Conversations has been a constant reminder of the widespread confusion throughout the global church. I have seen evidence of cessationism and its impact. I've heard the tales of disillusionment and defeat. Experience continues to be held at arm's length in the name of theology. We need to address the problems that Luther faced, deal with the dilemma of Joseph Smith and learn from the story of the murdered abortion doctor. We need to maintain the vital role of the Scriptures while still allowing the Spirit to speak as powerfully to us as he did to those in the first century.

***

Some people find theology a daunting topic. Perhaps it is because we tend to complexify what is really rather simple. Theology is simply our ideas of how God works. This is why this chapter, though theoretical, is so important. Whether we realise it or not, our thinking about hearing God starts with our theology of Spirit and Scripture.

In this chapter we've seen that there are four different approaches to the contemporary revelatory experience. These diverge at the point where Scripture comes to the fore. Either we see *continuity* with the experiences of the biblical characters or we see *discontinuity* with them.

The fourth theological framework, 'this is that', allows us to emulate the revelatory experiences of the early church while preserving the unique and foundational role of Scripture. Part II of this book unpacks this position further by exploring the fundamental questions of how we hear, recognise and respond to the voice of the Spirit. There is no competition between Spirit and Scripture. You do not need to subvert one for the sake of the other.

Bringing experience and theology together also allows us to address the theological and ministry problems that threaten the potential of our prized New Covenant gift. Some of these solutions will become apparent in Part II. Others will be addressed in Part III, 'Strategies for Building the Church Who Hears God's Voice'. There *are* answers to our questions. There *are* solutions to our problems. Good theology always works.

Part II

A Theology for Hearing God's Voice

'As the fully embodied Word, Jesus filled in the blanks of the prophets' words. Every contemporary Spirit experience must be seen through his eyes. Why look back to the prophets' time when they looked forward to ours? Why look into a shadow when we have perfect light?'

5

The 'Knowable' God

A mass child sacrifice

In 2019, in a coastal area of northern Peru, archaeologists discovered the largest child burial site ever found. Lying beneath a lonely plot of desert sands were the skeletons of 227 children between the ages of 4 and 14. The archaeologists dated their find to the time of the Chimu tribe 600 years ago. They tell us that the children were all ritually killed at the same time.[1]

It was a gruesome find. Autopsies indicate that the children were all stabbed in the chest. Some of the skeletons showed signs of the heart being excised. For us, the thought of 227 sets of parents offering their sons and daughters up to be massacred is unfathomable. How could they do it?

The chilling scene only makes sense when you understand how the gods were viewed in societies such as that of the Chimu. In ancient tribal communities, the gods were many and everyone was religious. But the gods were not like the lofty moral deities we imagine today. These gods tended to act more like oversized humans. They got into bad moods, fell in love and fought one another.

It was also understood in these societies that the gods controlled everything that happened. Each god was designated responsibility for a particular aspect of the natural world. Knowing this, the way to do well in life was to keep the gods happy – particularly the one you needed at the time. So, if you wanted a baby, you turned to the fertility god; if you needed a healthy crop, you looked to the rain god; if you longed for a lover, you turned to the deity of love. Having made your choice, you would bring your offering to the temple where the god was said to dwell. The type of offering depended on the magnitude of your request; you could bring food, animals or, if you were really desperate, your children.

So, people had a 'relationship' with the gods, but it was difficult to know what these deities were thinking. The gods weren't always predictable. The main way to work out what mood they were in was to watch for signs in the world around you. If the crops were flourishing, you knew the gods were happy. But if times were difficult, and famines, droughts or earthquakes ravaged the earth, you knew the gods were angry. In such cases, the only way to rectify the situation was by making sacrifices.

This appears to be what was happening in the Chimu community on that terrible day 600 years ago. Archaeologists believe that the 227 children were sacrificed in order to stop disasters linked to the El Niño phenomenon – a weather event known to trigger flooding and landslides in the area. You can only imagine the Chimus' desperation as they brought their children to the altar by the sea. They faced an impossible choice: the destruction of their village or the slaughter of their children.

It is against this backdrop that the God of the Bible shines most brightly. Like the Chimu, the people of the Ancient Near East worshipped many gods. In the beginning, there was no reason to anticipate that Israel's Yahweh was any different from the gods of the other nations. But time showed that to be far from the truth. Over the course of biblical history, God revealed his true nature to those who were listening.

In this chapter, we look closely at how the Scriptures present God as One who *speaks back*. Yahweh's nature stands out among the gods of the ancient pantheon. His faculty of language has two major outcomes for God's people: first, God becomes personally knowable, and second, relationship with him becomes the basis for partnership. The offer is there. Whether we accept it or not has always been in question.

The God who speaks back

There is a scene in the Old Testament that highlights God's nature perhaps more clearly than most. In the story, Elijah had just won a decisive victory over Israel's King Ahab and Queen Jezebel (1 Kgs 19). A contest by fire on Mount Carmel was held to determine which god was the most powerful – Baal or Yahweh. Elijah's God had won and Ahab's prophets were humiliated. Enraged at their loss, Ahab and Jezebel set out to take revenge.

Elijah runs for his life and escapes to a cave near Mount Horeb. There, we find him depressed, disillusioned and alone.

The cave sets the stage for the main point of the story. Here, Yahweh chooses to reveal himself. He says to Elijah: 'Go out and stand on the mountain in the presence of the LORD, for the LORD is about to pass by.'

A great wind follows. It tears 'the mountains apart' and 'shatter[s] the rocks', but God isn't present in the wind. Then there's a great earthquake, but God isn't in the earthquake. Finally, there is a fire, but God isn't in the fire either (vv. 11–12).

So how does Yahweh wish to be known?

In the stillness that follows, God *speaks*. He first comforts Elijah and gives him reassurance. Elijah is not alone. Then he tells him what to do (vv. 12–18). This is a God who knows Elijah personally. Yahweh reveals himself as a *voice*.

Elijah's revelation in the cave becomes even more pronounced when we remember Israel's earlier encounters with God. Before this, God had revealed himself with fire, wind, earthquakes, thunder, lightning and smoke. These phenomena were all in keeping with ancient expectations for a theophany. So, when the Old Covenant was given at Sinai, God spoke out of thunder, lightning and smoke (Exod. 19:9; 20:18–19); in the wilderness, God spoke from a fire at night and a cloud during the day (Exod. 13:21; Num. 9:15–19; Ps. 99:7); and during the showdown with Ahab and Jezebel, God acted by fire (1 Kgs 18:24). Yet, for Elijah, God used none of these phenomena to reveal himself.

At the cave, God placed the spotlight on his true nature. If the traditional marks of a theophany express God's *power*, his voice expresses his *personhood*. This God was known by a voice that was personal, intimate and identifiable. Tangible expressions of power may be a quality of God's persona, but they are not the means by which he chooses to be known. Instead, God is distinguished by his personhood. Yahweh the Creator – the God of the Bible – speaks back.

We see the theme of a talking God threading in and out of every story in the Bible. From the very beginning, God reveals himself by interpersonal communication. It has been estimated that one third of the Hebrew Scriptures is taken up with God-conversations.[2] The phrase 'God said' and its variations appear up to 3,800 times in the Old Testament alone! Time and time again, Yahweh's activity is expressed by a voice. It is this quality that is contrasted with the rest of the ancient pantheon. The Bible writers even mock the deficiency of the other gods: they 'have mouths, but cannot speak'; 'eyes, but cannot see'; they have 'ears, but cannot hear' (Ps. 115:5–7). They are like 'a scarecrow in a cucumber field' because they cannot talk (Jer. 10:5). So distinctive was the communicative nature of Israel's God that the Deuteronomist asks in wonderment: 'Has anything so great as this ever happened, or has anything like it ever been heard of? Has any other people heard the voice of God speaking out of fire, as you have, and lived?' (Deut. 4:32b–33).

The knowable God

The idea of a God who speaks back changes the way we relate to God. Language is the means by which we can be known. It is the vehicle by which relationship is possible. This is one of the reasons we enjoy watching our children grow older. As our toddlers learn to express themselves beyond cooing and crying, we get to know who they really are. We discover their thoughts and personalities and how they really do take after Grandpa Bill. We get to know them personally.

As God is omniscient, we take it for granted that God *knows* us. But the faculty of speech makes him *knowable* to us. When we hear his voice, we learn of his thoughts. We begin to understand what motivates him. At Mount Carmel, Elijah could only guess at what God was thinking. The display of fire revealed *what* God was doing, but not *why* he was doing it. But when Yahweh *spoke* at Mount Horeb, Elijah was able to know the wisdom of the Almighty in the midst of his desperation. And once he knew Yahweh's thoughts, he could cooperate with them.

This means that, as in any relationship, the way to know Yahweh personally is to hear his voice. God's words are an expression of his being. As the saying goes: 'A person is only as good as their word.' When we hear God's voice, we understand his character.

The connection between hearing God's voice and knowing him personally goes well beyond Elijah's story. It is the basis for all God's activity in biblical history. We see it at the beginning, when the opening scene sets the stage for God's ideal with Adam and Eve (Gen. 3:8). This unfettered communication continues in the lives of the patriarchs as God speaks to reveal his thoughts for national and global blessing. The relationship between God and Abraham, Isaac, Jacob and Joseph is all predicated on two-way conversation (e.g. Gen. 18; 28:10–22; 37:5–11).

This pattern continues with the establishment of Israel. With each defining moment in the nation's history, God's voice is paramount. At the exodus, Moses' leadership and friendship was based on 'face to face' conversation (Exod. 33:11; Num. 12:6). When the original terms of the covenant were drawn up, it involved hearing God's words and cooperating with them. Then, before crossing into the promised land, the people were reminded that listening to God would enable them to know God's presence (e.g. Josh. 3:9–10). Even the wilderness wanderings became meaningful because of their intent to help Israel hear and obey God's voice (Deut. 8:2–3). It was because God spoke into the future that the people could know who he was (Isa. 43:9–10).

The corollary was also true. If the Israelites *didn't* attend to the divine voice, they couldn't know God personally. This was the tragedy of the wilderness. The people hardened their hearts and didn't listen to God, and as a consequence didn't know his ways (Heb. 3:7–10,15; 4:7). We see it again in the time leading up to the monarchy, when

Israel experienced God's silence; as a result, young Samuel is described as 'not knowing God' (see 1 Sam. 3:7). Similarly, pre-exilic Israel did not 'know' God because they did not anticipate a response to their questions (Jer. 2:6–8).

When we move forward in history, we see the truth of a knowable God most completely in the person of Jesus. When we've seen Jesus, we've seen the Father (John 14:9). John's gospel describes Jesus as the living Word of God (John 1:1). The manifestation of God's word in the 'flesh' (John 1:14) demonstrates God's relatability. When Jesus spent time with his disciples, children, lepers, strangers, and even his enemies, he showed us the motivation of the Creator. At the heart of the Christian God is *personal relationship*. It is in knowing God that we experience fullness of life (John 17:3).

God's call has always remained the same. 'Listen to my voice!' This was at the heart of all God's dealings with Ancient Israel and it remains his heart for all creation. As it was in Israel's day, so it is in ours: God's heart is that *everyone* – 'from the least of them to the greatest' – would know him because they had heard his words for themselves (Jer. 31:34). By his very nature, God is a communicator. His heart to be heard reflects his desire to be known.

Today this personal relationship is accessible to us by the Holy Spirit. When we choose to follow Jesus, we receive the Spirit and the ability to hear God's voice for ourselves (Acts 2:16–17). Like Elijah, we do not need to guess at our circumstances to know what God is thinking. We do not need to appease God by our rituals and sacrifices. Instead, we are invited into a personal knowledge of God that grows through listening and attending to his voice. We can *know* the Creator!

Promotion to partnership

There is more to our relationship with God than knowing him. Knowing God becomes the basis for *partnership*. This ensures that the emphasis is never about *doing* as much as it is about *being*. Our Spirit-led activities find their basis in the context of genuine relationship. We do God's work because we know him, not the other way round.

Some people are only in your life to get a job done: the technician who comes to fix your Wi-Fi; the taxi driver who takes you to the airport; the supermarket attendant who tallies your groceries at the checkout. They perform their function and you pay their fee. There is no need for further conversation because the 'relationship' is based on a task. It is shallow and transactional. You're not likely to see them again.

When we talk of our relationship with God, we sometimes conceive it in transactional terms. Since God has paved our way to salvation, we respond by doing things for him. We obey the commandments, undertake good works, fulfil the Great Commission. But this is not the type of relationship envisaged by God. Our works of service are always understood to be a *product* of genuine relationship. It begins with knowing God personally. This takes us beyond the transactional.

Jesus himself distinguished between these two types of relationship. He likened the first to the relationship between a master and a servant. The master gives the instructions. The servant fulfils them. Tick. Job done. The second type is envisaged as a friendship. This relationship is defined by the things God *tells* us: 'I have called you friends, for everything that I learned from my Father I have made known to you' (John 15:15). Unlike the servant, the friend knows what he is doing. The difference is the level of intimacy. God not only shares *what* he is doing, but *why* he is doing it. God is not interested in transactional relationships. His heart is to share his thoughts with us (Jer. 33:3). It is this type of intimacy that paves the way for true partnership. When we hear his voice, we get to know him. When we get to know him, we're invited to partner with his plans. Personal relationship becomes the context for service.

It all starts with God's words. As the prophet Amos affirmed: 'the Sovereign Lord does nothing without revealing his plan to his servants the prophets' (Amos 3:7). God speaks to those who are listening. We hear his words and make a choice. Either we cooperate with them and witness their miraculous outworking, or we disobey them and they are passed on to someone else. God-speech is the basis for all

God's working on earth. His words are the vehicle of interaction with humanity, transmitting his will, authority and power.

Biblical history records this process time and time again. It begins at creation. Where other creation accounts have the gods jostling for power, Yahweh merely speaks. When he does, the chaos obeys. Light appears. Water is divided from land. Life teems on earth. The word of the Lord calls creation into being and orders it according to his nature.

From there, God speaks to call Adam and Eve into partnership by giving them responsibility to steward the earth (Gen. 1:26–28). While sin breaks their relationship with him, it doesn't change the process. God speaks to bring the solution in the form of a nation that carries his words into the future (Gen. 12:1–3; 15). The pattern remains as God speaks to the judges, kings and prophets. Then, when Jesus comes, the Old Covenant pattern continues: Jesus does nothing without first hearing from the Father (John 5:19). It is then in the light of Christ's revelation that we become co-workers (1 Cor. 3:9; 2 Cor. 6:1), partnering with the Spirit in Christ's mission.

Whenever God speaks, God's people are faced with a choice. Will they opt to partner with God to bring his plans to earth, or will they refuse? When they do, God's plan succeeds. When they don't, the plan fails. The repeated calls of the prophets remain: 'Hear and obey . . . hear and obey . . .' No sacrifice or offering is a substitute for this process (see 1 Sam. 15:22; Jer. 7:21–23).

God's plan B

God's offer of intimacy and partnership is not always easy to accept. I can still remember the sense of trepidation I felt when I first prayed for God to speak to me. I had been excited at first. Raised in a church that believed God had stopped speaking with the completion of the canon, hearing God's voice for myself was a wonderfully new and fantastical idea. I wondered how the God I had read about in the lives of Abraham, Moses and Paul might reveal himself in mine. But I also feared what God might say. What if he sent me to a place I didn't want to go? Or asked me to marry someone I didn't find attractive?!

Oddly, humanity has always feared direct communication with God. Even though hearing God's words is the way to know and partner with him, there is something terribly intimidating about experiencing them for yourself. Our fears are not totally unfounded. 'Getting to know' the supreme deity has profound repercussions on our lives.

Reticence towards hearing God directly has been around since the time of Moses. Back then, God had been speaking with Moses as a 'friend', but his intention was to open up the relationship to the entire nation. The book of Exodus records the sad outcome. God offered to speak directly to the people, but they rejected his offer. They insisted on staying 'at a distance', telling Moses: 'Speak to us yourself and we will listen. But do not let God speak to us or we will die' (Exod. 20:18–19).

It's a tragic scene. Fear drove a wedge between God and his people and prevented them from experiencing friendship with him. Israel's rejection ultimately led to God's 'Plan B'. Instead of receiving God's communiqués directly, Moses became an intermediary. Now God's people could only hear from God *through him*. This became the norm for all communication. Moses heard from God and told 'the people what the LORD had said' (Num. 11:24).

The events at Sinai marked the beginnings of the prophets' vocation under the Old Covenant. After Moses, others followed. Figures like Samuel, Jeremiah and Amos all became God's 'mouthpieces' in the tradition of Moses. Scripture tells us that God put his words 'in their mouths' (see Jer.1:5,9) and they spoke them forth or 'prophesied' them to the people.

This sad concession had significant ramifications for the people of God. It meant that under the Old Covenant, the main way – if not the *only* way – to hear from God was via a prophet. This made for a second-hand relationship with God. It meant that the vast majority of Israel were unable to know God for themselves because they couldn't hear him directly and personally. As the psalmist later reflects, Moses knew God's ways, but the people had only seen God's deeds (Ps. 103:7). Like those in the surrounding nations, the Israelites could only guess at God's thoughts. They could not truly know him.

This is why Israel's prophets looked forward to the New Covenant with such anticipation. They were the ones who had experienced the benefit of direct access to God's voice first hand. Moses himself had seen a glimpse in the early days of the nation's founding, when the Spirit was poured out on the seventy elders and they began to prophesy. You can almost hear the frustration in his voice when he said: 'I wish that all the LORD's people were prophets and that the LORD would put his Spirit on them!' (Num. 11:29).

After Moses, there were other prophets who caught the same vision. In the sixth century BC, Jeremiah prophesied a time when God's words would be written directly on people's hearts. No longer would they need an intermediary to 'say to one another, "Know the Lord," because they will all know me' (Jer. 31:34). Likewise, the prophet Joel prophesied the day when the Spirit would come and they could all hear from God in the same way as he did (Joel 2:28–29). Isaiah too declared that one day God's words would for ever be in the mouths of his people. This powerful truth would apply to every generation and would never end (Isa. 59:21).

An invitation to higher ways

Today the prophecies of Moses, Jeremiah, Joel and Isaiah have all been fulfilled. Jesus died to remove the barrier of sin in the human–divine relationship and then sent his Spirit so that we could all hear God for ourselves. The invitation to access the divine voice remains. We can stay at a distance or we can draw near. We can choose to rely on others for a second-hand understanding, witness the wind, fire and earthquakes from afar, or come close enough to hear the still small voice. We can be content with the mystery or we can press in for understanding.

It is true that the invitation to know God for ourselves is difficult to accept. After all, God is the Creator, the one who is above all things. In the words of Isaiah, 'As the heavens are higher than the earth, so are my ways higher than your ways and my thoughts than your thoughts' (Isa. 55:9). We are aware of the grandness of heaven's wisdom, the complexity of the world around us and our minuscule place in relation to it. Isaiah's oracle becomes a source of comfort in times when we cannot comprehend events in the world around us.

Yet, if you look more closely at the passage, you'll see that we are missing the point. Like one of those mirrors at the circus, we've been reading Isaiah's oracle through a distorted lens. His words are not a concession to the *limits* of human knowledge, but an invitation to the *expanses* of divine knowledge. The oracle had been given to Israel to explain God's perspective on the confusing state of the world around them. They had not understood that God's heart was for all nations, not just their own. So he spoke to call them out of their human perspective and into his. In effect, God had been saying, 'Yes! My ways *are* higher than your ways. But I want you to *know them*!' (see Isa. 55:2–3).

It's an extraordinary invitation. God calls us into the heavenly boardroom in order to share the insights of the world beyond ours. But this is not just about getting our questions answered or having our problems solved. God has a greater motivation in mind. He wants us to know not only *what* he is doing but also *why* he is doing it. We are invited to know his *ways*.

Knowing the 'why' behind an action puts us at a distinct advantage. When we know the thinking behind an act, we gain motivation to serve the bigger picture. We can anticipate how to respond in circumstances that are similar. This takes us beyond mere functionality. As we understand what is happening behind the scenes, we gain access to higher levels of thinking. We get to know the Person as well as the mission.

***

This is the dynamic God offers his people. It is the difference between a master–servant relationship that is largely transactional and a friendship that invites secrets to be shared. God's plan is for us to know the master's business (John 15:15). His desire for us is to partner with him in the context of personal relationship.

Here, we face a choice. Like the Israelites of history, we can opt to remain at a distance. We can piggyback on the relationship of others and be content with a relationship that only sees God's deeds from afar. And, like the Chimu, we can resort to guessing at the thoughts of God by trying to read the circumstances and offering our good works to change them.

Or we can draw near and listen for God's voice. His thoughts *are* above our thoughts. His ways *are* above our ways. That is why God offers us the Spirit. God wants us to *know* his ways (1 Cor. 2:9–10). This doesn't mean we will always know the 'why' for every situation, but the mystery should drive us into a deeper knowledge of God. His ways can be known. As Paul prayed, may we know the mysteries of God (Col. 2:2–3)! The call to God's people continues today as it did for the ancients: 'Listen, listen to me, and eat what is good, and you will delight in the richest of fare. Give ear and come to me; listen, that you may live' (Isa. 55:2–3).

6

The Covenantal Upgrade

A domestic call

Brian cuts the figure of the typical surfer guy. With his bleached blond hair, sun-kissed skin and stocky frame, it always looks as if he's just emerged from the waves. Brian made a decision to follow Jesus as a young man and since then has served God wholeheartedly, often volunteering at his church in the coastal town of Kaikoura in New Zealand. He had even been offered the senior pastor position at one point, but felt neither skilled nor qualified to take it on.

One morning, Brian was going about his normal routine when the Holy Spirit spoke to him: 'Make the bed.'

Brian was taken aback: 'But why?'

Brian's wife Lisa had always made the bed. She did a superb job of it too. It was an elaborate operation involving three layers of pillows and the careful placement of several cushions. Why would God ask him to make the bed when his wife was doing it so well?

Brian's protestations went unheard in spite of his angst. Eventually, he went to his wife and explained that he would like to take on the job of making the bed. Would she show him how? Lisa smiled as she detailed the process. First the sheets and duvet must be straightened so there were no creases. Then the pillows had to be propped up at the right angle so that they wouldn't topple over. Next came the sham cushions followed by the signature cushion – all positioned so that the labels didn't show. Finally, the throw rug was to be laid at the base so that it covered one third of the surface area – not too little so that it slid off the end, but not too much so it messed with the proportions.

Brian's early attempts were decidedly pathetic, but they improved as the days wore on. After a month or so, Brian's bed-making was as his good as his wife's.

A year later, God spoke again. The senior pastor was retiring and Brian was asked if he would take the position. 'Now you are qualified,' God said.

Brian was appointed leader of his church at the age of 51. Since then, the church has flourished and a host of people have been touched by Jesus. The dramatic testimonies of former drug addicts, gang members and rebels have become the talk of the town. Personally, Brian is thriving. He is still making the bed.

Under the Old Covenant, God spoke to the prophets about matters of global blessing, rituals for worship, and the rise and fall of nations. How could it be that now, God was speaking about making a bed?

Brian's story reveals something of the dynamics of New Covenant God-speech. The coming of Jesus signalled a definitive shift. Not only could everyone now hear from God without the mediation of a prophet, but the *function* of God-conversations in the contemporary church became clearer in the light of Jesus' ministry. Jesus' advent not only addressed the problem of sin; it also introduced an upgrade in the 'hearing God' experience. In this chapter, we look at the nature of this upgrade and why Brian's experience makes perfect sense in the light of it.

God's plan A

When you put yourself in the position of the disciples, it's difficult to imagine that anything could be better than having face-to-face time with Jesus. Three years of personal tutelage. Daily object lessons and one-on-one mentoring. Open access to divine wisdom on contentious issues and current affairs. It would have been easy for the disciples to hear God's voice. As God's word in the flesh (John 1:1,14), everything Jesus said was the direct word of God. The disciples could talk to Jesus about God's kingdom as they were walking down the streets of Jerusalem. They could ask him questions about their personal lives over meals of bread and olives. They could listen to him preach about salvation on the temple steps. Hearing from God was straightforward with Jesus in their midst.

So, we can only imagine the disciples' horror when Jesus announced he was leaving. 'But, Lord, how are we going to hear from you? How will we know what to do?'

It was a legitimate concern. Jesus was about to commission his disciples to take the good news into the whole world. The disciples' job was to lead a movement that would have worldwide repercussions. But they had never seen a church before. They didn't know how to take the gospel into new nations and cultures. They barely understood what Jesus had already said.

Of course, Jesus knew this. He knew his disciples would have questions after he left. He also knew they couldn't handle all his answers at once (John 16:12–13). So he began to outline the details of the new arrangement – one that had been promised long before. Instead of hearing God's words directly from him or from a prophet, they would hear them from the *Spirit*. God's words would no longer be confined to a physical person in a geographical location. The Spirit would remain with the disciples so they could receive God's communication whenever and wherever they went. Just as Jesus had led them into truth while he was on earth, now the Spirit would guide them 'into all the truth' after he left (John 16:13).

After announcing the imminence of the New Covenant, Jesus went on to complete his earthly mission. By his death and resurrection, he conquered the power of sin and evil, and opened up the way to relationship with the Father. Then, a week after his ascension, the long-awaited moment arrived.

It was among a small crowd of Jews in Jerusalem on the Day of Pentecost that the words of Jesus and the prophets were finally fulfilled. Many miraculous phenomena took place as the Spirit was poured out that day, but the pinnacle of them all was the gift of direct revelation: 'this is what was spoken by the prophet Joel . . . "Your sons and daughters will prophesy, your young men will see visions, your old men will dream dreams'" (Acts 2:16–17). The words of Peter's sermon proclaimed the essence of the New Covenant – the ability to hear God's voice. *Everyone* could now hear from God for themselves. Just as the prophets received the messages of God in 'dreams' and 'visions' and spoke them forth as prophecy (Num. 12:6), now 'sons and daughters', 'young and old', could do the same. No longer was a prophet needed to hear from God. All those who chose to follow Jesus could experience relationship with God *first hand* (Jer. 31:33–34). This was the moment everyone had been waiting for. Moses' long-awaited wish. The longings of Jeremiah, Joel and Isaiah. The promise had finally come to pass.

It is no coincidence that this moment took place during the Feast of Pentecost. As the second of the three great feasts in the Jewish calendar (along with Passover and Tabernacles), this day was widely believed to commemorate the giving of God's words to Moses at Mount Sinai hundreds of years before. We even have the familiar theophanic signs of wind and fire to remind us that Pentecost was God's answer to Sinai (Acts 2:1–4). This was God's return to Plan A. Where once the word had been delivered via another person, now it was delivered directly to everyone. Where once it had been received via a tablet of stone, now it was received by the heart (Exod. 31:18; Ezek. 36:26).

In the weeks that followed, we see the outworking of this new arrangement in the activity of the early church. The Spirit spoke to the disciples wherever they went. As promised, they were reminded of the truths Jesus had taught them and they heard about what was 'yet to come' (John 16:13). Thus, the Spirit spoke to bring salvation and healing in Jesus' name (Acts 9; 1 Cor. 14:25) and to give instructions about the church and what it should look like (Acts 10). The Spirit spoke to lead mission into new areas such as Cyprus (Acts 13:2) and Macedonia (Acts 16:9) and to new people-groups such as the Ethiopians (Acts 8:26–40). The Spirit spoke about personal situations to bring people into closer relationship with God (2 Cor. 12:1–10) and to show them how to respond to new challenges (Revelation). Each time, the message of Jesus was applied by the Spirit to new places and situations. Each time, it was consistent with what Jesus had already said. Whenever the Spirit spoke, it furthered the ministry and mission of Jesus.

Of course, the beauty of the New Covenant is that the Spirit's voice is not limited to the first-century church. The same Spirit who spoke to the early disciples is now speaking to us. As Peter proclaimed, access to divine revelation was not just for those gathered in Jerusalem. The Spirit who was 'on their lips' (see Isa. 59:21) would be on the lips of their children and on all the generations to come (Acts 2:39). Today, the promise applies to us. We can all hear the continuing voice of Jesus. We stand in the tradition of Moses, Jeremiah, Isaiah, Peter, Philip, James and John. Like them, we can know God for ourselves and partner with his plans. To know God is to hear the voice of the Spirit. It's the essence of being a New Covenant Christian.

A covenantal upgrade

When I first heard about the promise of the New Covenant, I found it difficult to imagine that I could hear God's voice in the same way as the biblical greats. As a child in Sunday school, the heroes of faith – particularly those in the Old Testament – seemed larger than life: Noah, who heard from God about building a boat a hundred years before a flood; Joshua, who heard from God and marched around a city to see its walls fall; Moses, who heard from God and parted a Red Sea. When I read their stories, they rolled off the tongue so smoothly. It seemed easy for them. They heard from God, they acted on it, and miracles happened.

Yet the events of Pentecost also show us that the covenant under which the Old Testament greats operated was horribly deficient. As God's Plan B, it was inefficient and substandard. Jesus came to usher in a new era. He announced that the new schema would be superior to the old (John 16:7). It was even preferable to spending face-time with Jesus! The biblical characters under both covenants reiterate this truth (e.g. 2 Cor. 3:7–18; Heb. 8:6–11). Our covenant is a definitive upgrade.

There are two important ways the New Covenant is an improvement on the Old. The first has to do with the impact God's voice has on our lives. The second has to do with our ability to discern it.

God with us

Rowena was an actor who was struggling to find her place in the entertainment industry. She loved acting, but working as a Christian in the arts was difficult. There were so many challenging decisions: which roles to take and which to refuse; what was an appropriate compromise and what wasn't. Questions about where to draw the boundaries came with each new script. How was she to navigate the nudity clauses in the contracts and the roles that seemed to revel in evil? What's more, her fellow workers seemed unreceptive to her faith and there were very few Christians around. She wondered if she could handle the isolation from her faith community. Her questions eventually led her to reconsider her career. Should she continue acting?

Then Rowena had a vision. She saw herself standing on the edge of a high cliff, gazing out at the sea. The night was dark, but lit by a full moon. She watched as the light slowly moved over the surface of the water and began to dip below the horizon. Suddenly, the ocean began to shift. Giant waves of water rolled back to expose the ocean floor. There she saw countless numbers of fish carcasses.

When Rowena came to, she was filled with a deep sense of conviction: 'These are all the fish that nobody went to catch.'

Rowena knew then that the entertainment industry *was* the place God was calling her to. Her love of acting was now imbued with divine purpose. Yes, it could be dark, but there her light could shine. She was being sent where others couldn't go. Hearing the voice of the Spirit gave her a sense of calling. This was God's mission for her life.

Rowena's dream and others like it reveal the first benefit of the covenantal upgrade – the impact of God's voice *with* us. The Holy Spirit comes as the 'Paraclete' (see John 14:16) – one who 'comes alongside' and accompanies us wherever we go. That means the Spirit can speak to every individual in every situation to lead them into God's purpose.

The content of our God-conversations is best understood using the two categories Jesus spoke of with his disciples. As we've seen, the Spirit speaks first to *remind us* of the truths Jesus has already spoken (John 14:26). These truths are accessible to us today via the pages of Scripture. The Spirit speaks to bring them to life in our hearts; we learn about the truths of salvation, the nature of God's kingdom and the promise of abundant life for all those who follow. These gospel truths represent the climax of the salvation story and lay the groundwork for our faith.

But, as Jesus said to his disciples, there was much more to be said (John 16:12). Like us, the disciples were not able to hear everything at once. That role falls to the Spirit, who speaks about the second category of our God conversations: 'what is *yet to come*' (John 16:13). The Spirit speaks to continue Jesus' ministry by applying the gospel to our personal and particular situations.

In the Scriptures, we see how the Spirit spoke to continue Jesus' mission in places like Antioch, Philippi and Corinth. Today the Spirit continues to speak about how to live out Jesus' message on a drought-stricken farm, a surfing Kiwi town and an Australian city. This is where we see *how* the New Covenant is an improvement on the Old. For Rowena, the words of Jesus about becoming fishers of people (Matt. 4:19) were applied by the Spirit to the entertainment industry. For Brian, the truth of Jesus was applied to his work in Kaikoura. The Spirit speaks wherever we go.

Of course, our starting point is always Jesus' life and teachings. We learn from what he said and did, while recognising that Jesus remains clothed in first-century garb, speaking in Jewish idioms and addressing first-century issues. The benefit of the Spirit's presence under the New Covenant is that the Spirit takes those first-century realities and brings them into our time. As the Paraclete, the Spirit knows the distinctives of our world. Therefore, he is able to take the foundational truths of Jesus and speak them afresh into twenty-first-century contexts.

This also means that the Spirit provides us with strategies for how to deal with the challenges of our day in never-before-thought-of ways. Unlike the testimony of Jesus, who remains locked into the first-century Greco-Roman world, the Spirit is able to apply the wisdom of Jesus to radically different contexts. Furthermore, because the Spirit knows us individually, he is able to provide tailor-made wisdom to *every person*. In Rowena's case, the Spirit was able to assess her ability to withstand the pressure of the entertainment industry and counsel her accordingly. But Rowena's story is not everyone's story. For someone else, the Spirit may speak about deferring their acting career because the pressure would overwhelm them. The beauty of 'God with us' is that the Spirit is able to apply the wisdom of Jesus to every situation.

Ultimately, the incarnation of Jesus enables us to place our contemporary Spirit-messages into their proper context. We can now clearly anticipate what the Spirit says and why the Spirit says it. 'Hearing God' experiences will always further the ministry and mission of Jesus in our lives. They will be *Christocentric* in their content and function and always point back to the foundations of our faith – the life, death and resurrection of Jesus.

A Jesus-shaped template for discernment

There's a second reason why the New Covenant is superior to the Old. The coming of the Spirit on all people means that we can *discern* God's voice more clearly than the Old Covenant prophets.

Discernment under the New Covenant has two advantages. To begin with, universal access to the Spirit means that we can now test our experiences in conjunction with others. Under the Old Covenant, the prophets are described as people with a lone 'voice', calling 'in the wilderness' (Isa. 40:3; John 1:23). Alone and isolated and dressed in their hessian garb, they often seemed disconnected from the rest of the world. Because there were so few of them, there were limited ways of checking their experiences. You had to put a lot more trust in the prophet back then because only they had access to God's voice, making the set-up open to subjectivity and abuse. Today the outpouring of the Spirit on everyone provides the safety of multiple witnesses. More than one person can confirm a revelation. (We explore this feature of the New Covenant in detail in Chapter 12).

The second reason for our improved discernment ability under the New Covenant is perhaps even more pronounced. We can hear the Spirit more clearly because we have the full revelation of God's nature in Jesus.

The full significance of this can be seen in one of our most famous God-talking stories – God's call to Abraham to sacrifice his son (Gen. 22:1–19). The Scriptures tell us that Abraham didn't question God's command. He got up early the next morning, saddled his donkey and began the long trek up Mount Moriah with his son. Today, when we look back on the story, we laud Abraham's obedience, but we should also realise it wasn't totally unexpected. Yahweh's command was consistent with the worship rites of all the Ancient Near Eastern gods of his day. Contemporaries like Molech and Baal freely demanded child sacrifice as an act of worship. Abraham had no way of knowing that his God was any different.

Of course, as time wore on, Abraham got to know more of God's nature. When God interrupted the sacrifice at the altar, his ways became clearer to Abraham. While Yahweh has always preferred obedience over sacrifice (1 Sam. 15:22), at the time Abraham could not have known that. Then, as time went on, God's people were able to see more of what Yahweh was like. They learned that child sacrifice was not only *unnecessary* for Yahweh – it was *detestable* (e.g. Deut. 18:10). They began to understand that the shedding of children's blood (and animals) was *never* consistent with God's nature (Ps. 40:6; Jer. 7:22–23; Hos. 6:6) but was only a concession to their limited perspective. With each revelation came more understanding. The lens through which the people viewed God slowly shifted into focus.

Then, when Jesus came, the image crystallised into perfect clarity. The Scriptures tell us that Jesus is the exact 'image of the invisible God' (Col. 1:15). Because of the incarnation, we know precisely what God is like. Jesus' three-year ministry gives us a tangible demonstration of God's true nature. The way he touched the leper, multiplied the bread and set the sinner free – all communicate God's personhood in vivid detail. Today we know God's character more fully than the Old Covenant prophets. They saw a shadow. We see in light

(Col. 2:17; Heb. 10:1). They saw a black-and-white outline; we see in multicolour detail.

The knowledge of God's nature makes it far easier for the church to recognise the voice of the Spirit. Under the New Covenant we have a Jesus-shaped template by which to discern our experiences. Since the Spirit is the continuing voice of Jesus, we can know with clarity the kinds of things the Spirit would say and why he says them.

***

When we return to Brian's story, it's now possible to see why God spoke to a middle-aged man about making his bed. A Christocentric perspective of Spirit revelation gives us the framework to understand his experience. Would Brian submit to God's call in the mundane things of life – where no one else could see? Would he develop a heart to serve others? The Spirit spoke to continue the ministry of Jesus in Brian's life. Knowing his strengths and weaknesses as well as the needs of the church in Kaikoura, the Spirit tailored the message to bring Brian's life into alignment with God's greater purpose.

This is the power and beauty of the New Covenant. Today, the Spirit speaks as the continuing voice of Jesus. The same Jesus who walked the earth two millennia ago is ministering to people today via his Spirit (John 16:7). He is still drawing, revealing, healing and releasing us with words that are creative and life-giving (John 6:63). The words he speaks are like bread to our bodies and food to our souls: Jesus said we *couldn't* live without them (Matt. 4:4). Hearing God's voice is not a spiritual discipline or a special gift; it is the essential staple of all our lives. It is the mark of a true follower of Jesus.

The template and model for all contemporary God-conversations begins and ends with the person and teachings of Christ. When we think about what the Spirit says and why it's said, our starting point must always be Jesus. As the ultimate standard and fullness of revelation, his life and teachings set the foundation for everything the Spirit continues to say.

7

How to Hear the Voice of God

Waiting in the tree

Our story of farmer Jarrod didn't begin with his dream of the canola field. It began a week earlier when, desperate for a breakthrough, he took the day off to hear from God.

It had been a blistering hot morning and Jarrod took shelter in one of the giant trees in the back paddock. Gazing over the withering fields, he poured out his heart to God: 'Speak to me; I need to hear from you.' Then he waited. And prayed. And waited again. The shadows grew longer as the sun sank in the sky. Still Jarrod refused to give up: 'I'm not getting out of this tree until you talk to me.' But the day wore on with no word from God. Eventually it got dark and Jarrod was hungry. He climbed down from the tree and returned to his house, weary and despondent.

A week later, Jarrod joined a group of friends at a Christian business conference in a nearby town. During the worship time, he experienced a vision. He saw himself high above his farm, as if he was looking through the lens of a drone. Below him, he could see the paddocks, the dusty soil and his struggling cattle. Then, he saw himself perched in the boughs of his prayer tree, crying out to God. In that moment, he knew God had heard his prayer. He knew God had been there with him in the tree. The dream of the canola field followed a few nights later.

How do we hear God's voice? It would be easy if there was some sort of formula: 'Follow these three steps; recite this prayer; spend an hour in meditation each day.' But hearing God's voice doesn't work like that. There is no set of steps to take, no well-worn procedure. The experience of hearing God occurs in the context of relationship, and every relationship is different. What works for one person does not necessarily work for another.

However, there are *conditions* that help to facilitate hearing from the Spirit. Jarrod's story gives us a hint of what they are. In this chapter, we look at how to hear God's voice. We discuss the interplay of personality, gender and gifting, and how, like Jarrod, we can position ourselves to hear from God more clearly.

The non-discriminatory Spirit

Have you ever noticed that some people in church seem to pick up on what God is saying more easily than others? In my experience, it always seems to be the older women, who spend a good deal of time on their knees. Or there are the mystical types who have the spiritual senses of a well-trained sniffer dog and seem able to tune in to the atmosphere with the flick of a switch. It appears that some people are better disposed to mystical experiences than others.

And they probably are. Psychological research suggests that certain personalities are better suited to hearing God's voice. 'Prayer skills' may even be *learned*. In 2012, American psychological anthropologist Tanya Luhrmann published the findings of a year-long ethnographic study of a Charismatic church in California. Her goal was to carefully examine the phenomenon of hearing God's voice. Luhrmann tells of one aspect of the study, where she tested the sensory skills of a group before and after a prayer training course. The course was based on the Ignatian prayer exercises and included a form of contemplation that involves focusing on mental imagery in prayer. A typical exercise takes you into a gospel scene. You picture yourself as Zacchaeus in the tree, or Mary at the foot of the cross. Then you answer a series of questions that develop your imaging faculties: 'What do you see? What do you hear? What do you feel, taste and smell?'

The results of the study were telling. After the course, participants reported better focus and sharper imagery, as well as more 'unusual' prayer experiences. As Luhrmann describes it, their minds had 'learned to sense a presence for which there was no ordinary sensory evidence'.[1] These skills of 'inner-sense cultivation' involve the development of mental muscles and the ability to pay attention to what lies on the boundary between thought and perception: 'between what is attributed to the mind – internal, self-generated, private and hidden from view – and what exists in the world'.[2]

Luhrmann also employed a psychological tool to measure how nature, colour and music are experienced by different people. She concluded that this trait of 'absorption' is central to spirituality and that there was a correlation between the levels of absorption and how God was experienced.[3] Her work suggests that the ability to 'hear' God's voice is related to our psychological make-up and inner sensory skills.

Recent studies in the field of neurology provide further support for the connection between 'hearing God' experiences and biology. After observing a particular area in the brain that registers high electrical activity during religious or spiritual experience, American neuropsychologist Michael Persinger and neurologist V.S. Ramachandran concluded that our brains have a built-in spiritual centre, which they termed the 'God spot'.[4] Their studies showed that people with artistic and creative abilities have a greater propensity for spiritual experiences.[5] They are also quick to explain that their observations neither prove nor disprove the existence of God or whether humanity can communicate with him. What is clear is that the differences in our make-up do contribute to the intensity and frequency of spiritual experiences.

The ability to hear God's voice may also be influenced by our gender. In general, women seem to find it easier to hear from God than men. In the Catholic tradition, Hvidt notes that the majority of key prophetic figures in history have been female.[6] In my own ministry, women have tended to be both more interested in hearing God's voice and more likely to experience it. Perhaps this is a product of their relational bent and penchant for language. Even the biblical testimony seems to hint at this, with a fascinating story about Samuel's parents, Manoah and his wife, at the time of the judges. While Manoah's wife heard the voice of God with ease, her husband constantly struggled (Judg. 13:1–25).

At one level, the ability to hear God's voice appears to favour certain biological traits and personalities. No doubt such people could be described as 'gifted', using the apostle Paul's terminology. But does that mean that some of us miss out?

Ironically, if I were measured on Luhrmann's absorption scale, I would probably rate relatively low. I am not the person who stands on a platform prophesying over the crowd or intuitively picking up on the spiritual atmosphere. I am a thinker – the analytical type, sceptical by nature and always in my head. This is part of the reason why, in the early years of my ministry, I struggled with my call. My cerebral, 'left-brained' personality seemed an awkward mismatch for a ministry centred on revelatory experiences! Of course, I am not alone in this. Whenever I tell my story to an academic audience, most of them nod enthusiastically. It is a relief to know there is nothing wrong with us.

At the same time, my testimony is one of consistently hearing from God in clear, definitive ways. We know that the Spirit of Pentecost *is not discriminatory*. The ability to hear from God directly has been given to us *all*, irrespective of age, gender or personality. God is able to cater to the limitations of our psychological make-up. The Spirit's communicative ability always transcends our human ability.

So we return to our original question: if not skill or gifting, personality or gender, what is the key to hearing God's voice?

The eyes of the heart

While the Scriptures do not provide us with specific answers to our question, we do know that hearing God often occurs in an atmosphere of prayer and worship. Many of the incidences of God-speech in the early church began in this way. For example, the early disciples were assembled in Jerusalem waiting together on God when the Spirit fell (Acts 2:1); Peter was on his rooftop praying when he experienced the vision of the unclean food (Acts 10:9); and the Antiochian church leaders were praying and fasting when they heard God speak about commissioning Paul and Barnabas (Acts 13:2). But there were also times in Scripture when the Spirit seemed to interrupt people while they were actively doing something else (Acts 8:26). At times, the Spirit spoke when people were at their least attentive – while they were asleep (Acts 12:6–7; 27:23)!

In my early attempts to hear from God, I would pack up my Bible, journal and picnic blanket and head to the hills near my home. The day often ended with a dozy nap in the sun and not much else. A week would pass, and then suddenly the Spirit would speak while I was brushing my teeth. This trend has continued for the rest of my life. I don't usually have my most profound moments of revelation when I'm seated in prayer on my sofa. Mostly, they have occurred when I've been stuck in traffic, jogging on a trail or standing in the shower – when my thoughts have been a million miles away.

When we speak about how to hear God's voice, we do not start with a well-designed formula or a set of skills. The answer has more to do with what is happening internally rather than what we are doing externally. Hearing from God begins with the *position of the heart*. We turn our hearts to *actively* seek God, believing in faith that he will speak to us. Jarrod's story illustrates this posture. His simple act of waiting in the tree provided the conditions to hear from the Spirit. The prayer, 'Speak to me', became the entry point because it was an expression of faith. Jarrod's spiritual ears were tuned in, and this alerted God to a heart that was ready to receive.

We may ask ourselves then: why didn't God speak while Jarrod was waiting in the tree? It was another week before God spoke to Jarrod at a conference and then another few days before inspiring the dream. Jarrod's testimony reminds us that it is always God's prerogative to *speak* and our prerogative to *listen*. God speaks to us when he wants to – we do not *make* him speak by our own efforts. Instead, we position our hearts to hear and, in faith, listen for his voice. We make a decision to wait in our own trees, wherever they may be.

This was the heart posture Jesus was seeking when he was on the earth. Jesus was constantly on the lookout for those who were listening. Like any good teacher, he knew that openness and readiness are essential prerequisites for learning. This was part of the reason for his frequent use of parables (Matt. 13:13–14). His constant refrain, 'Whoever has ears, let them hear' (e.g. Matt. 11:15), was a call to his audience to open their hearts.

Of course, many times, people didn't have ears to hear. They 'heard' Jesus' words, but they didn't receive his message. The Gospel writer Matthew tells us that when Jesus taught the parable of the sower, many walked away, having heard with their physical ears but not understood with their spirits (Matt. 13:1–23). Jesus never did explain the meaning of the parable to the crowd. Only those who came back and *asked* received an explanation. Jesus had all the treasures of the kingdom, but not everyone cared to discover them.

Why did Jesus make his message sometimes difficult to understand? Why shroud it in story and metaphor? This is because spiritual truths *cannot* be received by the mind. They must be revealed by the Spirit and accepted by the heart. Jesus was looking for hearts that were open. As the apostle Paul reminds us, the person without the Spirit perceives God's truths as foolishness. The natural mind cannot understand them because they can only be discerned through the Spirit (1 Cor. 2:14). Spiritual 'sight' comes through the 'eyes of the heart' (see Eph. 1:18). Hearing God, then, doesn't require a skill of the mind or a facility of the intellect. It requires an attitude that is expressed in faith and activated by seeking.

Ultimately, this heart posture will always lead to *action*. The key to hearing God is a heart that wants to know and love him. This love is expressed in doing what God says. Jesus said that God would show himself to those who listened *and* obeyed (John 14:21). Sensitivity and clarity come when our hearts are set to follow (John 10:27). This involves a conscious 'yes' at every point. It requires us to follow even when we don't want to. Our prayer must always be: 'Lord, speak to me. Make it clear and, if you do, *I'll do whatever you say.*'

Mystics in convents and mothers in homes

In day-to-day terms, what does this heart posture look like? The typical ideal is to take out blocks of time from our schedule to seek God. Indeed, this model was given to us by Jesus, who regularly extracted himself from the crowds to pray (Luke 5:16). The pattern has further been reiterated by the mystics of history who spent hours of time in prayer and contemplation. Some of them retreated to caves in the desert for months at a time. Even in our time, monks and nuns can spend up to eight hours in prayer each day.

But what of the parent with a young toddler who is unable to take time out in this season of their life? What of the businessperson working 15-hour days when the deadlines are pressing? Those with religious vocations have the luxury of uninterrupted time most people can't access. Does this mean that the everyday person can't hear from God?

If we say that hearing God's voice requires a certain amount of time, we miss the point. Devoting time to seeking God is one *expression* of faith. It is an action that *reflects* the position of the heart. While there is enormous value in taking time out to hear from God and we should pursue that, it is even more important to position our heart. The grace of hearing God is not determined by the number of hours spent seeking. When we start with this frame of reference, we can turn our relationship with God into a work and end up striving. Rather, access to the voice of the Spirit is made through the act of spiritual pursuit. While this will usually express itself in more prayer time, it is not always negated by the lack of it. God can still speak to the frantic parent and the overwrought businessperson when their hearts are fully turned to him.

In the God Conversations seminars we've conducted in the past, time was allocated in each session to listen to God. During these times, people often heard God's voice. But for others, God spoke while they were brushing their teeth that night or driving to work later that week. As in Jarrod's story, God didn't always speak at the designated time. The Spirit speaks whenever he chooses. Our constant is a posture of listening. Sacrificing a Saturday to attend a seminar and choosing to wait all day in a tree attracted God's voice because it reflected a seeking heart. In turn, this opened ears to hear and eyes to see.

Once we've set our hearts to seek, we make the most of every opportunity to lean in and attend to what God is saying. This is what makes corporate gatherings so important. Worship times in our church communities give expression to a seeking heart and create a regular rhythm for channelling our focus. Hymns and songs provide the ideal opportunity to tune our ears and posture our hearts. We come with a constant prayer: 'Spirit, speak to me.'

Our corporate worship times can then overflow into private moments, whether they are designated prayer times or unrelated activities. Our hunger to hear lingers as we go about our day-to-day lives, ever conscious of our communion with the Spirit. We can play worship music, journal our prayers and pray in our spiritual language if we are able to. All of our waiting and listening cultivates an inner life with God, creating space for his voice and sensitising us to Spirit activity. Whether God speaks or whether he is silent, these times have their greatest value in preparing our hearts to respond to whatever God says. When God does speak, we are ready to follow.

In our times of waiting on God, faith calls us to rest and patience. We learn to trust that God not only knows what to say but also when to say it. Young people in particular may struggle with this. I often see them in church, screwing up their faces in angst, *willing* God to speak. But faith takes a seat in the lounge and says, 'You know where to find me.' God *will* speak, and when he does, we need to have ears to hear.

Continuing the conversation

Melissa is an information technology (IT) consultant who struggles to hear God's voice. When she shared her story with me, she spoke of her endless frustration and disappointment: 'What's wrong with me? How can I hear God's voice?' I felt her angst as I've felt it in the lives of so many who have told me their story. But then, as we continued to talk, she told me about a dream she had had six months earlier.

In the dream, Melissa saw a long gold chain lying on the ground. She knew the chain was precious to her. Then suddenly a snake appeared and began pulling the chain away from her and burying it in the ground. Immediately she pulled the chain back and recovered it. But then the snake grabbed it again, coiling around it even more tightly. The chain had almost completely disappeared when Melissa fought to retrieve it again. When she woke up, the thought came: 'Don't let the devil steal your treasures.'

Afterwards Melissa and I talked about her experience together. As she thought about what was happening in her life at the time, it became clear the dream was from God. Her life seemed to be an endless struggle of feeling depressed and defeated. In the dream, God was revealing the source of her problems and how to deal with them. It was an appropriate message for what she was going through. But since then, Melissa had heard nothing more.

And yet, there was more to be said. Reflecting on the dream, I asked Melissa about the links in the chain: 'What treasures do you think they represent? If the snake represents the lies of the enemy, what lies are you listening to? And more importantly, what are your strategies for retrieving the chain?'

The key was to *continue* the conversation. This is what it looks like to actively seek God's revelation. It was more than a one-off experience. For Melissa, there was more to learn. A two-way relationship calls us to seek and *keep seeking*, to ask and *keep asking*. Communication requires listening and talking, listening and talking – often over a period of time. God doesn't usually give the full picture at once. The key is *our response* to what we've heard. We listen and ask, listen and ask.

A good example of this kind of tenacity is in Zechariah's God-conversation in the early years after the Babylonian exile. Zechariah had seen an image of two olive trees and a seven-branched lampstand, but the meaning of the vision wasn't clear. 'What are these?' he asked the angel. 'Do you not know what these are?' the angel replied. 'No . . . What are these . . .?' (Zech. 4:1–14). And so the conversation continued, like a tennis match back and forth. It took a number of questions before Zechariah finally received full understanding of God's plan for rebuilding the Temple. Zechariah was only able to understand God's message because he continued the conversation. He sought truth and kept seeking it.

***

Melissa's story is a common one. People may have had an initial encounter with the Spirit, but there is more to be said. Like the disciples with Jesus, we need to go back and *ask* so that more will be given. As we've seen, this takes neither intelligence nor skill. It doesn't require a special gifting, theological knowledge or ministry status, since the Spirit has been given indiscriminately to all.

All that is required is a heart that seeks. Whether this involves some dedicated time out, or extended contemplation on what God has already said, a posture of faith calls us to wait in expectation. We need to 'seek' so that we may find, and 'knock' so the door will be opened (Matt. 7:7–8). For those who seek God with all their heart, he will certainly be found (Jer. 29:13).

8

How God Speaks (1): The Incarnational Spirit

Feet of maggots

It was the early hours of Christmas morning when Nicola had a dream she will never forget. In the dream, she saw herself as a child with her brother at the local shopping mall. Nicola's brother was determined to buy her a Buzz Lightyear toy for Christmas, even though she didn't want one. Nicola protested vehemently, but her brother was insistent, dragging her from store to store in pursuit. Finally, he found the little robot figurine, bought it and handed it to her in triumph.

Then the scene changed. Nicola saw herself sitting on the floor of a tiny mud house with a dark-skinned woman she knew to be her mother. Suddenly, her mother began beating her with a long metal stick while screaming hysterically. Nicola cowered in the corner terrified, but her mother wouldn't stop. Fearing for her life, she ran out of the house.

Outside, the vile smell of sewage smarted in Nicola's nostrils as she sprinted down the narrow streets away from her home. She could hear her mother bearing down on her as she darted around the potholes. Suddenly an excruciating pain shot up her legs. Exhausted, she stumbled and fell face down in the dirt.

Lying on the ground, Nicola looked to see what had caused the pain. To her horror, the soles of her feet were covered in open, weeping sores. She winced as maggots crawled out of the wounds and the stench of rotting flesh filled her stomach. In the distance, she could still hear her mother's footsteps getting closer. Panic surged through her body and she yelled out to no one in particular, 'I told you I didn't need a Buzz Lightyear. I just need a pair of shoes!'

At that, Nicola woke up. Then she began to weep. The weeping continued on and off for three weeks. In her home. At the supermarket. Down the street. The groaning was so intense, Nicola couldn't explain it; she just knew her heart was breaking. Deep inside, a sense of grief raged for all the injustice around her. Every time she saw a child in pain or a teenager lost on the street, the crying would start again. In time, the tears subsided, but Nicola knew something significant had been birthed within her heart.

It was another nine years before God spoke again about the child in the slum. Nicola and her husband were working as the youth pastors in a well-known church in the English town of Bath when the message came: 'The time is now!' A number of prophecies followed. First, from an old friend Nicola hadn't seen in twenty-five years: 'You're supposed to be in Africa'; second, from a fellow conference speaker: 'You have the green light to go to Africa'; and then from another friend: 'I saw a vision of you in a land of red dust and sunshine.' The final seal came when an elderly woman Nicola had only met once gave her a photograph and said: 'God told me you would know what this means.' The photo was of an African child whose feet were crawling with maggots.

Three months later, Nicola, her husband and two children packed up their home in Bath and moved to Uganda. There, in one of the poorest places on earth, they committed their lives to the rescue and restoration of children and families. Today Nicola heads up Every Life International, an organisation that oversees ministry in Uganda, Kenya and the UK. Nicola and her team walk alongside people in their everyday lives, loving, serving, praying and supporting them wherever they can. Part of their ministry involves distributing hundreds of shoes to the children in the slums.

How does God speak? Nicola's story demonstrates how. God speaks to us *by his Spirit.* He speaks creatively in ways that change our hearts and motivate us to action. As the Spirit spoke to those in the early church, so the Spirit speaks today to continue the ministry of Jesus.

In this chapter, we examine the different modes of God-speech and how they are received. We start with how the Spirit speaks through Scripture and then look at the forms of Spirit communication outside Scripture. The Spirit is a masterful communicator who incarnates his message in a variety of ways.

Spirit, Scripture and biblical roulette

As we've seen, the starting point for all our God-conversations is Jesus. Jesus said that the Spirit would remind us of the truths he had established (John 14:26). These truths have been faithfully recorded and passed on to us via the Scriptures. Thus, the Spirit speaks first to illuminate the teachings of the gospel to us. Whenever we read Scripture or hear it preached about, the Spirit speaks to those with open hearts. This revelation grounds us in the foundations of our faith, providing us with understanding about the nature of our salvation, the fullness of God's character and how to live according to kingdom ways.

What does this look like in practice? We may have had one of those experiences where we've been reading our Bible and a verse has 'jumped off the page'. Or we've been sitting in church listening to a sermon and the Spirit wrests our heart with conviction and opens our eyes to something new. Or perhaps we've been going about our day-to-day duties when a passage from Scripture comes to mind. The Spirit constantly calls us back to the foundations of our faith and inscribes the truths of the gospel on our hearts in order to form us into the likeness of Jesus. The 'God-breathed' words (2 Tim. 3:16) that were once spoken, and are now written, continue to speak afresh into the lives of every person who is open to reading them or hearing them. God's words of truth and life retain their power to transform people and draw them closer to him.

This is also why, whenever we preach about or read the Scriptures, we pray for the Spirit to illuminate them for us. We pray that God will speak through them. As the Pharisees showed us in the first century and university professors of literature show us today, it is possible to read the Scriptures and *not* receive revelation (John 5:39–40). The mere act of Bible reading or Bible study does not equate to Spirit transformation. As we've seen, the work of the Spirit requires a certain posture of the heart, not an appropriate level of IQ.

The Spirit may also use Scripture to speak in ways that depart from its original meaning. We see some precedent for this among the New Testament writers as they outwork the New Covenant in the light of the Old. Matthew, for example, makes copious use of Old Testament prophecies in ways that move beyond the meaning they had for their original audience (e.g. Hos. 11:1 in Matt. 2:15, and Jer. 31:15 in Matt. 2:18). Similarly, Paul makes use of Abraham's story in ways that Abraham would never have conceived and that are later described as inspired (1 Cor. 10:6,11; 2 Tim. 3:16). Each time, God was speaking through Scripture.

God has used Scripture in creative ways in my own life. I can vividly remember how, in the early days, God used an image from Scripture as an analogy for my impatience. At the time, I had been trying to 'organise God' into my calendar: 'If you could just perform your word next month, then I can do what I need to do the following month.' My attempts to force God's hand were met with a vivid dream. In the dream, I woke up to discover my house had been broken into. My first instinct was to check the time. I checked the clock by my bed, but the hands were spinning wildly and I couldn't read them. Frustrated, I looked to the digital clock on the other side of the room. But all the digits were scrambled, and again I couldn't read them. 'What time is it?' I kept asking in the dream. Then I found myself wondering, *How could a thief break into my home while I was sleeping? Surely, I would have woken up?* Then I actually woke up.

It was a vivid dream that seemed of little consequence until half an hour later when I turned to my daily devotional. The reading for that day was from the Gospel of Matthew: 'But understand this: if the owner of the house had known at what time of night the thief was coming, he would have kept watch and would not have let his house be broken into. So you also must be ready, because the Son of Man will come at an hour when you do not expect him' (Matt. 24:43–44). God's message rang out loud and clear. Even though I didn't know God's timing, he was asking me to keep 'getting ready' in faith. I must be *awake* to his promises and cooperate with them to see them fulfilled.

My 'thief in the night' dream is a good example of the Spirit's creative use of Scripture. The Spirit used a passage to speak into a situation that had little to do with its original meaning. Jesus' words in Matthew were given to the disciples to prepare them for his second coming, not impatience with my situation! However, the Spirit used them to speak and, in doing so, caused me to reflect on the words Jesus had already spoken. When the Spirit uses Scripture in this way, it always links us back to our foundation in Jesus.

At the same time, these kinds of experiences should not be labelled authentic *just because* they draw on a passage of Scripture. This approach can lead to a kind of biblical roulette where we 'cherry-pick' an isolated verse to suit ourselves. Such manipulation of Scripture has been identified as a common practice in some of our churches.[1] Too often, people treat the Bible as a sort of magic book to dip into when they need a 'lucky treat'. Like the ancient practices of reading animal entrails or searching for omens in the sky, the selection of random Bible verses becomes a means of divining our personal agendas. Scripture clearly warns against these kinds of practices (e.g. Deut. 18:9–15). Instead, revelatory experiences that draw on the Bible in creative ways must be tested in the same way as all our extrabiblical encounters (see Chapters 10–12).

Spirit communiqués

Once we are grounded in the foundational truths of the living Word, Jesus, we are well positioned to hear the voice of the Spirit *apart* from

Scripture. As Jesus promised, the Spirit speaks beyond the truths he established in his incarnation, taking the message of the gospel and applying it to contemporary situations (John 16:13). God speaks directly to us via the Spirit.

These 'Spirit communiqués' are difficult to describe if you haven't experienced them yourself. It's a bit like trying to articulate how it feels to be in love. The experience is invisible to the natural eye, but still very real.

When I first set myself to hear God's voice, I anticipated some sort of earth-shattering, out-of-body encounter, which is why my early experiences were such a surprise. One of those moments came after dinner with friends. I had just parked my car in the driveway of my home when an unexpected thought entered my head: 'Someone is going to break into your car tonight.' It was such a random idea and I wondered why I should be thinking it. I had never had my car broken into, nor been concerned about the possibility. The idea seemed completely unfounded, so I promptly ignored it.

When I returned to the driveway next morning, I discovered someone had broken into my car the previous night. When I went to open the door, I found the lock dangling out of its socket and all the contents of the glove compartment scattered on the floor. Nothing was stolen (as a university student, there was nothing to steal) and the culprit was never found. There seemed to be no point to the episode other than learning what the voice of the Spirit sounded like. The surprise was that the voice in my head sounded exactly like my own.

It was a similar sort of experience when I first heard God in a dream. When I woke up the next morning, it didn't occur to me that the dream was from God. Even though it felt uncannily appropriate, it still felt like any other dream. I didn't realise it was God until afterwards when the Spirit repeatedly confirmed it in other ways. Like the voice in the car, I hadn't recognised it, because it had come to me on the stage of my mind. The Spirit had sounded just like my thought – and yet it wasn't my thought.

Similar descriptions emerged from the participants in my PhD study. The voice of the Spirit 'sounded' like one of their 'own thoughts', but was distinguishable by its tone, content and the fact that it 'came out of nowhere'. People said things such as: 'I never use that word', or 'I don't think like that', or 'It had never entered my mind before'. Most times, the encounter was *internal*, like 'an inner witness' or 'a conversation in your head'. Some described it as coming from 'deep within' their spirit, heart or soul. A number of times, the voice was reported to have spoken in the first person. Sometimes the message came as an idea or a single word, while at other times it was in the form of complete sentences. Often a question was posed.

In Scripture, we do not get many detailed descriptions of *how* God spoke. Most of the time, the author just says it was a vision or dream and gets straight to the content. It is our contemporary experience that seems to indicate that Spirit-speech is most often 'internal'. The voice of the Spirit comes largely on the 'stage of our minds'. Another way of saying it is our *imagination*.

I may have lost some of you when I used that term. Typically, when we see the word 'imagination', we associate it with the world of our fanciful thoughts. But this is not its original meaning. Imagination is the faculty of our minds that forms mental images, ideas or concepts that are not present in our natural senses. It is the place of our 'mind's eye'.

God's voice does not *originate* in this place, but it is *received by it* here. As theologian Greg Boyd describes it, imagination is the 'main receptor to the spiritual world'.[2] The biblical character Daniel alludes to it when he refers to his revelations as 'visions that passed through my mind' (Dan. 7:15). The Spirit's voice comes like a thought, but it is not *our* thought. It comes as a dream, but it is not *our* dream.

These experiences can be as mild and faint as a passing idea, so subtle we may not even notice them, or they can be loud and clear as though someone is yelling in our ear. The common feature is often the *spontaneity* of the voice. The voice of the Spirit interrupts our thinking and transcends it. It comes 'all of a sudden' because you didn't think of it yourself.

Occasionally, the Spirit's voice takes us beyond the 'internal' to the 'external' or natural realm. We may have a physical reaction to God's voice that leaves us reeling. We see this a number of times in the lives of the biblical characters. Both Daniel and John were left shaken physically and emotionally by their God-conversations (e.g. Dan. 10:8).

Some God-conversations may also involve entry into the *spiritual* realm. 'Out-of-body' experiences occurred for Isaiah, Ezekiel, Paul and John. At other times, a spiritual experience may also break into the physical realm, such as when Peter and the apostles saw an angel break them out of jail (Acts 5:19–20). Some call these 'open visions', because of the easy access between the spiritual and natural realms. In my research, this level of intensity was only experienced by a few individuals. It seemed to come at crucial moments – when people were experiencing extreme hardship or about to face a difficult season.

Whether internal or external, subtle or loud, the Spirit speaks to us on the stages of our mind. It is a spiritual voice that is able to find its way into our hearts and lives.

As to the modes of revelation, we see that God is able to draw on all the human senses. Here we turn to experiences in Scripture, where God's revelatory forms may be categorised in three ways: Spirit pictures, Spirit words and Spirit senses.

1. Spirit pictures

We start with the most common way God speaks in Scripture: Spirit pictures. Today we know them as 'dreams' that come when we're asleep and 'visions' that come when we're awake. But in biblical times the two words were interchangeable, which is why scholars often use the term 'dream-vision' to describe them.[3] This is also why dreams are often described as 'visions of the night' (Gen. 46:2; Job 4:13; 20:8; 33:15; Isa. 29:7; Dan. 2:19; 7:7,13). Irrespective of the receiver's level of consciousness, this mode of revelation comprises any experience that is *visual* in nature. It involves a spiritual seeing as opposed to a spiritual hearing. As Jeremiah asks: 'But which of them has stood in the council of the LORD to see or to hear his word?' (Jer. 23:18a). We *hear* God's word, but we can also *see* it.

For some of us, the use of picture language can appear a little obscure. In reality, it is the easiest form of communication available. For example, when we teach our children to read, we don't give them a dictionary! Pictures are easy to read. When we visit a foreign country, we can respond to a traffic light or follow the red cross sign to a hospital without knowing the local lingo.

Scripture tells us that when it comes to revelation, dreams and visions are God's modus operandi. It is how he describes his own communiqués (Num. 12:6; Hos. 12:10; Acts 2:16) and is the most common form of inspired speech in Scripture. Even angelic appearances are commonly described as 'visions' (e.g. Luke 1:11,22; 24:23; Acts 8:26–40).[4] Indeed, the most pivotal points in biblical history began with a dream-vision.

We see God speak in dream-visions throughout the biblical narratives. First, in the lives of the patriarchs: Abraham's covenant is sealed by a dream of a blazing torch passing between animal sacrifices (Gen. 15); Jacob's transformation is accessed via a visionary stairway to heaven (Gen. 28:10–17); and Joseph's future is illumined through a dream of celestial beings bowing down in deference (Gen. 37:9–10). Then, as the nation of Israel forms and Moses establishes his leadership, multiple visions guide the people into their next phase of development (Exod. 19:1 – 34:30). God's visual communiqués then continue into the period of the judges and kings, with Gideon's dream of the barley loaf (Judg. 7:13,14), Micaiah's vision of the heavenly council (1 Kgs 22:19–28) and Solomon's request for wisdom (1 Kgs 3:5–15). Later, dreams and visions feature prominently in the lives of the prophets. First, there are the pre-exilic messages: Amos's vision of Israel as a basket of summer fruit (Amos 8), Isaiah's scene of the throne on high (Isa. 6) and Jeremiah's vision of a boiling pot (Jer. 1:13–16). Visual experiences persist into the time of the exile, with Daniel's dreams of four beasts (Dan. 7), Ezekiel's valley of dry bones (Ezek. 37:1–14) and Zechariah's vision of the olive trees and golden lampstand (Zech. 4).

The use of dreams and visions as a revelatory mode doesn't stop with the Old Covenant. It continues into the time of Jesus, beginning with the five dreams of the Christmas story.[5] Jesus goes on to experience significant visions during his ministry: at his baptism (Luke 3:21–22) and transfiguration (Luke 9:29–36). Then, after Jesus, dream-visions feature as the primary mode of divine communication in the New Testament church (Acts 2:16–17). Luke records twenty-one instances of visions and dreams in Acts, including Peter's famous dream-vision of the unclean animals (Acts 10:1 – 11:18), Stephen's vision of his welcome into heaven (Acts 7:55–56), Ananias's vision of healing for Paul's blindness (Acts 9:10–18), and Paul's dream of the man from Macedonia (Acts 16:9) as well as his vision of safety at sea (Acts 27:23–24).[6] Paul's experiences also include his visions of the third heaven where he heard 'inexpressible things' he was unable to share (2 Cor. 12:2–4). Finally, the most detailed description of a dream-vision series can be found in the last book of the Bible, with its colourful scenes of a blood-stained lamb with seven horns (Rev. 5:6), saints wearing white robes washed in blood (Rev. 7:14) and a drunken prostitute riding a scarlet beast (Rev. 17:1–7).

A lamb with seven horns

One of the distinctives of Spirit pictures as a mode of revelation is their use of *symbolism*. Objects, people and scenes can all be used to represent an abstract concept or idea. Think about John's visions in the book of Revelation. For those who have never experienced God speaking like this, the first read can be confusing. With all those images of winged creatures, coloured horses and multi-headed dragons, the book seems more like a scene out of *The Lord of the Rings* than a piece of sacred literature! The scenes only make sense when you understand that the images are not meant to be taken literally. Lambs do not have seven horns and seven eyes. Robes that have been washed in blood do not come out white. Each of these images acts as a symbol that represents a particular meaning.

Of course, not all God-dreams are symbolic. Scripture tells of a number of dream-visions that reveal *literal* scenes of realities that have yet to manifest in the natural realm. The vision of Ananias praying for Paul's blinded eyes is a good example (Acts 9:10–12). But in general, literal dreams are the exception. Most dreams, whether from God or other sources, are symbolic.

A first-century rabbi once said that a dream uninterpreted is like a letter unopened. Because dreams and visions typically use the language of symbolism, they require *interpretation*. Like Jesus' parables, the message is not apparent at first glance. The visions of Revelation, for example, have been understood in a myriad of ways (many of them unhelpful). However, the process of interpretation is not as complex as it first seems. The starting point is an understanding that imagery is a *language* and, just like any other language, it is intended to be understood.

Like all good communicators, the Spirit employs symbols that befit the setting and audience. The biblical testimony provides plentiful illustrations of this. For the Egyptian pharaoh, the image of seven skinny cows was an effective way to communicate the message about a coming famine in an agrarian society dependent on livestock (Gen. 41:17–25). For Zechariah, the vision of a golden lampstand was an appropriate way to send a message about the Second Temple since he was intimately familiar with temple furnishings (Zech. 4:1–14). For John and the seven churches, the threat of a seven-headed dragon (Rev. 12:3,9; 13:1) was a clear connection to those who lived in the shadow of the famed seven hills of Rome,[7] and when you knew that horns were the ancient symbol of strength, it wouldn't be hard to see the clever irony of a slain lamb made strong in sacrificial weakness (Rev. 5:6).

Once we understand how picture language works, it is not difficult to interpret our visions and dreams. God speaks *not* to obscure his message, but rather to make it *abundantly clear*. But as with any language, understanding takes practice. We know that characters like Daniel and Joseph were skilled in dream interpretation (Gen. 41:12,14; Dan. 2:25–28). The goal is to learn the language of symbolism so we can all understand God's messages for ourselves.

The power of a picture

The scenes in our dream-visions are often elaborate and sometimes confusing, so why would God favour this mode of communication? It's a good question and an important one. Unfortunately, Scripture doesn't provide us with specific answers, but I'd like to propose three: 1) Spirit pictures are an effective form of communication; 2) Spirit pictures have potential for transformation; and 3) Spirit pictures (particularly dreams) have the ability to communicate beneath the conscious level.

Let's begin with the first: effectiveness of communication. Think about it from God's perspective. You have a message. What is the best way to deliver it? Consider an example from the time of Israel's exile in Babylon. God's people are languishing in despair after the devastating destruction of their home. How would you comfort them? God could have sent a message in simple black-and-white wording: 'I will restore your future.' But instead, he created a scene: A desolate valley. An array of dry and brittle bones strewn across the valley floor. A wind that stirs up the dust and shifts the bones into formation. Flesh that appears. Skin, muscles, ligaments and sinews. Bodies coming into alignment. They rise as a mighty army, tall and strong (Ezek. 37:1–14). The imagery is clear and powerful. A picture really is worth a thousand words.

The second reason dreams and visions may be favoured is due to their potential for transformation. The imagery in Ezekiel's vision does more than get the message across. Visual experiences leave a powerful impression on the brain with long-lasting effects. You can imagine how it felt for Ezekiel to watch the dry bones spring to life and then rise as a great army. The dream-vision can draw on all the senses so that it is experienced as real. Ezekiel would have seen it and *felt* it.

You see the same dynamic in Nicola's testimony. No one could fail to appreciate God's priorities after experiencing the dream of the child with maggots in her feet. The experience took Nicola into God's heart and allowed her to identify with the children she was called to serve. It ignited a powerful sense of compassion that compelled Nicola and her family to pack up their lives and leave them behind for the slums of Africa. God is a creative and masterful storyteller. He tailors his messages so that the hearer not only understands them cognitively but also feels them emotionally.

The impact of visual imagery has been further backed up by empirical research. It's said that approximately 65% of the general population are visual learners.[8] Neurologists also tell us that imagery is likely to stay with us long after we've seen it. Indeed, people remember messages with visuals six and a half times *more* than messages without them.[9] Marketers know this too. Advertising today focuses less on product information and more on the picture of a better life. Because the scenes stay with us, we find ourselves at the shopping mall buying things we didn't 'know' we needed. God has always done what neuroscience has only just discovered. His intention for Spirit-speech is to bring transformation, and visual imagery is simply the best way to do it.

A final reason God may speak visually is to communicate beneath the conscious level. This may be because we are 'hard of hearing', or because the message itself is difficult to receive. In these cases, dreams appear to be the most effective way of getting the message across. When we are sleeping, our minds are 'switched off' and we become more receptive to the messages we can't or don't want to hear in our waking lives. Why else would God put Peter in a trance to speak to him about the Gentiles (Acts 10)? Under normal circumstances the message would have repulsed him. Having been socialised his entire life to avoid Gentiles, he would not have even considered the possibility of visiting a Gentile home. The dream allowed God to gently present the concept to Peter by sidestepping his intellect, so that he was able to arrive at its meaning when some Romans knocked on his door. It was an ingenious way to introduce a new idea.

Personally, I love hearing God speak in dream-visions. Not only does it stir my imagination; it also offers a failsafe way to bypass a mind that is often too cerebral to pick up on the sensory cues when I'm awake. As we've seen, certain personalities have difficulty receiving the subtle nuances of Spirit communication. Dreams make God's voice accessible to those who are prone to over-intellectualising their experience. God has our full attention when we are asleep – even if we don't know it.

2. Spirit words

Sometimes God speaks without the use of visual aids. In Catholic theology, these *verbal* experiences are described as 'locutions' or 'auditions'. They are often likened to the 'still small voice' of Elijah's story. As a revelatory mode, Spirit words are less common than dreams and visions in Scripture. Oddly enough, the Gospel writer Luke subsumes them under the dream-vision category (e.g. Acts 9:10), a pattern that is in keeping with the Old Testament Scriptures.[10]

When I first set myself to hear God's voice, I anticipated an audible voice. By this I meant a voice that was external to my mind. I've since realised that the use of the term 'audible' is a bit of a misnomer. By definition, 'audible' means 'able to be heard'. God's voice is always able to be heard, but it doesn't mean that it is always external. As we've seen, most of the time, the Spirit's voice is internal. It comes on the stage of our minds. As a spiritual voice, you hear it with the 'eyes of your heart' rather than with your physical ears. It may seem 'quiet', because it comes amid your thoughts which no one else can access.

Sometimes when God speaks, he turns up the volume. God's voice is not always 'still' or 'small'. God may speak so loudly we can't miss it. The loudness of God's voice is designed to shock us into action. When Peter, James and John heard the voice of God at Jesus' transfiguration, they fell face-down to the ground, terrified (Matt. 17:5–6).

Even when God's voice is loud, it is not necessarily external. You may have 'heard' it, but someone next to you may not. As dramatic as Paul's experience on the Damascus road was, God's voice seems to have been largely internal. Not everyone heard it (though they did see its effects) (Acts 22:9 compared with Acts 9:7). The vast majority of God-talking experiences are *private*, designed to be received only by the individual. Rarely does God's voice break out of the internal, spiritual realm into the external, natural realm.[11]

In my PhD research, nearly every person who reported an 'audible' or 'out loud' voice was on the edge of a crisis. A man heard a voice yelling at him not to step onto the road. Seconds later a wayward truck rolled by. A woman heard her name being shouted so loudly that she woke up visibly shaken. The experience gave her the push she needed to leave a violent relationship that had kept her bound. These kinds of experiences are best likened to the parent who sees their child approaching an open stove – '*Stop!*' The occasion calls for an urgent bellow rather than a quiet word of calm. Even the volume and tone of God's voice meets the needs of the occasion.

3. Spirit senses

If the Spirit communicates in pictures and words, it shouldn't be surprising that God would engage the rest of our senses. There is less precedent for this in the Scriptures, but there is plenty of evidence in our contemporary experience to suggest that when the Spirit speaks, the senses of taste, smell and touch may be involved. In my own research, one woman reflected on the deep sense of comfort she felt when the scent of talcum powder filled her room. Another told how they picked up on the smell of a corpse when they met a person who was addicted to drugs and entangled in a web of toxic relationships. Another man told of how the entire left side of his body became numb and tingly as he approached someone for prayer who had just had a stroke.

Our senses are also involved when we experience 'impressions' that move us in some way. There are no actual words or pictures, but rather a 'hunch' or a sense of 'knowing' something. My prophetic friends tell me they experience this type of feeling when God wants them to prophesy. They are moved to speak, and as they do, the Spirit fills their mouth with a message for another person.

This kind of experience draws on our emotions. Like Spirit pictures and voices, Spirit senses arise independently of rational thought;

there is no reason why we are suddenly feeling sad, burdened or excited. There is no logical reason for phoning that person or performing that act of generosity, but we feel it anyway and we are compelled to act. Jesus may have experienced something like this when he was speaking to the teachers of the law; *immediately* he 'knew in his Spirit' what they were thinking (Mark 2:8). He sensed their antagonism and acted accordingly.

God's use of all the senses is not surprising given what we know about communication. Tone of voice, pitch, emphasis and body language all come into play. By its nature, communication is multifaceted. God is a masterful communicator who uses whatever mode is helpful in getting the message across. Whether the Spirit speaks in visions, voices or sensory impressions, God tailors the message to whoever he is speaking to.

The incarnational Spirit

Mark describes his experience of hearing the Spirit's voice as a new Christian. In a vision, Jesus appeared to him and said that if he prayed, his uncle Dave would be healed of bone cancer. When Mark later told his family that Uncle Dave would be healed, they laughed out loud. After all, the doctors said he had only days to live. Still, Mark set himself to pray, interceding throughout the night in the park outside the hospital. After three days, Mark's uncle suddenly began to recover. He went on to live on for another sixteen years.

Mark wasn't the only person praying for Dave. At the same time as Mark's vision, a friend of the family named Bett received an identical message. But Bett's vision was not quite the same as Mark's; instead of Jesus, she saw St Francis of Assisi. St Francis said that if she prayed, Dave would be healed. When Bett later told the family that Uncle Dave would be healed, again they laughed out loud. Still, Bett set herself to pray and, three days later, Dave suddenly began to recover.

What is happening here? For Mark, God spoke through a vision of Jesus. For Bett, God spoke through a vision of Francis. God *tailored his message to his audience.* When he spoke to Mark, a new Christian, the messenger was Jesus. When he spoke to Bett, a devout Catholic, the messenger was Francis. God adapted the form to the hearer. There was no compromise in the theological content – it was clear to both Mark and Bett that God was the source of healing – but the form was adapted for the sake of communication.[12] As a result of their encounters, both Mark and Bett interceded. Both witnessed God's power when Dave was healed. This incarnational approach shouldn't be surprising given that our God descended from a royal throne to walk the same dusty roads as his disciples. God's strategy is clear. He crafted the message to his audience so that it could be received.

The anthropologist Charles Kraft likens God's approach to that of a cross-cultural missionary.[13] It is as though he crosses over from the culture of heaven to the culture of earth. God speaks in the terms we understand – in English to the English, in Portuguese to the Brazilian and in childlike language to the young. Like a good teacher, he reduces profound and lofty concepts to the level of his audience's understanding.

In Scripture we see the incarnational ingenuity of the master communicator. Take a number of the Old Testament oracles. These were often delivered in multisensory forms and even acted out in theatrical ways that communicated powerfully to the audience. So, God's message was *felt* in the heartbreak of Hosea as he was betrayed by his prostitute wife (Hos. 1 – 3); it was *seen* in the exposure of Isaiah's nakedness as he paraded around the city (Isa. 20:1–6); and it was *smelt* in the vile defilement of Ezekiel's cooking fire (Ezek. 4:12–13).

This kind of incarnational ingenuity was also evident in my research. For one person, God spoke through Jesus as a lifeguard while she contemplated suicide in the surf. For another, Jesus appeared as a farmer dressed in overalls and a plaid shirt; this made God approachable because God knew she loved 'country stuff'.

***

These kinds of testimonies remind us of the God who reveals himself to whoever is listening. Our God is a creative genius. The Spirit crafts the message into whatever form is needed so that it is seen, heard and understood. He sends a dream of a child with maggots, an image of a desolate graveyard, a vision of a Catholic saint and a loud, disturbing shout – all with one intention: to get the message across. The *sounds* of God – the *forms* of his speech – are always subject to the message. God's priority is clear communication.

How does God speak? God speaks in ways that are not unlike our human modes of communication. Divine communiqués are diverse and creative, and appeal to all the senses. Just as God incarnated his message into Jesus' time, so the Spirit incarnates his message into ours. He tailors the message in such a way as to employ our language, the imagery we are familiar with and the settings we find ourselves in. Although God's modus operandi is a dream-vision, he can use *anything* to speak. Ultimately, his messages are always intended to be understood.

9

How God Speaks (2): God's Modus Operandi

An interstate move

When I first moved from Melbourne to Sydney in 2003, people would often ask me why I came. Occasionally I would speak plainly: 'God spoke to me in dreams.' Then I would watch as they rolled their eyes, changed the subject and walked away. Every time, I looked for some hint of understanding, but I rarely got it. I knew my experience was odd by everyday standards. Yet most of my new friends were Christians – many of them pastors – who believed in the ongoing voice of the Spirit. They were familiar with Bible stories such as that of Mary and Joseph, who left their homeland on the basis of a God-dream. And yet, when they heard mine, it was seen as strange and even suspect.

If you were to ask someone today, 'How does God speak?', it's likely that dreams and visions would be at the bottom of the list. Often they are not even on the list. For many of us, the idea of direct revelatory experiences is an unusual, if not uncomfortable, one. Dreams in particular are viewed as unstable and unreliable or, worse still, the penchant of the spiritually immature. You're more likely to hear that God speaks through Scripture, sermons, Christian books, nature and the 'wisdom of counsel'. In their own way, these are all valid forms of experiencing God. And yet, any careful Bible-reader will soon realise that the Bible itself shows that direct Spirit communiqués are the norm for hearing God. God's modus operandi has always been to speak in unmediated, experiential ways. As we've seen, this is true under both the Old and New Covenants.

So why is it that we think we cannot hear God's voice in the same way as the biblical characters? Why the aversion to the experiential communiqués that are so central to our most famous Bible stories? And why, in particular, the reluctance to accept God's *primary* mode of dream-visions?

Some of our aversion springs from the negative stories we've heard. People tell of seeing a flying pig with a top hat and think it has some sort of significance for their future. Dreams and visions are particularly prone to misuse and, as church leaders, we want to protect our people from the fallout. But most of our scepticism is due to a historic blind spot. The influence of both the Reformation and the Enlightenment on our thinking has meant that we no longer understand hearing God to be a directly inspired experience.[1]

In rejecting God's preferred form of communication, we suffer a devastating blow. Not only do we unwittingly render the revelatory experiences of characters like Abraham, Peter, Joseph and John 'unreliable', but we also miss the emphasis of Scripture and the pinnacle of the New Covenant itself. In this chapter, we look more closely at why we've rejected direct Spirit-experiences as a legitimate revelatory mode and why it matters. The church's difficulty in accepting the biblical forms of revelation has had wide-reaching ramifications on our understanding of revelation under the New Covenant. It has also led to a preference for *indirect* forms of Spirit communication, which limits the full spectrum of God-speech and can even lead to a manipulative use of Scripture. We start by looking at why dreams and visions in particular have been the object of our derision.

Our historic blind spot

Most of our biblical stories began while someone was sleeping. Jesus would have been murdered as an infant if not for a series of timely God-dreams. This so-called 'unstable' and 'unreliable' dream series forms the basis of the story we celebrate every Christmas. We believe the biblical story without batting an eyelid, yet struggle to apply the reality to our own. So why the disconnect?

Our theologies and traditions do not come to us in a vacuum. The gap between the dream-visions of our experience and the biblical experience can be largely explained by our theological and philosophical heritage. While the scriptural testimony is clear, Western cultures have struggled to accept visual forms of God-speech ever since the Protestant Reformation when spiritual experiences as a whole were rejected by the Reformers. This position was further reinforced during the Enlightenment in the eighteenth century.

Since then, the rise of Pentecostalism and Charismatic movements across the world has brought miraculous phenomena and spiritual gifts back into favour. But dreams and visions have yet to make the same renaissance into the life of the Western Protestant Church. Instead, they have been actively resisted. For example, when the writings of early church fathers (such as Augustine, Gregory of Nazianzen, Gregory of Nyssa, and later theologians like Synesius of Cyrene and John Cassian) were translated into English in the twentieth century, most of the references to dream-visions were completely left out.[2] In some cases, entire sections were omitted.[3] These are not isolated cases. History tells of our constant tripping up in this area. The first seeds of reticence were sown back in the fourth century when Jerome translated the Bible into Latin and dreaming was lumped in with witchcraft and divination.[4] These ideas were picked up again later by the great theologian Thomas Aquinas. With this neglect continuing into the modern era, it isn't surprising that today most Western Christians are more likely to associate dreams and visions with spicy pizza than divine revelation.[5]

The historic turn against dreams and visions also explains why we have unwittingly reinterpreted the meaning of dream-visions. Instead of being the primary mode of hearing God's voice, we have turned them into a metaphor to mean the *plans for your life*. We encourage people to 'have a dream' and 'dream big' because God's plans for us are good and we are destined to do 'great things' for him. Without realising it, we have substituted the sanctified human imagination for a God-talking experience.

It's a subtle distinction that is likely unintentional. There is nothing wrong with having a 'dream' or 'vision' for our life. We need to do all we can to engage our God-given abilities to build a life that is glorifying to God. But when Scripture mentions a vision or a dream, this is *not* what it means. Joseph 'had a dream', but he wasn't out in the fields 'dreaming' of his potential as a great leader. 'Having a dream' meant he fell asleep one night and saw sheaves of wheat bowing down to him. The symbolic scene pointed to a time when his family would submit to his authority. As the youngest son in a society that practised primogeniture (the leadership birthright of the eldest son), this was beyond *anything* Joseph could have imagined for himself. Joseph's retelling of the experience to his brothers only posed a threat because they understood the potential for dreams to bear a message from God (Gen. 37:11).

This is the case every time you read the terms for 'vision' or 'dream' in the Scripture. Divinely inspired visions and dreams are God's messages in visual form. They are instantaneous, divinely initiated experiences of God speaking. Take Proverbs 29:18 for example: 'Where there is no vision, the people perish' (KJV). This verse does *not* mean we need to have 'vision for our lives' or we will perish. It means we need to *hear God's voice* – or we will perish. It is better rendered 'Without *revelation*, people perish', as in more recent translations (e.g. NIV). Similarly, when we read Habakkuk 2:2, 'Write the vision, and make it plain' (KJV), it doesn't mean we should write out our plans and goals for the year. Instead, the prophet was to write down *what God had said*, so that it could be passed on and obeyed. Most importantly, when Peter announced on Pentecost that sons and daughters would have dreams and visions, he meant that all people, irrespective of their age or gender, could hear God's voice for themselves.

This historic blind spot has had devastating consequences on our theology. Our 'metaphoricalising' of God's primary revelatory mode has meant we have completely missed the thread of God-speech in Scripture and, therefore, the chief emphasis of the New Covenant.

Every time we preach Acts 2:16–17 as a motivational sermon for 'how to live your dream', we bypass the message of direct Spirit-communication. The promise that was so long awaited by the prophets is deftly and foully thwarted. Hearing from God becomes just one of many experiences in the Christian life, rather than the key point of the Spirit's outpouring and the primary means to dynamic relationship with God.

When we miss the biblical meaning of dream-visions, we also disconnect the experience of hearing from the Spirit from Christ's mission. We forget that the Spirit's outpouring is the fulfilment of Jesus' promise that the Spirit would speak to remind us of established truths and apply that truth in days to come. This leads to misguided expectations around what we expect the Spirit to say. Instead of anticipating the Spirit to speak within the framework of discipleship and ministry, those in our churches come to God expecting the Spirit to speak about their own agendas. But true Spirit-experiences will always lead us to the place where our prayers are redirected to kingdom purpose. The Spirit speaks in dreams to fulfil *God's* purposes, not ours. For our friend Nicola, having a God-dream meant giving up her own 'dream' of a quiet life in a big English country house for a ministry that cared for children who desperately needed shoes. While we dream up big plans for promotion, God may be sending us messages that tell us to make the bed for our wives.

Meaningless dreaming

Of course, dreams and visions are also fertile soil for misuse and abuse. I once heard a story of a man who claimed to have a dream about God's will for his church. During the Sunday service, he jumped onto the platform with a suitcase in hand and declared that the pastor's tenure was over and he was to take on the mantle. More than other modes of divine communication, dreams and visions seem to attract the weird and wonderful. Many of us have had to listen to wild tales of odd dreams full of 'meaningless' words, as the writer of Ecclesiastes describes them (Eccl. 5:7). In their eagerness to hear from God, people start attributing every dream to God, obsessively analysing every random detail.

In the same way that not every thought we have is from God, not every dream is from God. Dreams come 'when there are many cares' (Eccl. 5:3). Most of them are a reflection of the previous day – the processing of our thoughts in the subconscious realm. For our friend with the suitcase, his dream was probably a reflection of his misguided desire for power and position. Natural dreams reveal what is going on beneath the surface. This is why we dream of punching our boss in the face after a conflict in the office, or why we dream of standing naked in the exam room when we're feeling underprepared. Odd as these experiences may be, natural dreams are *healthy*. They should be understood as a God-given part of the healing process. As our physical mind comes to rest, our emotional self is being restored. Psychologists even tell us that if you repeatedly disturb someone while they're dreaming, they begin to exhibit symptoms of mental illness.[6] Therefore, attending to these kinds of dreams can reveal what is going on beneath the surface of our conscious lives and provide an aid for personal growth. Even a nightmare can point us towards wholeness.

However, there is also a darker side to our dreams. Jeremiah and Zechariah both make reference to those who prophesy false dreams (Jer. 23:32) and 'visions that lie' (Zech. 10:2). Other spirits can speak to us in our sleeping hours, perhaps even more than in our waking life. Every culture and society in history (apart from the modern West) has understood that the dream can act as a 'meeting place' with the Spirit world.[7] The Native Americans have their dream-catchers; the Chinese have their dream books; the Ancient Babylonians their professional dream interpreters; the Hindus their Upanishads and the Muslims their Qur'an. Even in the first-century Greco-Roman world, dreams were seen as a doorway into the spiritual realm. The ancient Temple of Asclepius provided sleeping chambers where you could reserve your bed overnight in anticipation of a visit from the god of medicine in your dreams. While God can speak in our dreams, so can the Enemy.

The solution is not to dispense with dreams entirely but to *discern* their source. The issue is not the mode of communication but where they come from. When Paul wrote of his visions of the third heaven to the Corinthians, he would have been aware of the practices of the Asclepian temple in nearby Epidaurus. Paul still held to the validity of God-dreams even as other spirits used the same form. The presence of the false does not dismiss the possibility of the true. But, as with any Spirit-experience, dreams must be tested for their authenticity.

It is clear that dreams and visions are God's preferred mode of communication in Scripture. A commitment to the truth of God's working in the past alerts us to his preferred way of working in the present. If God entrusted the biblical characters with the capacity to discern divine revelation in this way, he can trust us to do the same.

Sometimes we need a donkey

Even though the Spirit's revelation does not *require* the mediation of other people, God *can* still speak to us through them. One of my most profound 'hearing God' experiences came through a book. It was a well-loved title called *Hinds' Feet on High Places* by Hannah Hurnard and was recommended to me by a work colleague. At the time, I wasn't really interested in reading it, until the next day when I was visiting a friend. There on her coffee table lay the book, *Hinds' Feet on High Places*. I picked it up and asked my friend about it: 'Are you reading this?'

'No,' she said. 'When I woke up this morning, the Holy Spirit said to get it out for you, because you need to read it.'

That book changed my life. I still remember weeping as I turned the pages. The scenes vividly mirrored what had been going on in my own life; even the dialogue of the characters echoed my prayers. God used it to beautifully answer a number of questions I had in my life at the time.

The truth is God can use *anything* to speak! All creation is at his disposal (Ps. 19:1–2). He uses preachers and teachers, authors and bloggers, videos and films. He draws on nature as his object lessons. He creates visuals and metaphors and imagery to help us relate to what he is saying. The ravens who have no storeroom become a metaphor for his provision; the flowers of the field, a reminder of his careful attention to our lives (Luke 12:24,27). This is the beauty of the incarnational Spirit who crafts his messages in ways that we can receive. The classic Old Testament tale of the donkey speaking to a stubborn Balaam reflects the adaptability of God's speech to meet the situation (Num. 22:28–30). Sometimes we need a 'donkey' to hear from God. As in my own testimony, a tangible medium such as a book or sermon can be helpful. As we've seen, God is committed to getting his *message* across, no matter the *mode*.

At the same time, limiting God-speech to indirect means such as sermons, books and the counsel of others inhibits us from accessing the full spectrum of God-speech. These 'indirect' experiences are more likely to relate to what God has spoken in the past than the present. Such experiences are both valuable and necessary because they remind us of the truths that have been spoken (John 14:26), but, once the foundation is laid, where to from there? Jesus said the Spirit would be given to speak about issues *beyond* what he had spoken (John 16:13). Direct experiences mean that we can hear God's voice anew for personal and contemporary situations.

John, the author of Revelation, would have been grateful for this reality. When exiled on Patmos, he was still able to draw on divine revelation for his circumstances. As a prisoner of the state, John had no direct access to either the church or the Scriptures. Yet, through dream-visions, the Spirit was still able to speak. Because John was grounded in the truth of Jesus, he was able to discern his experiences appropriately and, as such, was able to access God's wisdom for his own life and the churches of Asia Minor, in the face of a potentially hostile Roman Empire. This is the beauty of the Spirit *with us*.

***

The biblical modes of Spirit revelation are employed for good reason. A commitment to the integrity of the biblical pattern calls us to remove our historic blind spot and revisit our understanding of how God speaks and why he chooses to do so. God's intention under the New Covenant has always been to provide direct access to God's voice. The Spirit is not confined to a sermon in a building, a preacher in a pulpit, or teaching in a book. *We* are the temple of the Holy Spirit. God's words are written on *our* hearts. We do not need another person to reveal the things of the Spirit (1 John 2:27; Jer. 31:34). God may speak wherever we are, whoever we are with, through whatever we have.

10

How to Recognise God's Voice (1): Getting It Wrong – and Right

The faceless women

Grace was a new Christian when she first started dreaming of a group of women she had never met. It was an unusual scene. For some reason, the women's faces were completely covered over. In one of the dreams, Grace saw a large sign – like the Hollywood sign – with a message in capital letters: 'Prepare yourself before you go.' The dream came repeatedly for three months. Frustrated, Grace shared her dreams with her brother. He explained that God spoke in dreams in the Bible: 'You may be hearing from God.'

During this time, a missionary visited Grace's church. Grace was riveted as the man shared about his ministry among the unreached peoples of the world. Then he finished his sermon with the words, 'Prepare yourself before you go!' Grace leapt out of her seat and immediately responded to his call for prayer. Afterwards, she volunteered her information technology (IT) skills with a local mission organisation. Some time later, she commenced a three-year study programme at a missionary training college.

Grace was part-way through her studies when a guest speaker named Patrick Johnstone visited the college. Johnstone had published a prayer guide called 'Operation World' that detailed the spiritual needs of nations all across the globe. During his message, he mentioned the need for help with IT. Once again Grace volunteered her skills. But when they met afterwards, Patrick didn't mention IT.

Instead, he asked Grace a question: 'Have you ever heard of the Uyghur people in Kashgar, Central Asia?' When she said no, Patrick began telling her about them. He talked about their history and culture and the lack of Christian witness among them. 'I think you really need to look into this,' he said, and the meeting finished. They never did talk about IT.

When Grace returned to her room that day, she happened upon a book that had been gifted to her by her sister the day she left for college. It was called *The Forgotten Tribes of China*. When she opened it, the page fell open to a photograph of a group of women whose faces were covered. Grace was taken aback. It was the faceless women from the dream! Finally, she understood why she couldn't see their faces. As Muslims, their heads were draped in thick brown burqas.

After graduating from her studies, Grace moved to Kashgar. There she began ministering to the veiled women of the city. She stayed for ten years, connecting with locals, sharing her faith and supporting local churches. Many of the women she spoke with had never heard the gospel before. Some had experienced dreams of Jesus and were keen to know more. Grace tells how she felt the sovereign positioning of God in her work as the people there treated her like family. This is where she belonged.

By far the most difficult part of having a God-conversation is *recognising* God's voice. 'How do I know it's God?' is one of the most common questions people ask. We've heard plenty of stories of those who got it wrong, but Grace's story demonstrates how we can get it right. It may take time (in Grace's case, seven years), but it's clear that throughout her journey, God was working to help Grace recognise his voice. Even for a new Christian, the Holy Spirit was able to get his message across. The reason should be obvious. God *helps* us to discern his voice so that people like the Uyghurs can be reached and his mission can be fulfilled. How else can we follow God's voice unless we first recognise it?

Most of the hazards in hearing the Spirit are wrapped up in a lack of proper discernment. The problem is never with God; we are the ones who muddy the process. While it is relatively straightforward to distinguish the voice of the Enemy from the voice of the Spirit once we are familiar with God's nature in Jesus, it is often challenging to separate God's voice from our own desires.

The next three chapters describe how to recognise God's voice, in detail. In this chapter, we start with two equally important attitudes that are needed from the outset: the confidence to know we can get it right, and the humility to know we can get it wrong. From there, we look at a model for discernment based on the narrative pattern of the early church. The three criteria outlined are easy to use and reflect the practices of the historic church and the Catholic tradition. We also take time to compare the New Covenant process of discernment with the Old to demonstrate further why the new regime is such an improvement. Finally, we look at the question of who is responsible for discerning the Spirit's voice.

Two essential attitudes

When it comes to recognising God's voice, we must begin with a 'posture of scepticism'. In other words, before we get it right, we need to humbly admit that we can get it wrong. We must take responsibility for our weaknesses and failings. This is especially important for those who are still learning to recognise the Spirit. Renowned Catholic theologian Karl Rahner put it this way: 'Where the supernatural, divine origin of a vision is alleged, this claim must be *proved, not presumed* . . . the burden of proof rests upon him who affirms a thesis, not upon him who doubts or denies it.'[1]

A sceptical approach is necessary because we know that while God's revelation is pure, we are not. Like clean water that becomes polluted when it flows through a rusty pipe, our flawed humanity contaminates what we hear. Our mindsets, desires and experiences all act together to create a 'fuzzy' filter through which we hear from God. As Paul says, we 'see in part' and 'know in part' (see 1 Cor. 13:9,12). Often God's messages become mixed with our own, so that we end up seeing what we want to see and hearing what we want to hear.

Our flawed humanity has always been the problem – today as it was in biblical times. Just as Jeremiah observed in his clash with the false prophets, we too are prone to speaking visions 'from our own minds' (see Jer. 23:16,36). Testing is and always has been necessary due to humanity's propensity for sin and manipulation. We should be slow to make any claim to divine inspiration. It is a fearful thing to put *our* words into God's mouth.

Along with the humility to know we can get it wrong, we also need the second attitude – the confidence to know that we can get it right. God's voice *can* be identified. Even in our weakness, God is able to put his words into our mouths (Isa. 59:21; Acts 2:17). Jesus himself said that his people would recognise his voice and, in doing so, be able to follow (John 10:27). The Bible characters give us further confidence, since they had no problem saying 'God told me'. Our most famous stories begin with: 'And the word of the Lord came to . . .' and 'God spoke unto . . .' In the New Testament, you're more likely to read: 'The Holy Spirit said . . .' God's voice *is* recognisable. So, we approach God with faith, knowing that the Spirit was given to speak to every person who chooses to follow Jesus.

Our confidence receives a further boost when we realise that God is fully aware of our frailties. God sees our propensity for mixed messages; he knows our fears and doubts. The writer of Deuteronomy echoes his empathy: 'You may say to yourselves, "How can we know when a message has not been spoken by the Lord?"' (Deut. 18:21). God not only recognises our weakness but also caters for it. He gives us a clear testing process to use and then he himself abides by it.

The Scriptures are clear that every claim to revelation – every voice we hear or vision we see – *must* be put to the test before it is responded to. This is the case under both the Old Covenant (Deut. 18:21–22) and the New (1 John 4:1; 1 Cor. 14:29). The testing process removes the filters of sin and self. It separates out the demonic voices that deceive and confuse. Like a fog burned off by the morning sun, it removes the fuzziness and makes it clear.

The need for testing applies particularly to those Spirit experiences that Jesus referred to as things 'to come' (John 16:13). These are the messages that go beyond what Jesus has already said in the Gospels and what is expressed in apostolic teaching (John 14:26). For example, when the Spirit says 'You are loved and valued', there is no reason to test the message, because these truths conform to what Jesus has already taught. We know they are valid because they have been tested by the early church through the canonisation process. But when the Spirit speaks of something future-oriented or unknown – say, a promotion at work or a new direction in ministry – it must be tested. This need for regulation applies every time the Spirit speaks beyond the canon.

Samuel the novice

Once we understand that we can get it both wrong and right, we need to implement the discernment process. Here we need to remember that this isn't always a cut-and-dried process. Recognising God's voice takes learning and improves with time and experience. This shouldn't be surprising, since discernment first and foremost is a *relational skill*. Ask anyone who has been in a long-term friendship or married for a length of time; it's clear that communication improves as we get to know the person. Over time, we learn to recognise their nuances of tone and body language. We pick up on their familiar vocabulary and distinctive cues. The same applies to the divine–human relationship. We learn to discern the Spirit's voice through the practice of listening and communicating.

The prophet Samuel is a good example of someone who learned to recognise God's voice. Samuel was one of Israel's foremost 'experts' in hearing God and became the prototype for all prophets to come. His ministry was attested to by kings and leaders, with Scripture saying that none of his words 'fell to the ground' (1 Sam. 3:19). Clearly, Samuel knew how to recognise God's voice. However, it wasn't always that way. The first time he heard from God, he didn't recognise it (1 Sam. 3:1–21). The biblical account tells us that it took three repeat experiences before Samuel recognised God's voice, and he still couldn't do it without Eli's input. Even for one of the biblical greats, the ability to recognise God's voice was not automatic. It took time and experience before God's voice could be reliably discerned.

We see the same journey of development in Gideon's story. When God called Gideon to lead the Israelites into battle against the Midianites, Gideon battled with major doubts about what he had heard. Admittedly, the call was absurdly irrational in human terms. The Midianites had been oppressing Israel for years and severely outnumbered them in numbers and weaponry. Gideon himself was lacking in confidence; a poor choice for leadership by any standard. The cost of Gideon getting his God-talking experience wrong was extreme; he not only risked his own life but also the lives of his troops and the survival of the nation itself.

Yet, in the midst of his doubt, God's commitment to clarity resounds. God actually *anticipates* Gideon's struggle to recognise his voice and provides a confirming dream through the voice of the enemy (Judg. 7:13–16): 'If you are afraid to attack, go down to the camp with your servant Purah and listen to what they are saying. Afterwards, you will be encouraged to attack the camp' (vv. 10–11). Even though today Gideon often gets a bad rap for asking God for multiple 'fleeces', in this part of the story God empathised with his doubt and actually initiated a process of confirmation.

We also see uncertainty in discernment in the life of the prophet Jeremiah. While he had heard from God before, Jeremiah had personally witnessed the possibility of error among the prophets opposing him (Jer. 28 – 29). Later, we find him wrestling with what he had heard. Could it really be God asking him to buy a field when the nation was about to be exiled by the Babylonians? With the armies camped just outside the city and the siege ramps stacked high on the walls, it certainly didn't look like it (Jer. 32:16–27).

It is clear that under the Old Covenant, the prophets were people 'even as we are' (Jas 5:17). Some got it right and some got it wrong. Proficiency in hearing God was acquired through experience and practice. The very existence of the 'Schools of the Prophets' established by

Elijah (1 Sam. 19:20; 10:10; 2 Kgs 4:1; 6:1,9) reveals the need for training and development under the Old Covenant.

Fast-forward to the New Covenant church and we see a similar dynamic. There were times when God's voice was clear and times when it wasn't. The story of Paul's trip to Jerusalem in the latter part of his life is often cited as an example of the potential for ambiguity. The issue concerned a proposed missionary trip to Jerusalem. Paul had heard God say he should go (Acts 20:22–23), but both Agabus and the disciples of Tyre claimed to hear God saying he shouldn't (Acts 21:4,10–12). Someone got it wrong! One thing they did agree on, however, was the likelihood of persecution in Jerusalem. Agabus specifically prophesied that if Paul went, the Jews would capture and bind him. As it turned out, Agabus was only partly right. When Paul eventually did go, it was the Romans who bound him, even while the Jews handed him over. The general gist was clear, even though the details were fuzzy.[2]

When we think about the overall process of gathering the New Testament Scriptures together, we see too that it mirrored our own discernment practices and, as such, was a messy and time-consuming process.[3] It took sustained effort to sift the false from the true, and conclusions weren't always unanimous. It wasn't until the fourth century that the canon was officially closed, and up until then, differences existed as to what should be included. A number of books went in and out before the final list was confirmed at the Nicene Council. The books of Revelation and 2 Peter were only added at the last minute. Then, during the Reformation, Martin Luther argued for James, Hebrews, Jude and Revelation to be ousted. Even today, the Catholic stream of Christianity has the Apocrypha and the Orthodox Church has 1 and 2 Maccabees. Our humanity means that discernment will always require humility and careful reflection.

Just because the Bible states 'The Lord says . . .' or 'The word of the Lord came to . . .' does not mean God's messages were always received smoothly. The biblical characters were as human as we are. Mistakes were made, learning was involved and testing was required.

The Scriptures are the *final* outcome of a discernment process that required careful regulation. While we know that God is an effective communicator, the onus is on us to grow in our discernment ability. The outcome won't always be perfect, but as any foreign speaker knows, communication is possible even with the basics. It all starts with a conviction that the Spirit is able to make it clear.

Trusting the Spirit

Whenever we feel that inviting sinful people to discern the Spirit for themselves is too risky, it is helpful to remember that after three years with the disciples, Jesus *left*. Jesus trusted the Spirit. He trusted the process. After laying the foundational truths in his incarnation, he handed on the ongoing revelatory work to the Spirit to work through the lives of his flawed disciples. Jesus did not feel under any compulsion to tell his disciples everything they needed to know. He left, knowing his disciples could get it wrong.

If we're honest, most of us wouldn't have taken that approach. If we were Jesus, we would have downloaded a lot more instructions. I, for one, would have talked more about the church and what it should look like. I would have given details on matters such as how 'Jewish' the Gentiles should be when they followed Jesus, how to organise church governance, the set-up for pastoral gatherings, and the like. I certainly would have given more insight into all those would-be controversial issues, such as the role of women in ministry, food offered to idols and slavery, that would soon confound the church. Then I would have provided an entire range of caveats and contingency plans for when things went wrong. I would have made it clear, and then I would have organised a scribe to write it all down.

But Jesus didn't. He relied on the Spirit to convey some of the most important truths for the church's ministry and mission. He relied on the *subjective experiences* of flawed individuals to communicate the specifics of how to incorporate the nations, how to behave under persecution and how to plan the most strategic routes for mission. In leaving, Jesus demonstrated greater faith in our ability to get it right than fear in our propensity to get it wrong.

Too often today, we act in the reverse. Our fears of getting it wrong overwhelm our faith in the Spirit to get it right. Most of our rejection of extrabiblical revelatory experiences stems from this fear. Our typical response is to shut it down, tighten it up, control it or deny it. Fear has always been an effective driver.

We must remember it was this same kind of fear that drove medieval leaders to prohibit the translation of the Scriptures during the Reformation. After all, if the common people could access the Bible in their own language, *they could get it wrong.* The people had no education and no ability to interpret what they were reading. In this, the medieval leaders were correct. People *did* get it wrong. Universal access to the pages of Scripture meant that anyone could make up their own interpretation. Anyone could take verses out of context and skew them to their own agenda. The result has been just that, with the proliferation of denominations as well as a litany of cults.

At the same time, fear of getting it wrong meant that generations of Christians were cut off from knowing God for themselves through the pages of the Bible. Imagine being banned from reading the words of Jesus, the Psalms and even simple passages such as the Lord's Prayer. As a lay person, you were executed for those kinds of activities during the Reformation.

Let history teach us this lesson: fear cannot be our driver. Yes, it is true that open access to the Spirit brings a whole range of risks. Yes, we can get it wrong, and we *will* get it wrong. But Jesus still left. He still sent his Spirit to be received in direct experiential ways. God's ways have always been to work with us in spite of our frailties.

***

In order to quell our fear of getting it wrong, we return to our original conviction that we *can* get it right. The breadth of biblical history is a demonstration of God's ability as a communicator. Then we need to embrace the testing process, understanding that it can take time and practice and that any one of us is subject to error. The next two chapters unfold a model of discernment that is simple but comprehensive. All it takes is the patience and humility to implement it. Above all, we need to trust in God's ability to make his messages clear over our ability to distort them. It's what Jesus did.

11

How to Recognise God's Voice (2): Would Jesus Say This?

How did Peter know it was God?

Peter was a young intern fresh out of training when he was commissioned by God to build the church. Full of zeal and energy, he was ready to take on his call, but he was also profoundly inexperienced. This was a whole new area of ministry and there were few models to draw from. So, one morning just before lunch, Peter set his face to seek God. While he was praying, God spoke in a vision.

It was an unusual scene. The heavens opened to reveal a large sheet. Laid out on the sheet was the midday meal. But it wasn't what Peter expected. Reptiles, birds, four-footed creatures. These were unclean animals! *Non-kosher* food. For a devout Jew, they were all ritually banned. Peter's stomach would have reeled at the spread. Then, to his astonishment, a loud voice beamed down from the heavens: 'Get up, kill and eat!'

His response was immediate: 'No! I would never eat unclean food!'

Peter was still pondering the scene when it came again – and again. Three times, he was presented with a table of unclean food. Three times the voice told him to eat it. Afterwards, Peter wandered around his house in confusion. How could a voice from heaven be telling him to break the law?

While Peter was still struggling to make sense of his experience, he heard a knock at the door. When he opened it, he would have experienced the same revulsion as in the dream. *Ugh.* Unclean Gentiles.

A Roman soldier and servants from Caesarea. To make it worse, they invited him to the home of their master, Cornelius. His internal response would have been immediate: *No! I would never enter an unclean house!*

The story unfolds as a defining moment in the church. Against all he had known, Peter accepted the Gentiles' invitation and travelled with them to Cornelius's home by the sea. There he preached the message he thought was reserved for the Jews to a group of Gentiles. As he did, the Spirit fell, producing the same phenomena as on the Day of Pentecost. The church of the Gentiles was born.

Today we celebrate these events as a matter of course. But too easily we forget the spurious nature of their beginnings. How did Peter know his vision was from God? His experience came while he was waiting for lunch. He prayed, fell into a trance and dreamt of food! What's more, everything about his experience defied what God had already said in Scripture. Laws about non-Jewish people had been practised since the time of Moses and were a binding part of the Old Covenant. Passage after passage told of the uncleanliness of the Gentiles. As God's holy people, Jews were to remain separate from them. Jews were not to enter Gentile homes. Gentiles were not allowed into the holiest parts of the temple. They were ritually unclean.

And yet, here is Peter claiming that the plan had changed because 'God had told him'. Suddenly Gentiles *were* welcome – not only at the Jews' table but also in their identity as God's people. Israel was no longer God's 'favourite' (Acts 10:34). You can only imagine the raised eyebrows. The intense degree of opposition from the 'Judaisers' later (e.g. Gal. 2:11–13) gives you some idea of the radical nature of Peter's new revelation.

Yet Peter had enough confidence to claim divine origins for his experience. He knew he could get it wrong (he had done so before [Matt. 16:23]), and the call to test the spirits was on him as much as it is on us. However, on this occasion, Peter *knew* that it was God, and he knew it well enough to act on it. His God-conversation became the impetus for a movement that would extend well beyond a minority Jewish sect to become the largest religion in the world.

As we've seen, the discernment of our spiritual experiences is crucial to discipleship as well as to the safety of our churches. As one of the most significant revelatory experiences post-Pentecost, Peter's vision of the unclean food provides us with a helpful model for recognising God's voice.

There are three criteria for discernment evident in Peter's story that should be used to test our own Spirit-experiences. These same criteria can be seen in the long-standing practice of the Catholic tradition (with some adaption).[1] They are: 1) Would Jesus say this? 2) Is someone else saying this? And 3) Are spiritual signs accompanying this?

In this chapter, we discuss the first and most important test question: would Jesus say this?

The first test question: would Jesus say this?

Let's revisit the story from Peter's perspective: how did he know his vision on the rooftop was from God? Peter knew he had been called to build the church (Matt. 16:18), but Jesus hadn't left him with specific instructions on how to do it. While Peter had been grounded in gospel truths about the character of God, the nature of God's kingdom, the way of salvation and the mechanics of Spirit-led ministry, he had never been told where to build the 'church', how to structure it or who to build it with.

Instead, Jesus had promised Peter and his fellow disciples that the Spirit would act as his continuing voice after he left. The Spirit would remind them of the truths Jesus had established (John 14:26) and then, as needed, speak about things to come (John 16:13). Peter's vision fell into the latter category. In this, Jesus had been clear: as his continuing voice, the Spirit would speak in line with what Jesus had begun. The voice would be consistent with the nature of God most fully revealed *in him*.

When the Spirit fell at Pentecost, the church was only comprised of Jews (Acts 2). So, if the Spirit's voice was consistent with Jesus, the question of the first test becomes: would Jesus say the gospel was for Gentiles too?

We see that when Peter later reflected on his experience, he 'remembered' what Jesus had said (Acts 11:16). Peter had spent three years of his life getting to know Jesus as 'the Word' in the flesh. Although Jesus' ministry was almost entirely with the Jews (Matt. 15:24), at times he did mix with Gentiles. He healed the Roman centurion's son (Luke 7:1–10) and exorcised a Gadarene demoniac (Matt. 8:28–34). He spoke of Samaritans as neighbours to be loved (Luke 10:25–37) and talked about God's heart for Gentiles even under the Old Covenant (Luke 4:23–27). Most significantly, his parting words were to preach the gospel to *all* nations and ethnicities (Matt. 28:18–20). The record is clear. Jesus' example was consistent with the vision on the rooftop. Yes, Jesus *would* say this. Peter's experience passed the first test.

As it was for Peter, so it is for us. Testing must always start with: would Jesus say this? All authentic contemporary experiences will be consistent with the life and teachings of Jesus. Our experiences will either be a reminder of the truths Jesus exemplified in his incarnation and now recorded for us in Scripture; or they will be about things to come that line up with God's nature in Jesus. Jesus is described as the 'image of the invisible God' (Col. 1:15) and the 'exact representation of his being' (Heb. 1:3). Therefore, every dream or vision, voice or impression should be tested against the question: 'Would Jesus say this?' All claims to revelation must pass through this filter.

In answering this question, we are not only considering everything Jesus *said* but also everything Jesus *did*. The beauty of the incarnation is that it *embodied* God's message. As the living Word, Jesus provided us with a vivid and tangible template for God's heart in multiple situations. This template transcends the words Jesus said to the actions he performed and the impact they had on others. When Jesus gathered children into his lap and reached out to a despised leper, he was sending a message about who God is. When he spoke with an adulterer and dined with a tax collector, he was communicating God's heart. When he stretched out his arms on the cross, he spoke the greatest message of all.

So, we ask, is what we're hearing consistent with Jesus' words of compassion, his touches of healing and his acts of sacrifice? Does it line up with his teaching on the kingdom, his provision for the hungry, his treatment of women, children and the poor? Does it bring the fruit of the Spirit – love, joy, peace, forbearance, kindness, goodness, faithfulness, gentleness and self-control (Gal. 5:22–23)? Does it encourage, comfort and edify people (1 Cor. 14:3)? These were the fruits of Jesus' ministry on earth and will be the fruit of his continuing voice today. As the angel of Revelation said to John, the testimony of Jesus *is* the spirit of prophecy (Rev. 19:10). Every authentic revelatory experience must be anchored in Jesus. This is our non-negotiable.

The more we understand the nature and character of God in Jesus, the easier it is then to recognise the voice of the Enemy. Whenever our experiences come with guilt, fear or condemnation, we can immediately dismiss them. Even when Jesus corrected the adulterous woman (John 8:1–11), his words brought truth and freedom, rather than judgement or shame. The life and teachings of Jesus must always be the filter for our experiences.

Having Jesus as the starting point for our discernment also makes the recognition of God's voice accessible to everyone. Even new Christians can discern God's voice when they have a basic understanding of who Jesus is. Children too can learn to answer the question: 'Would Jesus say this?' When I asked my friend Nicola how she teaches young people to recognise God's voice in the African villages where Bibles are few and literacy is rare, she said, 'Oh, that's easy. We just tell them the stories of Jesus.' If we want to recognise the Spirit's voice, we must first get to know the one who most fully embodies it.

A familiar voice

The link between the Spirit's voice and the life of Jesus makes the discernment process a highly personal one. Recognising God's voice becomes easier in the context of a personal, two-way relationship. In the same way that you learn to recognise the voice of a friend with time, you find it easier to recognise God's voice with a shared history.

This dynamic was demonstrated time and time again in my own research into the hearing God experience. When interviewees were asked how they knew it was God, they would say things like, 'Oh, I *know* that voice. I've heard it before.' People related to the *tone* of the voice as well as to the content. 'He's in a good mood,' one participant said. Even when the voice was firm and disciplinary, it was known for its gentleness. Sometimes, people recognised the voice because of its familiar vocabulary. Like any human relationship, the voice was recognisable because it came in the context of a relationship that had grown over time.

I was reminded of the value of familiarity in recognising God's voice when Ali, a member of our God Conversations prayer team, shared a vision she had for me. She had seen a life-size clock and I was standing in the centre of it. My arms were the hands of the clock and I was spinning round and round.

At first, Ali couldn't make sense of the vision, but I recognised it instantly. Both the imagery and topic of conversation were familiar. God and I had been discussing the issue of timing for the previous twenty years, beginning with the dream of the thief in the night I shared in Chapter 8. Back then, the hands of the clock had been spinning so fast I couldn't read them, and God was saying, 'You don't know the time, but get ready anyway.' In Ali's vision, my arms were the hands and *I* was the one spinning round and round. This time God was saying, 'You know the time', and to some degree, 'It's in your hands.' A month or so later, another friend had a similar vision. She saw me holding a clock: 'You're the timekeeper. You know the time.' It wasn't difficult to know the message was from God!

The basis for discernment of God's voice is our relationship to a *person*. God's voice becomes as familiar as the voice of a friend on the phone. Like secrets shared between two confidants and pet words reserved for lovers, recognition comes as a product of our shared and intimate history.

Our Old Covenant shadow

We've seen that the more we know Jesus, the easier it is to recognise the voice of the Spirit. Of course, the truest and most reliable record of Jesus' life and ministry is provided in the Scriptures, particularly the Gospels. We get to know Jesus' words and teachings by reading them deeply. However, this Christocentric approach to discernment raises questions about the rest of the Scriptures, and the Old Testament in particular. Don't we use *all* of Scripture to discern God's voice?

The answer is 'yes' *and* 'no'. When the Jerusalem Council eventually met to discuss the message of Peter's vision about the Gentiles, they were *selective* in their use of the Jewish Scriptures (Acts 15). The problem was that while some passages pointed to integration of the Gentiles, others didn't. The Jerusalem Council quoted Amos 9:11–12 to support their acceptance, but they could have equally argued against it using references like Exodus 19:5 and Deuteronomy 26:18–19.[2] The Scriptures as a whole were limited in their ability to judge Peter's vision because God's revelation under the Old Covenant was only a *shadow* of the New. Instead, the Council read the Scriptures through the eyes of Jesus – the ultimate measure of God's character and nature; the 'radiance of God's glory and the exact representation of his being' (Heb. 1:3). As the writer of Hebrews reminds us: 'In the past God spoke to our ancestors through the prophets at many times and in various ways, but *in these last days* he has spoken to us by his Son' (Heb. 1:1–2a).

As we've seen, the full revelation of God in Jesus is one of the reasons why the New Covenant is superior to the Old (1 Cor. 11; Heb. 8:6–11). All the words of the prophets, and indeed of the entire Old Covenant, point to him. This was Jesus' message to the disciples on the Emmaus road, when he showed them how *all* of the Scriptures concerned himself (Luke 24:27). Jesus is the goal, fulfilment and culmination of the law (Rom. 10:4). Because of Jesus' coming, we have far greater clarity hearing from the Spirit than Abraham, Moses or Amos ever did. His incarnation vividly demonstrates God's nature and gives us a kaleidoscope of scenarios by which to discern our experiences.

This perspective does not minimise the importance of the Old Testament. The way of salvation in Jesus is incomplete without the backstory of God's people Israel. The writings of the Old Covenant are sacred canon because they present the story of God. The whole narrative points to the climax of salvation history and Jesus' fulfilment of the covenant promises.

But when it comes to discernment, the Old Covenant experiences become less useful as a model for our own. Jesus' incarnation overshadows the revelation of God in the Old Testament. As the fully embodied Word, Jesus filled in the blanks of the prophets' words. It is therefore nonsensical to use their lens to discern our experiences. Why use a shadow when you have the perfect image? Why look back to the prophets' time when they looked forward to ours? (1 Pet. 1:10–12). What's more, there's real danger in using Old Covenant experiences as a reference point for our own. The story of the Roman emperor Constantine in the fourth century AD illustrates this. Instead of bringing encouragement, comfort and strength to people (1 Cor. 14:3), Constantine's visionary experience led to a gruesome bloodbath.

The cautionary tale of Constantine

When Constantine was proclaimed emperor of Rome in the early fourth century AD, Christians all over the empire breathed a sigh of relief. Under former leaders, Christians had been the butt of Greco-Roman society. After being scorned, persecuted and killed for entertainment in the great arenas, followers of Jesus viewed Constantine's conversion to Christianity as a long-awaited answer to prayer. Even though reports say that he had only a fledgling faith, with somewhat mixed beliefs, his decision meant that the persecution of Christians soon became illegal throughout the empire. Christians were to be treated in the same way as everyone else.[3] The edict marks one of the most monumental turning points in history, but tragically its impact wasn't entirely positive.

Constantine's story centres on a battle that took place at a pivotal point in his rise to power. It is said that when facing his rival Maxentius on the Milvian Bridge on the outskirts of Rome, Constantine prayed for help. His answer came in the form of a vision in the sky – an image of the cross and the words: 'In this sign, conquer.' Later, Constantine arranged for a symbol of the cross (the Chi Rho – the first two letters of the Greek word for 'Christ') to be painted on the shields of his warriors and went into battle. The armies clashed and Constantine won a decisive victory.

Of course, not everyone believes this popular retelling of Constantine's vision. Historians question its veracity, given the varying accounts, Constantine's somewhat rocky road to faith, and the way claims to divine revelation have been used to strengthen a leader's position.[4] But there is always the possibility that Constantine *did* see something in the sky. For our purposes, consider *how* the vision was discerned.

If Constantine had tested his vision against Old Testament experiences, he would have easily found precedent for his actions. Whenever the tribes of the ancient world confronted their enemies, they sought endorsement from their god. Here, the god would act as a 'banner' over their armies as they went into battle. The Ancient Israelites were no different; they too entered wars, slaughtered their enemies and proclaimed victory under the banner of their god Yahweh (e.g. Exod. 17:15–16; Ps. 18:34–40).[5] Like the ISIS terrorists today who fight in the name of Allah, an act of war was understood to be an act of worship in the name of Yahweh (Deut. 7:1–6).

But if Constantine had tested his vision against the New Testament, he would have seen the clarity that came with the coming of Jesus. Jesus showed us that God's way has always been to love your enemies (Matt. 5:44), turn the other cheek (Matt. 5:38–40) and do good to those who hurt you, even to the point of allowing love to nail you to a cross (Rom. 5:8). Under the Old Covenant, God's mercy and love were still evident (e.g. Lam. 3:22–23), but people could only see a 'shadow' of his true nature (Heb. 10:1). God was speaking, but the message was blurred through the filter of ancient thinking, so that the Israelites thought the successful killing of another person was a sign of God's presence. As God said, they thought he was 'exactly like' them (Ps. 50:21).

If Constantine had interpreted his vision in the light of Jesus, the 'exact representation' of God's being (Heb. 1:3), his interpretation would not have been more different. Now that God had spoken through his Son, Constantine could have seen more fully who God was. He could never have justified painting a cross on a shield as a weapon of war. He could not have plunged his sword into the side of an enemy soldier and proclaimed victory in the name of Jesus. Instead, he would have understood the power of bloodshed through Jesus' eyes. It would have come in the form of a man giving his life on a cross in love for the world (John 3:16; 15:13). The 'sword' would not be a weapon in a sheath at his side, but rather a message of good news in his mouth (Rev. 19:15; Eph. 6:17). The shield would be used, not to ward off the attacks of men, but rather the attacks of the real Enemy (Eph. 6:16).

This is the way God's voice had been understood for the three hundred years prior to Constantine. The early church knew that the sign of the cross called them to follow the example of Jesus. So, they healed the sick, sheltered the poor and demonstrated faithful witness to a kingdom of love, joy and peace – even in the face of persecution. Constantine's misguided interpretation of his vision marked a turning point in history and provided a precedent for religious wars and the formation of institutions that used coercion and power for their own gain for hundreds of years in the future.[6] This set the pattern that fuelled the Crusades, inquisitions and all the violence of the militant church to come. The heart of Christianity became detached from the heart of Christ. Ultimately it led to a terrible confusion about what God is like, the very thing Jesus came to clarify.

Constantine got it wrong because he didn't test his vision against the fullest revelation of God in Jesus. He failed to ask the first and most important question of discernment: would Jesus say this? As a result, instead of producing the fruit of the Spirit – love, joy, peace and the like (Gal. 5:22–23) – Constantine's revelation ended in a bloodbath. Use of the Old Testament narratives to discern our Spirit-experiences today suffers from the same problem. You could end up with people justifying marriage to a prostitute (Hos. 1:2–3), committing genocide (Deut. 7:1–6) or filing for divorce on the basis of race and religion (Ezra 10:11). An ex-pastor could rationalise the murder of an abortion doctor, and a terrorist could reason that God had told him to kidnap teenagers. Whenever natural disasters or calamities hit, people could say it was God's judgement on sin rather than drawing on Jesus' assessment of the situation (e.g. Luke 13:4).[7] Discernment becomes based on the prophets' shadowed lenses rather than Jesus' clear one.

Today when we say to test revelation 'against the Scriptures', what we actually mean is: test it against *God's character* seen in the Scriptures. And the best way to understand that is in the life and teachings of Jesus.

***

In some ways, it would have been easier for Peter and his disciples to connect the Spirit's voice with Jesus than it is for us. The memories would have been so vivid: the words he said, the sense of strength and hope in his voice, even the bittersweet feeling that came when he rebuked them. Since Jesus sent the Spirit to 'replace' him, the connection would have been natural and easy.

Today we haven't experienced Jesus on earth with us, but we do have the Scriptures as a true and reliable record of his life. In order to recognise the Spirit, we need to immerse ourselves in them and become intimately familiar with all that Jesus said and did. Like the first disciples, recognising the Spirit will be easier when we know Jesus.

After all, this is one of the main reasons Jesus came to earth. When we ask, 'What is God like?', Jesus says, 'Anyone who has seen me has seen the Father' (John 14:9). When we ask, 'How do I know it's God?', Jesus says, it will sound like me (Rev. 19:10). We need to always ask, 'Would Jesus say this?' Every vision, no matter what the context, *must* be seen through his eyes. Why look into a shadow when we have perfect light?

12

How to Recognise God's Voice (3): The Church and Signs

Bankrupt and burnt out

David was a successful businessman who lived in an exclusive suburb of Sydney with his family. As a committed Christian and churchgoer, he had always endeavoured to serve God with all his heart. One day David heard God telling him to quit his job and trust him for his livelihood. So he shared the news with his wife and resigned from work. Time went on and nothing happened. David continued to wait in faith for God's provision, but nothing materialised. The family savings began to shrink. David's marriage started to fragment. A few months on and he had nearly lost his home – and his wife.

Eventually David turned to his pastor for counsel: 'Why didn't God come through?' As they talked about it, the answer became clear. David had not heard from God at all. He had been suffering from a severe case of burnout. Instead of hearing the voice of God, he had heard the voice of his weary and anxious mind.

Like David, Aaron was committed to following God's plans for his life. Aaron too heard God telling him to leave his job and trust him for provision. So he resigned his position and waited to see what would happen. Shortly after, God spoke to him about an opportunity that took him down a new career path. Then a large sum of money came unexpectedly into his life. In time, Aaron's step of faith and obedience released new levels of blessing that extended far beyond his dreams and plans.

David and Aaron's stories highlight the need for more than just the 'test of Jesus' to discern our revelatory experiences. We've seen that everything the Spirit says is consistent with the nature and character of Jesus. But would the Spirit of Jesus tell a person to leave their job and trust their finances to God? Maybe, yes. Maybe, no. The question 'Would Jesus say this?' is not sufficient for situations like those of David and Aaron. When God speaks about topics for which there is no precedent in the world of the first century, more is needed.

This chapter describes the second test question for hearing God's voice: is someone else saying this? And the third question: are spiritual signs following this? As before, Peter's visionary experience with the Gentiles provides us with the best model to follow. Then, in our last section on recognising the Spirit, we look at the question of *who* is responsible for testing revelatory experiences.

The second test question: is someone else saying this?

David's story is an awful one, but it was completely avoidable. Ultimately, his failing was not in his knowledge of Jesus or his earnestness to heed God's call, but in his inability to discern it in conversation with others. His story highlights the crucial role of the church. We may not need others to *hear* God's voice, but we do need their help *recognising* it. The second test by which we recognise God's voice is found in asking: is someone else saying this?

We see the involvement of other people in Peter's experience. The first and most important test had been passed: Jesus *would* say that the Gentiles were to be embraced by the church. But there was more. While Peter was dreaming of the lunch menu from his rooftop in Joppa, God was speaking to Cornelius in his home in Caesarea. Through some uncanny timing, the Spirit spoke to bring them both together and they discovered God was speaking the same message to each one of them independently of the other (Acts 11:11–14). God made his message clear by speaking *twice*.

We see a similar scenario in Mary and Elizabeth's story. After hearing from the angel about an impossible promise, Mary turned to her cousin Elizabeth – a person who knew how it felt to carry a child born of God's promise (Luke 1:13). The divine origins of Mary's vision were affirmed when Elizabeth's child leapt in the womb and she prophesied: 'Blessed are you among women and blessed is the child you will bear' (Luke 1:42). Like Peter and Cornelius, the word of the Lord came to two different people on two separate occasions. Indeed, we see this pattern throughout the birth accounts. Zechariah, Elizabeth, Anna and Simeon all heard from God about Jesus independently of one another. Each one's testimony confirmed the other. As the saying goes, 'there is safety in numbers'.

This is also the pattern we saw in Nicola's story, Grace's story, and countless others I have encountered in my research and ministry. The scenarios were miraculously timed and divinely initiated. Each time, God spoke more than once to make the message clear. Like witnesses in a law court, multiple voices filtered out the distortions and helped verify the issue. Cornelius provided a witness to Peter. Elizabeth provided a witness to Mary. An elderly woman provided a witness to Nicola, and a missions speaker provided a witness to Grace. As a result, they were all able to respond in faith and see the divine purpose birthed.

This does not mean that God speaks to *everyone* about a particular matter. God is not a gossipmonger, scattering his morsels indiscriminately to anyone in range. He speaks to strategic people at strategic moments. He is more likely to operate through individuals than through the crowd. Consulting a 'multitude of counsellors' about any one revelatory experience usually only results in a multitude of opinions!

The courts of the Old Testament

The availability of Spirit-filled witnesses is one of the reasons why the New Covenant is such a substantial improvement on the Old. In ancient times, it was considerably more difficult to assess the source of a revelatory message. As we've seen, under the Old Covenant the Spirit came largely on the prophets – those who were specifically anointed to communicate revelatory messages on God's behalf. This meant you couldn't always find confirmation in the witness of others. So, in the days of Moses, Jeremiah and Amos, there was no equivalent to Elizabeth's prophecy or Cornelius's vision. Of course, this doesn't mean there was no means of discernment at all. God's messages still suffered pollutants and therefore required a process of assessment. The Old Testament text mentions three such tests, although as biblical scholars remind us, the lack of consistency across Old Covenant history makes it difficult for us to be too definitive about them.[1] They are worth outlining here to show how they compare with our criteria under the New Covenant.

The first test was the *test of fulfilment*. This involved the outcome of a prophetic message – if a revelation came to pass, you knew it was from God (Deut. 18:22). Jeremiah used this test in his argument with Hananiah over whose prophecy was correct (Jer. 28:15–17). He understood that a true word from God always contained the power to bring itself to fulfilment. However, this test had serious drawbacks. Sometimes a word could take decades to manifest and many of its hearers died before it did. That didn't leave much room for getting it right. The other issue involved the question of conditionality. A word could be from God, but it might *not* come to pass if people didn't cooperate with it, or, in the case of a warning, if they repented. The latter is what happened in Micah's prophecy when predictions about the destruction of Jerusalem failed because the people repented (Mic. 3:12). Similarly, Jonah's prophetic message to Nineveh didn't come to pass because the people changed their ways. As a means of discernment, the test of fulfilment had significant limitations.

The second test under the Old Covenant was the *test of the prophet*. This was essentially a character test. If a prophet showed evidence of holiness, their word could be trusted (Jer. 23:14), but if not, their revelatory messages were deemed suspect. This test seemed generally to hold, but there seemed to be some exceptions: a 'good' prophet could still get it wrong (2 Sam. 7:3; 1 Kgs 22:15) and a 'bad' prophet could still get it right (Deut. 13:1–3). Testing the prophet was helpful but not quite foolproof.

The third test was the *test of worship*. This related to the fruitfulness of the divine message in recipients' lives. If the message led you to worship the true God, it could be deemed authentic (Deut. 13:2–3; 18:15–20). This test was perhaps the most helpful, although again it was impossible to test the experience's source without waiting for the outcome.

The difficulties of testing God's voice under the Old Covenant highlight the benefits under the New. No longer is the experience of hearing from God relegated to the voice of one individual 'calling out in the desert', as prophets are often depicted (see John 1:23; Isa. 40:3). Now that *all* God's people have Spirit-access, God can speak to more than one. He can provide a witness through another person. This means that under the New Covenant, we can hear from God more clearly than under the Old.

The local church

The beauty of the New Covenant is that the church of Spirit-filled believers provides a witness to God's voice in the lives of others. But there is more to the church's role in discernment than providing a secondary revelatory experience.

Because our fellow Christians know the *general* ways of God, they are able to help us reflect on the voice of God in our *specific* experiences. The church helps us to discern God's voice by providing an objective perspective on our subjective experiences. This truth would have most likely saved David from near bankruptcy. Those who knew David would have been in a position to observe the stress he was under in his current employ. If they had been invited into the testing process, they would have been able to pick up on the signs of burnout and assess his claim to revelatory experience apart from them.

David's story also shows us that when we speak of 'the church' here, we are not talking about the entire community. We are referring to our inner circle – the people who know us well and who are familiar with our character and history, our foibles and blind spots. This relational knowledge places them in the best position to sort through the multiple voices and identify the divine one among them. Our confidants may not have heard from God directly, but because they know our story and because they know the ways of God they can offer a measure of wisdom. They should also be people who are willing to speak honestly and openly and challenge our perspective if needed. This is the type of consultation we see regarding the question of the Gentiles at the Jerusalem Council. After his visit to Cornelius's home, Peter shared his experiences with the wider leadership and they reflected on it together. When the final judgement was made, it was because it 'seemed good to the Holy Spirit *and to us*' (Acts 15:28).

It is clear that we need the church in order to recognise God's voice. While the senior leadership cannot be involved in every individual act of discernment, they must take responsibility for equipping their congregations to do the same. Even when we receive requests for discernment and dream interpretation in the online ministry at God Conversations, we nearly always point them back to their local church. People know they need help discerning their experiences, but they do not always know where to find it. Reflection must take place in the context of relationship, because it is the people who know and love us who are best equipped to help discern our experiences. While our revelatory experiences can take place at any place and any time, the discernment process always belongs in the church and, more particularly, in the safety of authentic and trusted relationships.

The third test question: are spiritual signs following this?

The final test for recognising God's voice involves a supernatural element. We know that God's words are an expression of his authority and contain the power to bring themselves to fulfilment (Gen. 1:3; Isa. 55:11; John 6:63). When God speaks, miracles follow. Therefore, we can recognise God's messages because they often come with manifestations of the Spirit that Scripture calls 'signs'.

We see a number of signs in Peter's story. They begin when Cornelius's servants arrive at Peter's home at the precise moment that Peter is contemplating his vision. Then, when Peter begins to preach to the Gentiles at Cornelius's home, the Spirit touches them miraculously in the same way as he had touched the Jews (Acts 11:15). Everyone sees that Peter's revelatory message was authentic because it was backed up by tangible indicators of God's presence.

Jesus also demonstrated the use of signs when he was on earth. When he spoke, 'signs and wonders' followed (Mark 16:20). For example, Jesus' words describing himself as the 'bread of life', and saying that those who came to him would 'never go hungry', were seen as divine when he multiplied the bread and fed them until they were full (John 6:35).

The pattern of signs following the word of the Lord extended beyond Jesus' ministry. Signs were a repeated form of divine affirmation throughout the book of Acts (2:19,22,43; 5:12; 6:8; 7:36; 14:3). They are also widely appealed to in the epistles (2 Cor. 12:12; Heb. 2:4).

Today, the idea of signs often has negative connotations. This is largely due to the way they can be manipulated to suit personal agendas. Too quickly, people read 'signs' into their circumstances as a way of finding certainty for their experiences and preconceived ideas. Psychologists have even given the phenomenon a name: 'confirmation bias'.

The beauty of genuine, divinely initiated signs is that they transcend confirmation bias. True signs cannot be misconstrued. They contain an element of the extraordinary that affirms the revelatory experience in ways that defy manipulation; for example, an aspect of foreknowledge comes to pass; previously unknown information is verified; a person experiences salvation and transformation; or a divine healing occurs. Spiritual signs cannot be humanly contrived. When God speaks, there will be something undeniably supernatural about it!

Signs have regularly followed the word of God in my own life. When God first spoke to me in a dream about moving to Sydney and working at Hillsong College, I had no idea that such a place existed. I was familiar with Hillsong *Church*, but did not know that a college had long since been part of their ministry. So my curious experience was written off without further thought. Then, that same day, I was lunching with a friend who for no reason started to talk about Hillsong College. 'But there's no such college,' I argued, while my friend proceeded to tell me otherwise. A year and a half later, through a series of serendipitous events, I found myself in Sydney and the scenes of my dream materialised. There had been no room for manipulation. God moved creatively and sovereignly to bring his words to fulfilment. Clear signs of the supernatural followed God's words all the way.

We see a similar dynamic in Jeremiah's experience back in the early sixth century BC. Signs were the means by which Jeremiah was able to discern his revelation to buy a field just outside Jerusalem. It shouldn't be surprising that at first he balked at the message; after all, the nation was about to be taken into exile. Buying the field was God's way of saying they would one day return to the land. But how was Jeremiah to know it was God? What tipped him off was a sign. God had included an element of foreknowledge in the prophetic message and, in doing so, created a ready mechanism for discernment: 'Your cousin Hanamel will make an offer to sell the field.' Sure enough, Hanamel arrived on Jeremiah's doorstep at the providential moment and offered to sell him the field. As Jeremiah said, then 'I *knew* this was the word of the LORD' (Jer. 32:8b).

These types of signs do not necessarily accompany *every* God-conversation. As God's voice becomes more familiar, there is less need for miraculous affirmations. But because God's words contain his power and authority, we should always expect an element of the supernatural to be involved.

Of course, not all extraordinary happenings are from God. Signs can be counterfeited by the one who masquerades as an angel of light (2 Cor. 11:14). Hence, the criterion of signs should always be applied in conjunction with the other two tests. Supernatural displays of power must always reflect the truth of Jesus (2 Thess. 2:9–12).

Who discerns?

Our last issue of discernment involves the responsibility for testing. Does it lie with leaders, the church or the individual?

Recently, I attended a conference hosted by a well-known prophetic ministry. It was full of inspirational teaching by reputable leaders who were experienced in handling the prophetic gift. However, in the opening session it was announced that during the conference, no one was permitted to prophesy. The very thing we had signed up to learn about, we were not allowed to do! The rationale was based on *who* was responsible for discernment. In this case, the answer was the senior pastor of a local church. Since this was an inter-church event and not all local pastors were present, it was thought that revelatory experiences could not be properly judged. Although the intention was good – to create an environment of safety and accountability – it meant the primary goal of the conference was partly undermined.

This scenario raises the question of who is responsible for discernment. We know that 'the church' in general should be involved, but how does it work in practice?

In his first letter to the Corinthians, Paul writes that when someone prophesies, the 'others' should weigh up what was said (1 Cor. 14:29). In the academic world, debates exist about who the 'others' were when he wrote those words. Was it the local church's prophets and those with gifts of discernment? Or was it the senior leadership? Or everyone in the church? The consensus seems to be that responsibility for discernment lies with *everyone*, even while the process remains unclear.[2]

The additional problem is that Paul's instructions to the Corinthians only relate to the public service. A pastor can be present when God speaks in the corporate setting, but what about when God speaks privately, when we're sleeping, taking a shower or driving to work? Some churches get around this by insisting that their congregants always consult with their leaders about their experiences. But, even if this kind of regulation were possible (increasingly onerous as the church grows in size), *should* it be the role of the leader to assess every experience? After all, this kind of set-up sends us back to the Old Covenant. It relegates the responsibility for hearing God to the clergy rather than to 'sons and daughters' and 'young and old'. There is a better way.

The answer to the question of responsibility for discernment lies in *who the audience is*. It depends on who is responsible for the message's outcome. If the message is for an individual, then the responsibility for discernment lies with the individual. If it is for the church, the responsibility lies with those who have responsibility for the church. This is why the discernment of Peter's vision did not finish at Cornelius's home. Although God's message was initially directed to Peter and Cornelius and their immediate sphere, it had ramifications for the entire church. Delegations were later sent from Antioch to investigate the matter (Acts 15:1–3). There were also other issues relating to circumcision and the law. Because it involved a larger audience, those who had jurisdiction over that audience – in this case the Jerusalem leadership – were responsible for its discernment. This is why a convening of the Council was necessary. Together, James and his team could reflect on the experiences of Peter and Cornelius (and others) and decide how to respond (Acts 15).

Compare this with another scenario in the life of the apostle Paul. As we've seen, when Paul was contemplating his final journey to Jerusalem, both the disciples at Tyre and the prophet Agabus prophesied that if he went, he would be handed over to the Gentiles (Acts 21:4,10,11). Fearful for his life, they urged him to reconsider. But Paul had already heard from the Spirit; he knew that trouble was imminent but that he was to testify to kings and influencers in spite of it (Acts 20:22–23). While Paul listened to the warnings of his local church community, he took responsibility for his own discernment and chose to go to Jerusalem anyway (Acts 21:12–14).

The desire to protect our church communities from poor discernment is a legitimate one. We need to do everything we can to prevent stories like David's. But the answer is not to confine discernment to church leadership. Instead, we must *train* our congregants to test their own experiences. We need to help them take responsibility for their own discernment, so that we do not rob them of the opportunity to grow as disciples and, in doing so, thwart the democratic intent of the New Covenant.

Where Joseph Smith got it wrong

In Chapter 3, we saw that many of the problems of revelatory experience came from a lack of healthy discernment. When we revisit the story of Joseph Smith and his visions of Moroni, we can now see clearly where it went wrong. Joseph's visions failed at the very first test. Would Jesus say that he appeared to an unknown pre-American civilisation with the keys to truth? Would Jesus say that his incarnation in the first century was insufficient to bring the gospel? No, Jesus would not. Joseph Smith made claims about Jesus that were not a part of the first-century apostolic witness as recorded in the New Testament documents. There was a good reason why the councils of the early church insisted that every canonical writer must have had close proximity to Jesus and/or been part of the first generation of the church. As we've seen, nothing can be added to the foundation that was laid in Jesus' incarnation, death and resurrection.

Joseph's visions also failed the second test: is someone else saying this? Every established church of the early nineteenth century rejected his claims. Even though there were claims to spiritual signs, these did not line up with the truths established in Jesus. Like so many in history, Smith's assertions transgressed the foundational truths of the gospel and contradicted the long-standing witness of the church.

***

A rigorous process of discernment is not optional for those who claim to hear from God. Our experiences are dubious and subjective. They are subject to our fleshly nature, individual agendas and corrupt filters. But by God's grace, we *are* able to get it right. When we see the activity of discernment in the early church, we see that God himself participates in the process. Through the incarnation of Jesus, the witness of the Spirit-filled church and the accompaniment of spiritual signs, God orchestrates our experiences in ways that help us verify a true revelatory message. Discernment is not difficult because the Spirit comes alongside to help us. Clarity *is* possible when we set our hearts to follow.

13

After God Speaks (1): The Making of a Disciple

The fast track or the slow?

Lola was a successful executive living in New York when she made a decision to follow Jesus. Her life was rich and exciting, filled with promising business opportunities, lavish parties, five-star dining and international travel. Then, in her early thirties, she was captured by God's gift of grace. Overnight her heart was changed and her one desire became to know God and live for him.

Lola was in church one morning when God spoke to her about her spiritual life: 'Would you like to do this the slow way or the fast way?'

Never one to dally, Lola responded immediately: 'The fast way!'

God's 'fast way' was to ask her to give away all her belongings. Lola didn't hesitate. She arranged for a charity truck to come to her home and packed it with her collection of designer gowns, handbags, artwork, furniture and jewellery. Then she gave away her job. Soon she found herself dressed in ripped jeans and T-shirt as a first-year student at Bible college. In the space of nine short months, her life had been completely dismantled.

Lola describes the next fourteen years as a wilderness of humiliation and obscurity. Rejection, unfair treatment and not being seen or heard was the order of the day. But through it all, she learned how to listen to the Spirit and respond to God's ways. She began to apply grace in the face of injustice and find her identity in Christ apart from human recognition and material rewards. By the end of the season, the foundations of Lola's life were completely reset and she was grounded in a deep contentment that came entirely from her relationship with God. Everything else had fallen to dust.

These days, Lola's life has shifted into a new season. She has unexpectedly found herself back in the world she knew before becoming a Christian. Parties, travel and fast-paced living fill her calendar. Ironically, every loss from the past has been restored exponentially. But Lola experiences them differently now. With a heart to serve others, she is committed to bringing God's kingdom of love and kindness to the wealthiest and most powerful spheres of society. Her heart beats for the lost, lonely and downtrodden, wherever they are.

Lola would say that even though it appears she lost everything, she has actually gained everything. She has tasted the richness of God's kingdom on earth, the ability to know God and how to fully live. Back then, if you had asked her how it felt to have a Prada handbag on her arm, she would say it was a symbol of prestige that made her feel good about herself. Now she would say it is a part of her 'uniform', connecting her with the mission field God has called her to. It's not hard to follow God, she reflects, even though the flesh can put up a fight. If you are surrendered to God, the circumstances you find yourself in don't really matter.

What happens after God speaks? Lola's story illustrates something of the journey the Spirit takes us on to form us into disciples of Jesus. The pathway will look different for each one of us, but the destination will be the same. In this chapter, we explore the goal of our God-talking experiences, how they are custom-made to lead us into wholeness and how they fill us with a type of knowledge that means we will never be the same.

The journey of discipleship

What is a disciple? For me, growing up in church, the process of becoming a disciple of Jesus was neatly summed up in a list of simple tasks. First, you prayed a prayer that agreed to a set of beliefs about Jesus. Then you went to church on Sundays, read your Bible daily, prayed as much as you could, and did your best to obey all the commandments.

And yet, as important as these activities may be, they are *not* what Jesus said makes a Christian. You can read your Bible from cover to cover and go to church every week for the rest of your life and it won't guarantee a healthy relationship with God (John 5:39).

Jesus' opening words to his disciples were 'Come, follow me' (Matt. 4:19). He described Christians when he said, 'My sheep listen to my voice; I know them, and they follow me' (John 10:27). For Jesus, the essence of being a Christian was to hear and heed the voice of God. This process involved taking up your own cross, denying yourself and losing your life in order to find it (Luke 9:23–24). The process of 'followship' didn't look the same for everyone – what Jesus said to the apostle Peter was different from what he said to the apostle John – but as the disciples responded to Jesus' words, they got to know God and his kingdom ways.

As it was for them, so it is for us. The journey begins with an understanding of our God-given potential for wholeness and purpose. Scripture tells us that we are divine image-bearers (Gen. 1:26–27) who are 'fearfully and wonderfully made' (Ps. 139:14). We are God's 'handiwork, created in Christ Jesus to do good works, which God prepared in advance for us to do' (Eph. 2:10). Those plans are custom-made, divinely designed and far beyond anything we can 'ask or imagine' (Eph. 3:20).

At the same time, we remain broken and sinful vessels. As a 'cracked jar' in the potter's hand, we are marred by the wounds of sin and selfishness (Jer. 18:1–6). To be effective in God's kingdom requires a restoration of God's image in us. This is the goal of discipleship. A mature Christian is one whose character reflects the nature of God in Christ. There will be less of the 'flesh' driving our motivations and more of the Spirit's fruit – love, joy, peace – in our behaviour. We will be like the One we are called to follow, but also like the one we were created to be. Ultimately, we will be *our true selves*. And when we are, we will be able to fully partner with God's plans.

The path of discipleship is a well-trodden one. It has been walked by all the biblical greats, the nation of Israel and by Jesus himself. The journey takes on its own distinctive shape in every person's life, but it shares a number of common steps. We first see them in the story of Ancient Israel. The journey begins with a rescue out of 'Egypt', where we experience salvation from oppression, evil and sin. The path then leads into the 'wilderness', a forlorn season that lies outside God's promises for destiny and fulfilment. Here, in this place of hunger and need, we learn to feed on God's words – his 'manna' – and abide by them (Deut. 8:7). This is not easy, as it demands constant surrender to God's ways above our own. Each step tests our hearts and calls us to relinquish our idols so that God's way of love and grace becomes intimately known. Sadly, not everyone makes it through the wilderness. Many choose to wander in the desert, lingering there beyond its time. Like the first generation of national Israel, not everyone reaches their promised land.

Significantly, we see the same pathway in Jesus' life. As the 'new Israel',[1] Jesus modelled the process of discipleship when he journeyed down the wilderness road and succeeded in all the places where the nation went wrong. Like Israel, his path included a testing of the heart. Would he follow the way of the kingdom or the way of the Enemy? Three times Jesus was tempted, and three times he chose to listen to God's words and submit to them. It is no coincidence that at every point of testing, he quoted from Israel's point of failure (Deut. 8:3; 6:3; 6:16). In doing so, Jesus reiterated the process for discipleship: hear God's words and obey them. As he said, we cannot live without attending to the words that proceed from God's mouth (Matt. 4:4). After the wilderness, Jesus went on to continue the same pattern, doing 'nothing' without first seeing what the Father is doing (John 5:19). The pathway finally led to a cross where the ultimate declaration of a disciple was made: 'not my will, but yours be done' (Luke 22:42).

The same journey of the wilderness and the cross is seen in the life of Jesus' followers. The twelve disciples spent three years learning to heed the voice of God in Jesus. This 'followship' process produced specific outcomes. We see what they are at Peter's commissioning, when Jesus asked him two simple questions: 'Do you love me?' and 'Will you love my people?' (see John 21:15–17). It was Peter's 'yes' to both questions that marked his readiness to minister.

When God speaks, he always calls us to respond. When we say 'yes', we become like Jesus. Our 'followship' produces love for God and love for people. This is the goal of discipleship and our qualification for mission. By our obedience to the Spirit, God brings transformation and the fruit of Christ's love in our lives (John 14:21). Our spiritual growth remains ever dependent on doing what the Spirit says.

A custom-made discipleship pathway

We've seen the ultimate goal of discipleship and its outcomes. But while the heavenly curriculum has the same end for everyone, the Spirit tailors the learning process to the individual. This is every teacher's ideal. When there's only one teacher and only one student, the curriculum can be individually customised. As supreme educator, the Spirit leads us on a bespoke learning journey that takes into account our weaknesses, is paced to our capacity and made to suit our learning style and personality. It is the ultimate in one-on-one teaching.

We see this Spirit-led, custom-made pathway in Lola's story. Her discipleship journey was designed to topple the idols of materialism and success and address her misplaced identity. It was a track designed to heal the brokenness of her heart and deal with the obstacles that stood in the way of her knowing God. All along, we see the call to take up the cross as the Spirit spoke to nail her sin to death (Matt. 16:24). For Lola, as for the apostle Paul, the desire to know Christ was an invitation to participate in his death (Phil. 3:10). Hearing from the Spirit will always lead us there.

This is why our 'wildernesses' will present themselves in vastly different ways. The Spirit may direct one person to give away their Prada handbag, while another is led to buy one. God may call one to the slums of Africa and another to the boardrooms of Wall Street. One person is asked to give up surfing, another instructed to take it up. Jesus did not tell every disciple to sell their possessions and give to the poor as he did for a certain rich man (Matt. 19:21). There is no one size that fits all. The Spirit speaks to kill off our individual idols in individual ways. For Lola, it was a love of status; for Joseph, it was probably a love of power; for Abraham, the desire for a legacy. The lessons are different, but the outcome is the same.

The wilderness is arrived at according to God's initiative and in his way. We cannot and do not need to carve it out for ourselves. Trying to walk in the footsteps of another person only leads to striving and condemnation. This is why each of us urgently needs to hear the voice of the Spirit for ourselves.

Ultimately, all of God's words will lead to a cross, where we experience the death of sin followed by resurrection on the other side (Matt. 16:25). This resurrection life is most fully expressed when we love our enemies, forgive those who hurt us and show generosity without expectation of return. We become like the One we follow (Gal. 4:19). We become like Jesus.

The one variable in this process is our response. The degree to which we grow is equal to the degree to which we say 'yes'. Lola chose the 'fast track'; her immediate 'yes' enabled the Spirit to work quickly. Not everyone could handle the radical dismantling seen in Lola's life, but we don't necessarily have to. The Spirit knows what to say and when to say it. All we need to do is to be faithful to what the Spirit is saying *to us*.

This means there's little point in hearing God's voice if we are unwilling to listen. A relationship can only go so far if just one party is committed. No matter how much God loves us, our growth ceiling will always be determined by our response. At the point where we say 'no', our spiritual growth will stagnate and we will continue to bear the wounds of our sin. We won't be any less valued or loved, but there will be limitations on the freedom we enjoy and ultimately on how God can use us. Our response to the Spirit is the key.

God has already proven his love for us on the cross. Jesus said we can reciprocate our love to him by following him. When we say 'yes' to whatever God says, he is able to reveal more of himself (John 14:21). This is the way we come to *know* God. But this knowledge is of a very particular type – and not what we've normally understood it to be.

Two types of knowledge

When I first set my heart to hear God's voice, I wondered what difference it would make to my life. As a 21-year-old graduate launching into adulthood, I needed clear direction for my future. I had also been looking for some sort of apologetic – a way of knowing God was real.

Looking back, I see that hearing from God did help navigate my decision-making. I also experienced the tangible evidence of God's existence that I had been looking for. But the most significant outcome of hearing God for myself was more subtle than both these things.

For me, the greatest outcome of hearing God's voice was a personal knowledge of God.

This knowledge was different from the one I had received through reading books and listening to preaching. I had read the Bible from cover to cover, listened to hundreds of exegetical sermons and memorised large chunks of Scripture. The result was that I knew a lot *about* God. But I knew him in the same way that you would know the Queen of England through the pages of a magazine. You can learn all about the UK's reigning monarch – her love of bright colours, her passion for corgis and horses, the highlights and lowlights of her reign – but it is not until you sit down and talk with her that you can truly know her. That kind of knowledge only comes with personal interaction.

Students of epistemology call this type of knowledge *experiential*. The Hebrew language of the Old Testament calls it *yada*.[2] *Yada* is the knowledge that stems from experience and is based on relationship.

It is most frequently depicted in Scripture in the form of people's stories. The other important feature of this type of knowledge is how it is obtained. Scripture teaches us that it comes from hearing God's voice and following it; it always involves *action*. The apostle John reflects this type of knowledge when he writes, 'We know that we have come to know him [God] if we keep his commands' (1 John 2:3). This is also why the narrator of Scripture says that Samuel didn't know God until he started hearing his voice (1 Sam. 3:7).

Unfortunately, when we think of knowledge – particularly those of us who live in the West – we don't usually think of it in the same way as the Bible writers. Unlike the Hebrew approach, we tend to reflect the Greek preference for cerebral knowledge (Greek *ginoskein*). As lovers of knowledge, the Greeks were steeped in rationality and intellectualism, which stemmed from the philosophy of Plato and Socrates. In the Greek tradition, knowledge involves a 'standing back' from something in order to objectively 'know it'.[3] It is *abstract* in that it can be separated from a person's story and obtained apart from one's response to God. It is the type of information that is recited in creeds and found in systematic theology books. It is useful, but it is not the type of knowledge associated with spiritual growth in the Scriptures. The difference is in the outcome.

Nava's story illustrates this well. Nava became a high-level quadriplegic when she was hit by a car at the age of 5. Her injuries left her with no movement below her neck, and she became permanently dependent on medical apparatus to breathe and a high-tech wheelchair to get around. Then, as a teenager, Nava decided to follow Jesus as a result of the witness of her nurse. Ever since, you will find Nava in the front row of her local church on Sundays.

One night not long ago, Nava had a dream. In the dream, God told her she was going to have problems with her medical insurance. Having recently learned at one of our seminars that God spoke in dreams, she took careful note of it. That week, Nava's dream manifested when her insurance company defaulted on a claim. Because of her dream-experience, Nava knew exactly what to do. She followed the leading of the Spirit and trusted God's message from the dream.

It took a month, but the situation resolved itself. When I asked Nava what difference her experience had made, she said, 'I have never felt so loved.'

Nava had been in church for years. She had sung all the songs and heard all the sermons. If you had asked her about her spiritual life before the dream, she would have said she was loved by God. But after hearing God's voice and seeing it outworked in her life, she *knew* it in a different way. The knowledge was experiential because she had lived it. Before, she knew God loved everyone (John 3:16); now she knew that God loved *her*. The truth was no longer abstract because it was part of her story. From the depth of her being, she had felt God's love and would never be the same. The difference came because she had heard from God.

Servant and master

Someone may then ask: if experiential knowledge comes from hearing God, what role does cerebral knowledge play? Here, we need to remember that *ginoskein* has value, but only when it is maintains its place as secondary to *yada*. The apostle Paul reinforces this priority in his writings to the Corinthian church. He contrasts the Greek concept of knowledge with the knowledge received by Spirit revelation (1 Cor. 3). As a 'Pharisee of the Pharisees', Paul had obtained great reservoirs of cerebral knowledge under the rabbi Gamaliel, but he also knew this type of knowledge had a tendency to 'puff' people up (1 Cor. 8:1–3). Compared with the 'surpassing worth' of knowing God personally, it was the worst kind of 'garbage' (Phil. 3:8). In contrast, knowledge from the Spirit is worth losing everything for. Even though it doesn't always make sense intellectually, it is the wisdom of God (1 Cor. 1:20). This is why when Paul prayed for the Ephesians to know God better, he prayed for them to experience the 'Spirit of wisdom and revelation' (Eph. 1:17).

So, while it may be helpful to learn about the path of Paul's missionary journeys, the customs of Ephesus and the tenses of *koine*

Greek, we must never confuse this kind of knowledge with what the Bible itself calls knowledge. Cerebral knowledge must never be elevated above experiential knowledge. This was the failing of the Pharisees who 'studied the Scriptures' but had never heard God's voice (see John 5:39–40). Instead, *ginoskein* must retain its rightful place as the servant, not the master.

This truth was reinforced for me in the early days of doing my PhD. I had been staying with my mum in Melbourne while on a study intensive. During the week, I had spoken harshly and made my mum cry. Even I was shocked at the meanness of the words that came out of my mouth. Afterwards I was deeply convicted: 'Learn to love your mum,' the Holy Spirit said. In that moment, it struck me how useless my twelve years of theological study would be if I refused. No amount of Bible knowledge could substitute for surrender to the Spirit's voice. My PhD knowledge was only useful in service to a PhD in love.

We can see again why it is so important to hear God for ourselves. Second-hand knowledge can never take the place of first-hand revelation. That's why the gift of the New Covenant Spirit is so life changing. As Jeremiah said, it would allow for personal, direct knowledge of God (Jer. 31:33–34). God's words would be written internally on our hearts, not externally, on tablets of stone (2 Cor. 3). We could all know God for ourselves.

This perspective allows us to better situate the role of teachers. When the apostle John wrote, 'You do not need anyone to teach you', he was reminding us that the Spirit is in charge of the learning process (1 John 2:27). We don't 'need' human teachers, because 'God's anointing' is what 'teaches us all things'. Human teachers shed light on revelation, but they cannot impart it. They help articulate what we have experienced, but without revelation 'knowledge' of God becomes an empty shell of abstractions.

This means that although we value the work of teachers, scholars and educators, the accumulation of knowledge must never become the mark of spirituality. Hearing and obeying must always precede the cognition of abstract concepts. Even the work of secular psychologists shows us that there is minimal direct link between cognition and behaviour. Those who are competent in moral reasoning are not necessarily moral in their actions.[4]

This is why a preacher can be standing on a platform, an expert in biblical insight, but committing horrendous sin behind the scenes. Like the Pharisees, we can know a lot but still be resisting the voice of the Spirit. The height of our 'spirituality' is always in the experiential knowledge of God, which comes from hearing and obeying.

***

Thomas Aquinas was one of the theological heavyweights of church history. His enormous collection of writings, *Summa Theologica*, is one of the most comprehensive and profound works of theology the world has seen.[5] Years of his life were spent developing the systems of thought and rationalism that would go on to shape theology far beyond his lifetime. But near the end of his life, Aquinas had a significant revelatory experience and ceased writing as a result. When urged to continue, he said: 'I can write no more; such things have been revealed to me that all I have written seems as straw, and I now await the end of my life.'[6] After spending a lifetime gaining the knowledge that comes from human intellect, he recognised its place in the light of the wisdom that came from the Spirit. Aquinas's conclusion was not too dissimilar from that of the apostle Paul, who viewed everything 'a loss because of the surpassing worth of knowing Christ Jesus' (Phil. 3:8).

This understanding of the importance of experiential knowledge has profound ramifications for our world. It means that the path of discipleship is available to all, not just to those who have the privilege of being educated. The depths of God's wisdom are accessible to everyone, no matter their educational status. This was just as good news for the 'unschooled, ordinary' disciples (Acts 4:13) who listened and followed the voice of God as it is for us. To receive the Spirit's revelation, we need to be neither educated nor intelligent. Rather, we must 'remain in him' (1 John 2:27). Whether poor or rich, young or old, the defining factor in our spiritual growth is whether we say 'yes' or whether we say 'no'.

14

After God Speaks (2): Bringing Heaven to Earth

An impossible opportunity

The story of how I planted my church is not a typical one. When the opportunity was first presented to me, everyone advised against it. It wasn't hard to see why. The plan was to replant a church in St Kilda, the red-light district of Melbourne. The community had been pioneered over ten years earlier but had since deteriorated to a handful of people. Our 'team' was a tired remnant of five or so who were still tending the wounds of a church that had fallen apart. We had no money – the church was thousands of dollars in debt – and I was a single woman in her early thirties, alone, inexperienced and scared. This was not something I wanted to do.

The only 'hitch' was that *God had spoken*. There had been a dream, a vision and three different prophecies. All were precisely timed. All were piercingly accurate. In spite of the obstacles, the call was clear. This was God's plan for the church in St Kilda.

The question then became: how would I respond? My answer would be crucial to seeing God's promises come to pass. His words for this church contained the power to bring themselves to fulfilment, but on their own they were not enough. They required my cooperation and participation before they could manifest.

This is how God works. From the beginning, humanity was appointed to be 'ambassadors' who would steward the earth on his behalf (see Gen. 1:26–28). God looks for faithful partners who will hear and respond to his call. God *will not* do it without us.

In this chapter, we look at the role of our response in the divine–human partnership. As in the case of discipleship, our response is crucial to bringing God's plans for the kingdom from heaven to earth. We see that hearing from God is the starting point of a process that involves active participation, confrontation with the Enemy, and an underlying faith in the God whose word overcomes all.

God's words in our mouths

When God spoke to the Old Testament prophets, the narrators of Scripture often describe it as God 'placing' his words 'in their mouths' (e.g. Deut. 18:18; Isa. 51:16; Jer. 1:9). The same image is used when Jesus is pictured riding a white horse with a sword in his mouth (Rev. 19:15; also 1:16). God spoke and the prophets echoed his words. This is what it meant to 'prophesy'. The original terminology (Hebrew *nâbâ*; Greek *prophéteia*) simply meant to 'speak forth' or 'proclaim' the mind of God.[1] The prophets were essentially *mouthpieces*. They heard from God and proclaimed what he said.

Having God's words 'put in our mouths' can sound a little demeaning, as if God was treating people like robots. But this is not what it meant. To prophesy was not only to echo God's words but to *agree* with them. Agreeing with them also meant *obeying* them. Prophetic speech is always equated with action. It means bringing our whole selves into alignment with the revelatory message. Our actions must follow our words. Only then can God's words materialise in the natural realm.

God's words come with an inbuilt deposit of faith to believe what has been spoken. As Paul wrote, faith comes from hearing the message (Rom. 10:17). Faith is activated when we receive God's words and agree with them. When we speak them out, we are declaring that God has the power to bring circumstances into alignment with them.

This process of active partnership defines what we mean by having faith. Faith can never be about conceding to a set of beliefs or a creed. It isn't about *trying* to believe something intellectually. Faith is about making a choice to receive the word of the Lord when it comes. It involves hearing and obeying; receiving and prophesying; listening and doing. This is the essence of faith, without which it is impossible to please God (Heb. 11:6).

As the 'father' of our faith (Rom. 4:1–12), Abraham provides the model. Receiving the promises of God (Gen. 12:1–3) meant that Abraham had to leave his homeland and venture into a new one (Heb. 11:8–10). It meant identifying himself as 'father of many' when he was father of none (Gen. 17:5) and offering up Isaac in sacrifice while believing for his resurrection (Heb. 11:17–19). It took time – one step after another over a period of at least twenty years – but God's words to Abraham could not have been fulfilled without his cooperation (Rom. 4:16–25). Throughout the entire process, Abraham 'carried' God's words in his mouth. By his actions and faith, he *prophesied* a child to an infertile womb, a settlement to an inhabited land and a blessing to the nations.

This same process is depicted in the ministry of Ezekiel during the exile. After the devastation of their home and city, God's people were crushed and despondent, and completely cut off from their homeland (2 Kgs 24:14). But as God had said through Jeremiah, he had a plan to 'prosper' them with 'a hope and future' (Jer. 29:11). God would bring them back to their promised land. This return began with a revelatory message to Ezekiel – the vision of dry bones. 'Can these bones live?' God had asked. With the answer yet lingering, Ezekiel is told to prophesy. When Ezekiel speaks forth God's words of life and hope, the dry bones come together. Flesh appears and life begins to flow. This was not just a spiritual object lesson. The vision was given to manifest reality. Ezekiel's role was to prophesy the vision to the exiles so they would act in accordance with it. It took time, but the word of the Lord was eventually fulfilled when King Cyrus announced the exiles' release. Leaders such as Joshua and Zerubbabel then acted on the word of the Lord, and against all odds it came to pass (Ezra 1:1–4; 2:1–2).

Thus, we see time and time again that hearing God's voice becomes the entry point to the miraculous. All the heroes of faith heard from God, cooperated in faith and saw the word of God manifest (Heb. 11). When Noah heard God warn him about the flood, he built an ark and was saved. When Abraham heard God prophesy a lineage, he moved to an unknown land and fathered a miracle child. When Gideon heard God speak about victory, he overcame the Amalekites with his meagre troops. Every release of power started with hearing from God.

The same pattern applies to us. As the prophets heard from God in visions and dreams and then prophesied, we too can hear from God in dreams and visions and prophesy (Acts 2:16–17). In prophesying, we are declaring the will of God over our circumstances. As we speak and act, the power of God's words is activated. Note that Ezekiel's dry bones did not come to life until he spoke. This was not mere gesturing. The Spirit's power was only released when Ezekiel agreed with God's words. His faith triggered the manifestation of the promise. In the same way as creation was called into being, and the word of God became flesh in Jesus, God's words create their own reality. When we echo his words, we are participating in that reality. Through faith and obedience, the word of the Lord is fulfilled.

It was this process that enabled me to rebuild the flailing church in St Kilda. In spite of the situation, my feelings of inadequacy and our glaring lack of resources, I decided to believe what God said, and acted on it. I received the words that God had placed 'in my mouth' and prophesied them through my speech and actions. As I did, provision flowed and the vision unfolded. Step by step, our needs were met with abundance and ease. I was offered an office free of charge in a neighbouring suburb and an inexpensive flat to live in nearby. Money came through a new part-time job that complemented my pastor role perfectly. Cheerleaders came alongside to encourage and provide support. Mature leaders even arrived in the church via explicit directives from God. It took time, faith and perseverance, but the outcome was a thriving church. Lives were changed and a loving community was built. That season still remains as one of the best in my life.

Hearing from God is an invitation to participate in God's plans. It is an unspeakable privilege to see with God's eyes and then work with him to experience his miracle-working power. When we respond with a right heart, we become partners in the process of bringing God's kingdom to earth. Hearing from God becomes an opportunity to be a part of the solution.

The fight of faith

Of course, heeding God's words doesn't often bring *instant* success. Even though God's words are the most powerful on earth, fulfilment doesn't come automatically. In between the promises and their manifestation, we deal with an enemy who rallies to oppose them. This enemy has a level of jurisdiction over the world that doesn't exist in heaven. Jesus called Satan the 'prince of this world' (John 14:30) and Paul described him as the 'ruler of the kingdom of the air' (Eph. 2:2). Until God's kingdom comes in full, the Enemy will resist the process. There will always be a battle to bring God's will from heaven to earth. Carrying God's word in faith and seeing it to fulfilment will take some fortitude.

The Enemy is familiar with the divine strategy. As soon as God's words are out of his mouth, they attract opposition. From the Enemy's words to Adam and Eve in the garden: 'Did God really say . . .?' (Gen. 3:1); to the doubts of Israel: 'God won't provide as he said' (see Exod. 16:28); and then to the temptation of Jesus: 'If you are the Son of God . . .' (Matt. 4:6), every demonic attack comes against the truth of what God has spoken. It starts with the seeding of doubt, then manifests itself more aggressively in our circumstances. Circumstances reverse. Things go wrong. We are tempted to compromise as the Enemy assaults God's faithfulness to his words. The battle becomes a matter of holding on to what God has said.

Here we reckon on God's unwavering character. His word is as good as his nature. As it was said to Balaam: 'God is not human, that he should lie, not a human being, that he should change his mind. Does he speak and then not act? Does he promise and not fulfil?' (Num. 23:19); to Jeremiah: he is 'watching to see his word is fulfilled'

(Jer. 1:12); and to Isaiah: It 'will not return to [him] empty but will . . . achieve the purpose for which' it was sent (Isa. 55:11); by himself he has 'sworn . . . in all integrity a word that will not be revoked' (Isa. 45:23a). God's *faithfulness* is our foundation and battle cry. His words are more powerful than any enemy.

Thus, in the journey to fulfilment, God's words become our weapon. When the Enemy attacks, we wield them in defence. This is why the word of the Lord is described as a 'sword' in the epistles (Eph. 6:17; Heb. 4:12) and why it was in Jesus' 'mouth' rather than his 'hand' in John's Revelation (Rev. 19:15). Whenever the Enemy attacks the plan, we fight back with God's word. As in the case of Timothy, we are to 'fight the battle' in 'keeping with the prophecies' made about us (1 Tim. 1:18). We are not only to remember them but also to stay in position in accordance with them. No matter what the Enemy does, God's words contain the power to rise above it.

The ability of God's words to bring themselves to fulfilment in the face of attack is powerfully illustrated in the life of Joseph. As soon as God speaks about Joseph's future as a leader, circumstances reverse. The word of the Lord looks increasingly unlikely as Joseph is thrown into a pit and sold into slavery by his brothers. Then, as time passes and Joseph rises to prominence in Potiphar's house, the word of the Lord looks as though it is coming to fulfilment. But again, it comes under attack through the accusations of Potiphar's wife. The Enemy's victory seems complete when Joseph is seen languishing in an Egyptian prison. Yet even then, God's words prevail. Like a weighted punching bag that refuses to be knocked down, Joseph rises again with the pharaoh's intervention. In the end, it is a prophetic experience that propels Joseph into his destiny. Through it all, Joseph is sustained 'till what he foretold came to pass, till *the word of the LORD proved him true*' (Ps. 105:19).

This is the power of God's words. As the perfect expression of God's character, they *must* come to pass (Luke 1:37). Obstacles and delays cannot defy the One who is faithful (Job 42:2). The word of the Lord merely finds another way. When the Enemy attacks and Plan A fails, God's Plan B springs into action. When the Enemy attacks again and

Plan B fails, God's Plan C comes to the fore. God's ability to perform his word in spite of attack, delays and reversals is a testament to his sovereignty. It was not God's will for Joseph to be falsely accused (Gen. 39:11–19); neither was it God's purpose for his brothers to hate him (Gen. 37:4). Yet, each time, God was able to use the evil of humanity to perform his word. In his creative genius, God wove enemy attacks into the fabric of the story so that Plan C ended up looking like Plan A. Thus, Joseph was able to conclude that whatever was meant for evil, God can use for good (Gen. 50:20; Rom. 8:28). This is the staying power of the word of the Lord.

The only variable in this process is our faith. We are called to *fight* according to the words we've received. Our faith is based on the character of the One who cannot lie and has the power to perform what has been spoken. When we receive the word and act in accordance with it, we never lose. No matter how ferociously the Enemy attacks, how long the delays and how cruel the detours, the word of the Lord is always able to bring itself to pass.

When we say no

We know that God is always faithful to his word, but what happens when we say no?

In 1865, Abraham Lincoln had a disturbing dream. He saw his body lying in state in the White House. Afterwards, Lincoln discussed the dream with his friends. He explained how, when opening his Bible that morning, the pages had strangely fallen open to the story of Jacob's dream. Then it kept happening: every time he turned a page in his Bible, he seemed to encounter a passage about God communicating by dreams.[2] Tragically, Lincoln did nothing to respond. No attempts were made to add to his security detail. No changes were made to his routine. A few days later, Lincoln was shot in the head by a Confederate sympathiser.

In the same era, another man had a foreboding dream. You may know him today as the composer of 'Amazing Grace' – John Newton.

But you may not know of the dream he had twenty years before the writing of his famed hymn. In the dream, Newton saw himself being presented with a choice: either to retain his Christian faith as symbolised by a precious ring, or surrender it to the Enemy. If he opted to let go of the ring, the result would be destruction and torment for many. The dream was so real that it left him shaken for three days. Yet, when the effects wore off, Newton did nothing to heed it. The 'ring' was lost.

In time, the dream bore itself out as Newton entered the slave-trading profession, trafficking African people to the Americas and selling them into a life of subjugation and misery. Through it all, Newton hardened his heart to the faith he had known as a young man. While there was 'amazing grace' when he eventually repented, the intervening years saw thousands of slaves pay the price for Newton's decision to ignore the message of his dream.[3]

The concept of partnership with God offers us incredible privilege and opportunity, but it also places onus on our response. The divine–human relationship goes both ways. If God invites us to partner with his plans, our refusal to acquiesce has real consequences. The fulfilment of God's words *cannot* occur without us playing our part. That means we have power to alter the plan. The manifestation of God's words in our lives is always conditional upon our response. When we say no, God is compelled to change it.

This was the main point of God's message to Israel at the potter's house. As the potter was shaping the clay, God asked, 'Can I not do with you, Israel, as this potter does?' (Jer. 18:6a). If the nation was not willing to be moulded and shaped, God was forced to change the plan (Jer. 18:1–10). God had good plans for his people, but they would need to be adjusted if they did not become like soft clay in his hand. This approach not only applied to the Israelites. In Jonah's day, God's words were redirected when the people of Nineveh repented, and the city wasn't destroyed (Jonah 3:10). The clay of the Ninevites was soft enough to redirect God's plan.

When God speaks, we always have the freedom to say no. But we must remember that our 'no's' have consequences. When we refuse to heed God's words, his plans cannot be fulfilled in and through us. As we've seen, this does not mean we are loved any less. The clay jar will always be of immense value to the potter, for it is for 'flawed jars' that Jesus died (see 2 Cor. 4:7). However, it does mean that cracks will remain, making the vessel less useful for God's purpose.

Faithful God and unfaithful humanity

The prospect of human participation in God's plans opens up a co-nundrum: how does God remain faithful when we are faithless (2 Tim. 2:13)? How do God's words *not* 'return empty' (Isa. 55:11) when we have the power to void them through our lack of faith and cooperation? This question lies at the heart of our debates over free will and predestination.

The answer is found in clarifying our understanding of the future. Do we believe in fate, whereby the future is sealed? Or do we believe the future is open and we can therefore change it?

These same questions existed in Bible times, and the Jews and Greeks gave different answers. Both groups believed they could access future information from the spiritual world, but this is where the similarities ended. You might be able to know the future, but could you change it? The Greeks said no. Everything was fated. You could hear from an oracle about the future harvest of a successful crop or the coming birth of a healthy baby, but once you knew, the crystal ball was set. The Hebrews, however, saw it differently. God knew the future, but it wasn't all predetermined. This was largely due to God's relational nature. The primary reason for Yahweh's revelatory acts was to *engage participation*.[4] The future was never fated, because it relied on covenant partnership with God's people. God was always faithful to do what he said, but this never nullified the free agency of others. They could either agree with him – or not.

This mindset means that divine plans can be redirected. When God's people don't comply with his word, God passes them on to someone who will. God is not a liar. His word still achieves its purpose, but at a different time or by a different method. In this way, God retains his faithfulness, even when people may not retain theirs.

We see this 'promise transfer' several times in Israel's history. The first king of Israel, Saul, is a prime example. God had anointed Saul for kingship and spoken clearly about his reign (1 Sam. 9 – 10). But later, Saul chose to disobey God's voice in his dealings with the Amalekites, and God had to pass his kingship promises on to David (1 Sam. 15:11–28). The truth of the muddled situation is seen when Samuel declares that God is 'not a human being' who would 'lie or change his mind' – *even when it looks as though he just did* (1 Sam. 15:29).

We see a similar pattern in the life of Moses. God had called Moses to lead his people out of Egypt and into the promised land (Exod. 3:1–10). Moses' obedience meant that the nation was able to escape from Egypt and into the wilderness. But this was also where the manifestation of the promises came to a resounding halt. After a time in the wilderness, Moses disobeyed the word of God by striking the rock. As a result, God's promises for Moses were passed on to Joshua, who carried them into the land (Num. 20:1–12; Deut. 34:1–4).

The ultimate transfer of God's word is seen in the story of national Israel. Where the people of Israel disobey (Heb. 3:16–19), Jesus picks up the charge, succeeding at every point of their failure. He becomes the 'new Israel' who overcomes the forty-day wilderness trial and enters God's inheritance such that the 'promised land' of Israel becomes the 'promised land' of the whole world (e.g. Rom. 4:13; Eph. 6:2–3; cf. Exod. 19:2; Deut. 5:16). God actually uses Israel's disobedience to expand the promise and, in so doing, fulfils his word.

The two-way arrangement between God and humanity places enormous significance on our response. When we say no, there are real and serious consequences. But we must also remember that where there is sin, there is grace. Plan A may be nullified by our disobedience, but, in God, there is always a Plan B. His grace goes beyond our failings and our 'no's'. At the very moment we respond, the Potter is able to redirect the plan. There is always another chance to say 'yes'.

Friendship over dictatorship

We've seen what happens when we say yes, and what happens when we say no. God has his part to play and we have ours. The challenge comes when we try to reconcile the two.

You may have met someone who refuses to do *anything* without God speaking. It can make the rest of us feel terribly unspiritual. It can also seem restrictive – more like living in a cage than an open field. But there are also those at the other end of the spectrum, who never seem to hear from God about anything in life. Decisions are made with a spreadsheet and calculator, and supernatural intervention is never incorporated into the decision-making process.

The divine–human partnership may be clear on paper, but in practical terms we're often confused by it. The waters are murkier when we allow for relational play.

When we say that hearing God's voice is the means to working with God, it does not mean that we need to hear God's voice about *everything* we do. Jesus said, 'I've come to call you friends, not servants' (see John 15:15). This is a friendship, not a dictatorship. The relational dynamic means that while we do what God says, our input is essential too. There is still human autonomy. Unlike the master–servant relationship which implies a one-way dynamic, a friendship involves working together for mutual ends. It enlists our desires, input and creativity. It does not mean that God directs every decision in our lives.

We see this two-way interaction in the apostle Paul's life. Even though the Spirit sometimes gave Paul specific instructions on his missionary journeys (e.g. to go to Macedonia rather than Bithynia [Acts 16:9]), there were plenty of times when Paul made his own decisions. Paul 'decided' to sail past Ephesus because he was 'in a hurry to reach Jerusalem' (Acts 20:16) and he 'thought it best' to stay alone with his team in Athens (1 Thess. 3:1). He 'decided' to winter in Nicopolis (Titus 3:12) and planned to visit the church in Corinth on his way to Macedonia just because he 'wanted to' (2 Cor. 1:15–16).

Hearing from God doesn't negate our choices, particularly once the trajectory of our life is submitted to God's purpose.

This set-up can be challenging to navigate because it means there are no set rules. Rather, it varies with each individual relationship. One person hears from God about where to live or who to marry. Another person hears nothing and makes a decision based on the best options. What works on one occasion may not work on another. There are times in my own life where following God has led down a narrow trail, while at other times it has been a six-lane motorway. Those on the motorway might say they prefer the trail, and those on the trail, the motorway, but we all need to stay faithful to the path we've been given. We must not flatten our relationship with God into a set of rules and principles. The Spirit is a person, not a machine.

I saw this dynamic when I first began praying about doing a PhD degree. At the time, God Conversations had been running successfully for a number of years, but there were still pressing theological questions. Completing a PhD was a massive undertaking – up to five or six years of study, requiring thousands of dollars and enormous slabs of time. The last time I had prayed about postgraduate study was for my Master's degree fifteen years earlier; back then, God had spoken clearly and miraculously provided the fees. Since this was a decision with even greater ramifications, I figured he would speak the same way again.

So I prayed, 'Should I do a PhD?' But there was no answer. I prayed again and nothing came. I continued praying, but as I did, I researched the details: how to pay the fees; which educational institution to study at; who would be my supervisor. I consulted with my ministry board and close friends. All the while I prayed, but still there was silence. With the new year fast approaching, it came time to make a decision. So I did.

God never did speak about my PhD. Looking back, I see that he had given me the resources to make my own decision. Instead of dictating his plan to me as if I was a child, he was calling me to dig deeper into what *I* wanted and what *I* thought was best in line with what he had already said. Unlike the days of my Master's, when I couldn't see God's greater purpose, I was in a far better position to make a good decision.

The beauty of the divine–human relationship is that it dignifies the roles of both parties. Just like in any relationship, both are involved. Even though, as flawed humanity, we remain the lesser partners, God by his grace is constantly calling us up.

When we partner with God, servanthood ends and friendship begins. It's a relationship that is motivated by love rather than fear or control. Sometimes God speaks; sometimes he doesn't. Sometimes he says, 'This is what I want you to do.' Other times, 'What do you want to do?' We do what God says because we are submitted to his will in love. With his supernatural power and our natural abilities, together we bring God's kingdom from heaven to earth.

***

I've often said that hearing from God is one of the most thrilling experiences on earth. There is nothing quite like knowing that the God of all heaven and earth has taken time to communicate personally. It is both thrilling and humbling. But it is also weighted with responsibility. The experience signals the need for active response. Will we believe what God says? And will we believe it enough to prophesy it and act on it? Our response will require a step of faith that will take us beyond our comfort zones. Often, it will call for a choice to elevate God's words above those of the crowd. When we do, there will be always be a battle involved.

Hearing God's voice is the place where our convictions meet reality and where intangibles will confront impossibilities. This is *faith*, and the kingdom of heaven requires it. When we hear the Spirit and act on it, we will learn what it means to know that it is only by faith that we 'conquer kingdoms', 'administer justice', 'shut the mouths of lions', see our 'weaknesses turned to strength' and 'gain what was promised' (see Heb. 11:33–34).

15

When the Prophet Comes to Town: The Role of Prophecy and Prophets

As one of the keynote speakers for a large church leadership conference, Sue was standing in the front row of the opening meeting when the speaker announced, 'God is showing me a phone number: 027 448 316. Who does it belong to?'

Sue's face flushed red when she realised it was hers. Too embarrassed to put her hand up, her friend dobbed her in: 'It's Sue's! Over here!'

The next moment, the speaker was standing in front of Sue smiling. Then he began to prophesy: 'You are not going to keep going round and round the mulberry bush,' he said. 'The Lord is raising you up as a voice in this nation. He has given you a vocabulary to reach people within the church as well as beyond it – into businesses, workplaces and boardrooms.' He then proceeded to tell her that soon she would release a resource that would impact the nation.

The prophet's message was spot on. He didn't know that the draft for Sue's new book lay waiting at the publishing house ready to be launched in the new year. He wasn't familiar with her heart to speak into the lives of those beyond the four walls of the church. And he certainly didn't know that Sue's home was called Mulberry House.

Sue was both encouraged and bemused. She had never received a prophecy like this before. This man had spoken about things few people knew – matters that reflected the desires of her heart. The prophecy gave vision and direction for years to come.

There is nothing quite as spectacular as seeing a genuine prophet in action. Sue experienced a phenomenon similar to that of the Corinthian church, when the 'secrets' of a person's heart were revealed and the crowd saw that 'God was really among' them (1 Cor. 14:25). Personally, I love those moments. There is something about the thrill of witnessing the disclosure of information in ways that demonstrate God's omniscience. For the person receiving the prophecy, the depth of God's intimate care and knowledge is for ever instilled. True prophecy brings strength, encouragement and comfort (1 Cor. 14:3). God really does know our innermost thoughts – and our phone number.

At the same time, this phenomenon has created serious problems for the church. It can be seen most clearly in prophetic conferences around the world. When the prophet comes to town, crowds of people rush to the meetings, hankering for a 'word of the Lord'. Like prophecy junkies, they push to be first in line.

It's difficult to blame them. Who wouldn't want to hear from God? Who wouldn't want to know what the future holds? The desire to gain knowledge from the spiritual realm is a shared human trait that doesn't only exist in the church. You can see it in the queues at New Age gatherings, where the lines for psychic readings are the longest and people eagerly hand over wads of cash in anticipation.

The problem with this scenario is that although it powerfully demonstrates God's ability to speak, it can also inadvertently limit our inheritance under the New Covenant. People begin to look to the prophet to hear from God, and those who don't receive a prophecy can feel overlooked and forgotten. This promotes dependency on the prophet and powerlessness among the people. The prophet can even become a celebrity. Instead of being inspired to know God for themselves, people register for the next prophetic conference.[1] This subverts the entire purpose of the Spirit coming on *all*. We have unwittingly returned to the Old Covenant.

If everyone can now hear from God for themselves, what is the point of prophets and the gift of prophecy under the New Covenant? In this chapter, we look at the role of these specialised prophetic giftings in the light of our universal inheritance in the Spirit. We also look at humanity's propensity to 'piggyback' on the shoulders of other people's relationships with God and how, as the church, we can overcome it.

Piggyback relationships

There is something in humanity that prefers to 'piggyback' on other people's relationship with God rather than our own. Humanity tends to default to a second-hand relationship with God. We have already seen this in the founding of Israel. God's intention had been direct communication with every person, but the people insisted on Moses hearing for them. This tendency to lean on a human mediator has persisted throughout history. American scholar Jon Ruthven points out our constant preference for the mediation of others, whether they be 'popes, saints, Mary, teachers and theologians or prophets'.[2] It is ironic that we who have been given a privileged hotline to heaven hesitate to use it. What makes us rely on the relationships of others when we have ready access to God's voice ourselves?

There are a number of reasons for our piggybacking tendencies. The main one is probably fear. As we've seen, this was the driver in the case of the Israelites. When God invited them into face-to-face conversation, fear kept them at a distance (Exod. 20:18–21). This trepidation appears to linger into the New Covenant. Even with the revelation of God's love in Jesus, the writer of Hebrews is compelled to remind his audience that they have *not* come to a mountain that was 'burning with fire; to darkness, gloom and storm' or to a sight that was 'so terrifying' that Moses 'trembled with fear' (Heb. 12:18,21), but to a 'mountain' with 'thousands upon thousands of angels in joyful assembly' (v. 22). Hence, there was no reason to 'refuse him who speaks' (v. 25).

What, then, are we afraid of? Our fear may stem from the possible exposure of our sin and failures. After all, the word of God brings conviction (John 16:8–11) and, as a double-edged sword, reveals the thoughts of one's heart (Heb. 4:12–13). Or it may be our fear of getting it wrong. We would rather trust the expert with a proven track record than our own experience. Laziness may be involved too; we prefer to trim off the cream of others rather than paying the price of milking it ourselves.

For leaders, the drivers are likely to be different. Typically, we fear the loss of control of our congregations. If we delegate the ability to hear from God to a select few, we can better control the messaging. When we set the limits, we retain the power. We see this tendency even in the Judaism of the first century. Ruthven shows that the scribes of Jesus' time were emphatic that the only way God could speak to people was through them. They alone considered themselves to be God's voice to the people through their interpretation of the Torah. This is the problem that Jesus confronts when he says that the Pharisees studied the Scripture yet had never heard God's voice (John 5:37–47).[3]

Yet, Scripture is clear that the Spirit alone brings revelation. The Holy Spirit is our teacher (John 14:26) and we do not need another (Heb. 8:11, quoting Jer. 31:33–34; 1 John 2:27). God's words have been placed directly in our hearts (Ps. 119:11) and mouths (Isa. 59:21). Given humanity's propensity for piggybacking, it is our role as pastors and leaders to point people back to their full rights under the New Covenant. Fear of exposure, fear of error and laziness will always pull people back into the shadows of the Old Covenant. We may not be able to impart revelation, but we can teach them how to access it. It is our job to turn them away from the shadow and into the light. At stake is the fullness of a first-hand relationship with God.

Learning from the experts

While all followers of Jesus have been given the grace to hear from God directly, the church has also been given the specialist gift of prophecy and the ministry of the prophet. I call people with prophetic giftings *experts* in hearing from God. So how do they fit into the new schema?

Prophecy is typically understood to involve hearing from God on behalf of another person (1 Cor. 14:3–5). Sue experienced the power of this gift at the church conference. The prophecy brought a profound sense of God's knowledge of, and purpose for, her life. The beauty of prophecy over direct experience is found in the way Christians minister *to one another*. All of the spiritual gifts are designed to orientate us towards others. So, we can pray healing for ourselves, but God may still choose to heal through the prayers of others. We can hear God for ourselves, but God may still choose to speak through the prophecies of others. As the body of Christ, we are called to be God's 'hands and feet' as well as his 'voice'. God is always at work through relationships and connections. He delights to use people to bless others. There are also times when we *need* another person to hear from God on our behalf. Circumstances and challenges may mean we can't hear clearly for ourselves. This is why prophecy is labelled the 'greatest' gift and the reason it should be eagerly sought after (1 Cor. 14:1–5).

At the same time, the prophetic gifting must never replace direct communication with God. Hearing from God is *not* a specialist gift for a select few; it is the universal inheritance for all. Where, then, do today's prophets find their place?

The concept of a prophet in the New Covenant is a carry-over from the prophets of the Old. The first Christians were Jews who took their cues from the prophetic traditions in the Old Testament.[4] However, the fact that everyone can now hear from God significantly changes their role. Unlike under the Old Covenant, we do not need to rely on someone else to hear from God on our behalf. Instead, those who are gifted in this area become the *trainers*. Paul's letter to the Ephesians tells us that as with all 'fivefold' ministries, the main role of prophecy is the 'equipping of the saints for the work of ministry' (Eph. 4:12, NKJV). If pastors are anointed to equip the saints to care for one another, teachers are called to equip the saints to teach one another, and evangelists are called to equip the saints to evangelise others, then prophets are called to equip the saints to hear from

God for themselves. This shifts the role of the prophet from being God's sole mouthpiece to being God's primary equipper. As experts in hearing from God, prophets and those with prophetic gifts are called to help everyone else hear from God for themselves.

Periscope training

God highlighted the training role of prophets to me early on in my ministry. At the time, I had been praying for a new home. Options at the time were limited given the competitive rental market in Sydney, and my income was already stretched. Then God gave me a dream. I saw myself being shown around a large house that belonged to a banker. It felt like a mansion compared to the two-bedroom flat I was living in. There was one particular area I saw clearly. It had white marble tiles on the floor, grand columns and French windows.

Then the scene changed. I was walking along a dirt road and came across a boy playing with a toy periscope. When he saw me, he told me it was broken and asked me to fix it. I saw the problem immediately: the two mirrors inside the periscope were fuzzy and you couldn't see the image when you looked through the end. So I took the old mirrors out, replaced them with clear ones and handed the periscope back to the boy. Then I woke up.

A few weeks later, I was talking with a colleague at work about my home situation. He told me about a friend who was looking for a house-sitter while overseas on a long-term business contract. His friend was a banker. When we visited the home a few days later, my colleague showed me around the house. It felt like a mansion compared to the two-bedroom flat I was living in! Then he led me to the back entrance of the house. It had white marble tiles on the floor, grand columns and French windows. I moved in a week later.

The periscope dream revealed God's abundant provision, but there was more to it than that. The periscope was a symbol of God's provision for us under the New Covenant. Periscopes enable us to see beyond what we can normally see. We use them to see over walls, and around corners and other obstacles. In the same way, God wants us to see into areas we can't humanly access. He wants us to see with *his* eyes. The problem is that our mirrors are fuzzy. As New Covenant Christians, we haven't fully realised the gift that is freely available to us; we have the periscope, but the image is unclear. This is where New Covenant prophets find their place. Our job is not to see through the periscope for others. Our job is to replace the mirrors, and then *hand the periscope back.*

The truth is that most people are already hearing from the Spirit; they just don't know it. All throughout my ministry, I've heard the comment: 'I didn't think I could hear from God, but now I realise I always have.' As in ancient times, the Spirit is speaking 'now one way, now another', but we are not 'perceiving' it (Job 33:14). The role of prophets, then, is to teach people to *recognise* the voice they're hearing. We do this by teaching them the truths and principles of the New Covenant. We show them how the Spirit speaks and how to discern their experiences. This is where prophetic giftings become so helpful, particularly for those who are learning. When we hear from God on behalf of others, we confirm what they are already hearing.

Recently a woman came to me for prayer, her face etched with frustration. 'Please pray for me,' she said. 'I've never heard God's voice!' So I began praying that she would have ears to hear what the Spirit was saying. As I prayed, I saw a stack of money bags in my mind's eye, so I began to ask God that he would give her strategies for how to use her finances.

Next day in church the woman ran up to me beaming: 'I heard God's voice!' Then she explained that recently she and her husband had come into a large sum of money. They thought they had heard from the Spirit about how to use it but were unsure if the message was from God. After my prayer, this woman realised she *was* hearing from God. My prophetic witness 'replaced her mirrors' and she could now see more clearly.

This is what it means to 'give the periscope back'. It involves empowering others to hear God for themselves. If we hold on to the periscope, we rob people of their inheritance and send them back to the Old Covenant. Of course, it's often easier just to use the periscope ourselves. As every parent knows, teaching children the skills of adulthood is messy and difficult; sometimes you just want to get the job done. But if we keep doing the job for our 'children', they will never grow up. They will continue to remain powerless and dependent on their parents.

Training people to hear God for themselves has a further benefit. It helps to address many of the problems surrounding the practice of prophecy. Prophecy, and in particular *personal* prophecy, is prone to serious abuse. When a speaker prophesies over a person from the platform with confidence and conviction, it's easy for that person to accept what they say without question, especially if he or she is a new Christian. This has led to countless problems in the church. Denominations have even shut the gift of prophecy down as a result – particularly as it relates to the 'supernatural' elements. Ministries in Australia, Canada and the United Kingdom have all minimised or prohibited the high-level revelatory and foretelling components of prophecy, only allowing content that includes 'exhortation for edification'.[5] In some cases, personal revelation in decision-making has been actively discouraged in preference to using 'sanctified common sense'.[6] The result is that we are no longer embracing the fullness of the New Covenant and the supernatural work of God among us.

If a person is hearing from the Spirit for themselves, they are less likely to be subject to the flaws of a prophetic messenger. As we've seen, the apostle Paul's ability to hear from God about his trip to Jerusalem meant that he was able to discern prophetic input from the disciples of Tyre and the prophet Agabus (Acts 21:4,10–12). Paul relied on his own revelation rather than being dependent on the prophecies of another. This should be our goal. When the prophet comes to town and prophesies over someone in the crowd, the ideal is that the person is able to turn around and say, 'Yes, thank you, I know. God gave me that same message last week.'

The expectation should always be that God will speak to us directly. We should never live our relationship with God through someone else. The people of God have waited for too long to go back on what was promised.

The prophet's sphere

The understanding of the prophet's role as trainer positions their sphere of ministry first and foremost in the local church. Like pastors, evangelists, apostles and teachers, God has appointed prophets and people who have prophetic callings in every church community (Eph. 4:11). We may not know who they are, their gifting may be underdeveloped, and we may not even call them prophets, but *they are there* because God has appointed them to be. Their role becomes crucial when we're building the church who hears God's voice.

There is also potential for a further aspect to a prophet's role. As people gifted with acute spiritual sight, God can use prophets to speak into wider spheres, communities and even nations. We see this in the early church, where the prophet Agabus foresaw a famine that would impact Jerusalem and the regions beyond. Agabus's prophetic ministry meant that the wider church was able to mobilise resources across the city and alleviate suffering in the Jerusalem community (Acts 11:27–30). Similarly, the revelations of John on Patmos provided encouragement beyond his own life to the seven church communities of Asia Minor (Rev. 1 – 3).

This long-range insight also enables prophets to play an important role alongside apostles in new ministries and initiatives. In his letter to the Ephesians, Paul speaks of the church being 'built on the foundation of the apostles and prophets, with Christ Jesus himself as the chief cornerstone' (Eph. 2:20; also 1 Cor. 12:28). In the early church, apostles and prophets played a pivotal role in extending the kingdom into new areas. Once the ultimate foundation had been laid in Jesus and expressed in apostolic teaching,[7] it was replicated in new contexts and places. In the same way, apostles and prophets should work together today to pioneer Jesus' ministry in new ways. The Spirit is always on the move, stirring ideas, creating opportunities and making advances in the Spirit realm. Here, the prophet sees where God is moving and what God is doing. Then, as a commissioned or 'sent-out one',[8] the apostle works with them to establish the new initiative. Together, they blaze new trails and make inroads for the kingdom.

***

We cannot build the church who hears God's voice without his prophets and prophetically gifted people to lead the way. This is why they play a key role in our discussion of the strategies for building the church who hears God's voice (see Chapter 20). It's not enough that prophets stand on our conference platforms or at special events. We need them in local church leadership, helping to guide decision-making, prophesying to the congregation on Sundays and encouraging our people to hear from the Spirit throughout the week. We need them in one-on-one conversations, guiding people through discernment and encouraging them when they are suffering delays and discouragement. We also need them to see the potential of new ministries and opportunities so that they can work with apostles to take the church beyond its current borders. Most of all, we need them to clear those fuzzy mirrors and hand the periscope back – to train and equip everyone to hear from God for themselves.

16

Resolving the Theological Problem (1): The Word of God

Customs breach

Aisha was on the third day of her Hajj, the pilgrimage to Mecca that all good Muslims aim to take in their lifetime, when she had a dream that would challenge everything she had known.

It was late in the evening and Aisha had lain down in her tent after an exhausting day. Together with her fellow pilgrims, she had completed the seven circuits of the Kaaba, the sacred black shrine in the centre of the city. As she lay there pondering the day's events, she suddenly heard a sound. She sat up to see an astonishing sight. Standing before her was a man dressed in a gleaming white robe. At first, she thought it was a visiting cleric, but she could see no opening in the tent behind him. Light from the man's clothing seemed to flow into her body and she felt an unearthly warmth and calm. Then the man raised his arm in greeting and she *knew* he loved her deeply. In an instant, she realised it was Jesus.

Over the next few months, Aisha had more visions like this one. Sometimes she only saw Jesus' face. Other times, he spoke to her. Each time, the message in his eyes was clear: 'Come with me.'[1] As a result of her experiences, Aisha made a decision to follow Jesus.

There are thousands of stories like Aisha's coming out of the Middle East. Missiologists estimate that between 30% and 50% of conversions to Christianity involve dreams of Jesus.[2] In Iran, one report says that 100% of them are due to dreams.[3] The experiences are often similar. There is a figure in white robes with arresting eyes, an intense feeling of love, and then, the call to follow. The dreamers are inexplicably drawn to Jesus, and afterwards embark on a journey to discover if he is more than just the prophet they have heard about in Islam.

Testimonies such as Aisha's happen in places where there are no Bibles or churches. In Mecca, you can't even get past Customs without a passport stamp proving your Islamic identity. Aisha's experience is not unlike the apostle Paul's on the Damascus road. Yet, for cessationist Christians, Aisha's story presents a conundrum. As we saw in Chapter 4, cessationists believe that the only way in which God speaks is through the Bible. How then could Aisha be led to follow Jesus without it? Sadly, they end up concluding that conversions like Aisha's are not legitimate, even when they lead to a radically transformed life and, in some cases, martyrdom.[4]

As we've seen, the relationship between Spirit and Scripture has been a theological problem throughout history. The issue is crucial because it has often led to a rejection of the Spirit's voice in order to preserve the sanctity of the Bible. For cessationists, this has meant that the Spirit's voice has been completely nullified; God has literally stopped speaking directly. For others – largely theologians in the Pentecostal–Charismatic tradition – God's voice has been watered down into a weaker form, such that contemporaries cannot hear God's voice as clearly or as effectively as the Bible-writing characters (the 'good but not as good' approach from Chapter 4). On the other hand, for the Friday Apostolics in Zimbabwe, preserving the ongoing voice of the Spirit has led to a rejection of the Bible.

The inability to resolve the tension between Spirit and Scripture has led to one or the other being rejected in some way. In this chapter, I show that there is no need for the rejection of either. Each finds its place when we remember *who* the Word of God is and where divine authority ultimately comes from.

Getting it in writing?

The underlying issue in the Spirit–Scripture debate is one of *authority*. If I claim to hear from God today, I am effectively claiming the same authority as the biblical characters in their day. As the argument goes, this places my encounter on the 'same level' as Scripture. Herein lies our problem. Most Protestant theologians say that the inspirational experiences that led to the writing of the Bible were 'special' and unrepeatable. Therefore, the spoken word of my contemporary experience must be invalid or at least inferior to the experiences of Scripture. In popular speak, the *rhēma* must be subject to the *logos*.

However, both these positions ignore a simple reality: in biblical history, God *spoke* before his words were written down. Although that sounds rather obvious, this truth lies at the crux of the theological dilemma. Our 'theological problem' is only a problem when we overlook the fact that the word of God was spoken before it was written.

To fully grasp the issue, we need to go back to the actual dynamics of revelatory experience and its relationship to the written texts of Scripture. We know that God has always spoken to people. Sometimes those God-conversations were written down, often because people were specifically instructed to do so (e.g. Exod. 17:14; Isa. 8:1; Jer. 30:2). Characters such as Isaiah, Jeremiah and Amos are known as the 'writing prophets' because they recorded the words they heard from God on tablets or papyrus. The primary reason for writing them was so that they could be passed on to the rest of their intended audience (e.g. Hab. 2:2). Today many of these prophetic words are preserved for us as Scripture.

However, not all of God's words in Bible times were written down. There were plenty of prophets who did not record their oracles, including the so-called 'non-writing prophets': Elijah, Elisha and Nathan. We also know that even when God's words *were* written down, this did not always occur at the time of the experience. Many prophecies were written long after they were spoken. God's words to Jeremiah, for example, were recorded twenty-three years after the fact.[5] We see a similar phenomenon in the New Testament. The book of Acts was written thirty years after the actual events and contained no reference to any written forms of the gospel.[6] Even though the apostle John wrote his revelations down in detail, many others didn't.[7]

The interplay of orality (what was spoken) and literacy (what was written) in the ancient world is a complex one. While the issues are too detailed to address at length here, what is clear is that the act of writing down God's words in biblical times didn't make them any more credible or authoritative. The spoken word of God had authority irrespective of whether it was recorded as text. This is because divine authority was always seen to lie with the speaker.

Today people often question the reliability of this set-up. How can you trust the spoken word to be passed on accurately without a bad case of Chinese Whispers (the 'telephone game')? Surely those messages would become distorted? Our concern exists largely because our modern world is so different from that of the ancients. Today, we live in a text-dominant society. For us, authority rests largely with the *written* word, with the spoken word holding considerably less weight. It would be questionable, for example, if a witness in a law court based their testimony on the fact that someone had 'told them' something without solid evidence to back it up. Our legal system usually only recognises agreements when they are transcribed, signed and dated. The written word guarantees its credibility and reliability.

But in oral societies, the reverse was true. It was the *spoken* word that typically carried more authority than the written. This is because literacy rates were low and the primary means of passing on information was oral. Even though the precise levels of literacy in the ancient world are widely contested,[8] we do know that in the main the emphasis was on hearing and speaking rather than on reading and writing. Traditions were passed on by storytelling and performance, not by books and printing. This transmission process was reliable because oral societies were set up for it. Fieldwork studies in oral societies today provide evidence of the inbuilt community mechanisms that ensured messages stayed true to the original.[9]

Not only did the spoken word carry more weight in oral societies than in textual societies; it was also often *preferred*. Plato, for example (drawing on the wisdom of his teacher Socrates), resisted writing because it didn't offer 'true wisdom'; it was only an 'image' of 'living and breathing words'. Written documents were thought to be unclear because they did not provide opportunity for questioning and teaching, making them vulnerable to manipulation and misinterpretation.[10] For Plato, 'Written words seem to talk to you as though they were intelligent, but if you ask them anything about what they say from a desire to be instructed, they go on telling you just the same thing forever. And once a thing is put in writing, the composition, whatever it may be, drifts all over the place' (*Phaedrus* §275d). This is why the oral world preferred face-to-face relationships as the main context for learning. Learning occurred through dialogue, interaction and questioning, rather than through study of written texts. It was the spoken word that counted.

It is this kind of approach that we see in both the Ancient Near East world of the Old Testament and the Greco-Roman world of the New. When we imagine the communities of Israel or the early church, we typically envisage them to be like ours, with every person holding a Bible in their hand. But in biblical times, reading was largely the preserve of the academic elite. The general populace couldn't have read the Scriptures even if they were widely available.[11] Thus we see that in Old Testament times God's words were passed down through storytelling and performance (the Passover meal is a good illustration of this [Exod. 12:1–28]). People *heard* God's words more than they read them, and the spoken word was privileged over the written. Even the prophet Jeremiah warned against the 'lying pen of the scribes' who could not be trusted over his oracles (Jer. 8:8)! Of course, this emphasis on the oral does not mean that written works were non-existent; they just served a different role. They were recorded for the sake of libraries and archives, but were not accessed regularly and certainly not by the average person.[12] That's why, when the 'Book of the Law' was discovered in Josiah's day, it was such a celebrated event (2 Kgs 22:8–10).

This same oral bent is true of the New Testament setting. While Jesus could clearly read (Luke 4:16–21), he spent the bulk of his time teaching his disciples through dialogue and preaching. Jesus left no books behind and it is unlikely that people took notes during his sermons. This was in keeping with the educational practices of the day. It is also why Jesus repeatedly asks people, 'Have you not heard?' rather than 'Have you not read?', and says to them, 'Those who have ears to hear, let them hear.' The same pattern is evident in the epistles. Faith comes through 'hearing' the word rather than reading it (Rom. 10:17). Again, this did not mean that written texts were unimportant. Jewish people were known as 'people of the book' because of their high esteem for the Scriptures. The Hebrew writings were understood to be sacred and were referred to regularly in the Temple and synagogues. Many young Jewish males were taught to read the Torah. However, we must remember that access to the Scriptures in the main was limited to the *educated* interpreters of the day – the Pharisees, scribes and Sadducees.

In order to properly understand the relationship between Spirit and Scripture, we must acknowledge the actual context from which our Scriptures came. Then we must recognise that the authority of God's words – whether spoken then or now – always remains.

The meaning of the 'word of God'

The understanding that authority derives from the speaker has implications for our understanding of the meaning of the 'word of God'. When you hear this phrase, what do you think of? It's likely that your first thought is the Bible. We often call the Bible the 'Word of God' because we want to honour the source of its inspiration.[13] However, it may be a surprise to discover that this is not the meaning used in the Bible itself. In fact, whenever you see the phrase 'word of God' in Scripture, its meaning is the *spoken* prophetic word, and then, the living word of God in Jesus.

We see this perspective throughout the Old and New Testaments. In the Hebrew Scriptures, the 'word of the Lord' referred predominantly to the inspired words of the prophets who were commissioned to pass on God's messages to the people.[14] To a lesser degree, it was used for the divine *commandments* spoken to Moses (Exod. 20:1–17) (the Hebrew term *děbārîm* is better translated 'word' in this passage).[15] Thus, when the narrators of Scripture tell us that Abraham kept God's commands or *torah* (Gen. 26:5 etc.), they are referring to God's oracles and ultimately to spoken revelation.[16] Similarly, when Isaiah declared that the word of the Lord would 'not return empty', he was referring to the prophecies spoken to Israel (see Isa. 55:11).

As we move into Jesus' day, the 'word of the Lord' continues to refer to the spoken word and, more specifically, the body of Jesus' teachings.[17] For example, when Jesus prayed to God about his disciples and said, 'I have given them your word' (John 17:14; 14:10), he was referring to the message he had brought them orally. When he spoke about the 'bread' of the word of God that we can't live without, he was referring to the word that came directly from his mouth (Matt. 4:4).

Then, in the early church, the meaning of the 'word of God' became associated with the person of Jesus and his message (John 1:1,14). This word continued to be expressed by the ongoing witness of the Spirit.[18] In Acts, for example, when the text says 'the word of God continued to spread and flourish' (Acts 12:24), it means that the *message of Jesus* continued to flourish. Similarly, when the writer of Hebrews refers to the 'word of God' as a living and active 'double-edged sword' (4:12), he is referencing the Spirit-inspired word, *not* the Scriptures.[19]

We also see that when both Jesus and the early church refer to the Old Testament Scriptures, they do not call them the 'word of God'. They use a different word: the Greek term *graphē*. Jesus himself made the distinction between Scripture (*graphē*) and his spoken word (*logos*) in his conversation with the Pharisees (John 5:37–40). *Graphē* is also the word used by Paul in 2 Timothy 3:16 in reference to the inspiration of Scripture. There are only two exceptions to this, but in both cases the phrase 'word of God' references oral statements that *preceded* the writings.[20]

It is now easy to see why the popular *rhēma–logos* schema doesn't work. In an oral society, there is no distinction between *rhēma* and *logos*. *Both* reference God-breathed, authoritative words. The idea that there is a phenomenological distinction between the two is an anachronism that we project onto the Bible because of our preference for written texts.[21] The early church did not conceive any distinction, and if they did, the *spoken* word (*rhēma*) would have probably held more weight!

All this means that in the context of the oral societies of the biblical world, a true word from God had authority regardless of whether it was written down. While the Hebrew Scriptures were authoritative and certain to be fulfilled, this authority was derived from the fact that God had originally spoken (Luke 4:16–21; Matt. 4:1–11; John 10:35), not because the message had been written down. We're reminded again that divine authority always originates with the speaker. God's character remains his signature and seal.

The downside of textualisation

Of course, we no longer live in an oral society. Between the time of the Bible and ours, the location of authority has shifted from the spoken word to the written through the process of 'textualisation'.[22] In textualised societies today, the written word carries more weight than the spoken. It is largely *because* of this process that the conflict between Scripture and Spirit arises. We start to think that the written word has more authority than the spoken just because it is recorded as text.

This assumption has a tragic downside for hearing the voice of the Spirit. This is because it tends to move our focus from present revelation to the past. Books and texts are designed to *preserve* a person's words. In our desire to emphasise what God *has said* through the pages of the Bible, we have inadvertently de-emphasised what God *is saying* through the voice of the Spirit. The gift of direct and unmediated revelation received at Pentecost is not promoted as part of the normal Christian life. This has led to the rise of teachers and theologians who focus on past revelation, and the corresponding diminishment of prophets who focus on present revelation. We see this same pattern in history whenever textualisation occurs. Old Testament scholar

William Schniedewind shows how it occurred in Israel after the exile when oral stories were collated and the scribes rose to prominence.[23] North American philosopher James K.A. Smith shows how the same process was repeated in the church of the third and fourth centuries when the New Testament was canonised. Smith warns that we are at risk of it occurring again in Spirit-filled churches today.[24]

When divine authority is seen to move from the speaker to the text, there is a tendency to focus more on the Scriptures than on the God who inspired them. It's a subtle distinction, but a crucial one. Knowing the Bible becomes a substitute for knowing the Spirit. Knowledge of God becomes associated with the ability to exegete a passage rather than obeying God's voice. This relegates 'God's word' to the domain of those who are literate and have access to education, and is a direct contradiction of the democratic intent of the New Covenant. God's plan was for everyone to have access to the Spirit's wisdom, from the professor in the seminary to the illiterate child in the remote village (Acts 2:17).

Understanding the process of textualisation allows us to see why some theologians remain suspicious of Aisha's conversion experience. When we say that God cannot speak apart from Scripture, we are defining the Word of God as a text rather than a person. Aisha's testimony reminds us that the Word of God is a living deity who is contained by neither a book nor a translation (John 1:1,14). Jesus is not paper and ink. Jesus both preceded the Bible and supersedes it. You can have the Bible but not have Jesus; you can have Jesus but not have the Bible. In Mecca, where Christians are prohibited and Bibles are banned, the Word of God can *still* get through Customs.

What began as a healthy desire to honour the biblical text has unwittingly led to a distortion of God's New Covenant intention. We have created an artificial distinction between the word of God spoken today and the word of God spoken to the early church by saying that the former is by nature inferior to the latter. Then, in using the 'word of God' for the Bible rather than in its New Testament use, we've substituted the Bible for Jesus and the continuing voice of the Spirit. This has created a competitive mindset that pits Scripture against

Spirit and mitigates the ongoing experience of hearing God's voice. Ultimately, it silences the Spirit's ability to speak powerfully today.

The resolution

There is a resolution to our conundrum. It lies in reminding ourselves of the true location of divine authority and the *biblical* meaning of the 'word of God'. When we recognise the fact that the word of God was spoken before it was written, we can form a better model. Here, we do well to model our language on the biblical pattern. The 'word of God' is first and foremost God's spoken and living word. It is God's character personified and the means through which God chooses to reveal himself to humanity. This word created the earth and sustains it. It was spoken through the prophets under the Old Covenant, embodied in the person of Jesus and continues via the Holy Spirit under the New. Through it all, the authority of God's words remains the same. This is because divine authority originates with the One who has spoken and continues to speak. The dynamic holds true irrespective of whether God's word is passed on via oral tradition or written documents.[25]

When we understand this reality, there is no conflict between the word of God in Scripture and the voice of the Spirit in our experience. This is because they both arise from the same origin. The Word and the Spirit are the *same Trinitarian reality*. They represent two living persons in the triune godhead. What the Spirit says today is consistent with Jesus, the Word of God, and with what the Spirit has already said in the Bible.

When we reorient our understanding of the Word of God to a *person*, it calls us to pay attention to the ongoing voice of the Spirit. Before God's words were ever written down, God was speaking. After God's words were written down, God is still speaking. The production of a text does not obstruct this living reality. The word of God spoken by prophets, personified in Jesus and continued by the Spirit is alive and active. Today that word of God goes by the Spirit where no one else can go – to pilgrims in Mecca, to people who cannot read and to places where the Bible is banned. God has never stopped speaking.

The uniqueness of the Bible

Where does this leave the Scriptures? As we've seen, a belief in ongoing revelatory experiences has led the Friday Apostolics in Zimbabwe to become 'Christians who don't read the Bible'. This is a treacherous path to take since it risks the disconnection of Spirit experiences from the foundation of Jesus. History tells of the tragic fallout of movements that lose this vital anchor.

It is significant to note that after Aisha's initial visionary experience, she happened upon a Bible via her cousin. On reading it, she was able to discover more of the life and teachings of Jesus. This pattern occurs regularly in testimonies like Aisha's. God's plan includes a vital place for Scripture. Recently, I heard a testimony from an Arab ministry leader who reported that before a quality Arabic Bible translation was in place, 90% of people came to faith through dreams, but afterwards, access to Scripture became the primary vehicle of conversion.[26] Whether spoken or written, the gospel message made its mark.

There's no question that the Bible is unique among books and central to the Christian faith. While originally the gospel was transmitted orally, we now live in a textual society where the written word is understood to bear more authority than the spoken. This makes the Scriptures our primary mode of transmission for the good news of Jesus. Today we are privileged to have the story of Jesus and the first disciples in one comprehensive collection. As the true and reliable repository of gospel teachings, our Hebrew and Christian Scriptures make us 'wise for salvation' (2 Tim. 3:15). They are inspired of the Holy Spirit and do not arise from human origin (2 Tim. 3:16; 2 Pet. 1:20–21). They are the one-stop shop for the core tenets of our faith.

What then makes the Christian Scriptures unique? As we've seen, the fact that the Scriptures are divinely inspired is not the primary reason they stand apart. There have been plenty of other Spirit-inspired experiences in history that were not included in the canon. The apostle Paul uses the descriptor 'inspired' to describe Scripture in 2 Timothy 2:16, but there were other documents from that period for which the same wording was used.[27] Some were even referred to as 'Scripture' at the time![28] A good example is the second-century bestseller, *The Shepherd of Hermas*. It was described as 'inspired' even though it wasn't included in the canon.

What makes the Christian Scriptures 'special' is their *content*. The Scriptures alone tell us the story of God as revealed in Jesus. They give us the backstory under the Old Covenant through Israel's history and the climax in the New. They are a true and reliable witness to the living Word of God. The reality of the incarnation, death and resurrection of Jesus as recorded in the Scriptures sets the foundation for our faith that can never be added to or removed from. The Scriptures then become the primary vehicle through which the Spirit reminds us of the truths Jesus established in his incarnation, death and resurrection (John 14:26).

Although the Scriptures become the main means by which the Spirit speaks the gospel to us, we also need to remember that the Word of God is *Jesus*, and Jesus is not the Scriptures. It is clear that not every word of Scripture is the direct word of God. For example, we would never describe the advice of Job's friends, the cynical questioning of Qohelet in Ecclesiastes or the imprecatory psalms of David as the 'word of the Lord'. Yahweh himself declared Job's friends to be in error (Job 42:7). Even Paul says explicitly that not everything he wrote was a direct word from God (1 Cor. 7:12). Old Testament scholar John Goldingay suggests that the use of this kind of language for the Bible is a 'category mistake'.[29]

When we conflate the meaning of the 'word of God' with Jesus *and* the Scriptures, we blur the distinctives of both. This has practical consequences for hearing God's voice. On the one hand, people begin to pull phrases out of Scripture as promises for their own lives without any consideration of their ancient context. This has the effect of dishonouring the Scriptures in that we are not taking seriously what

God actually said, who it was said to and why it was said. Scripture becomes 'flattened', as though every statement has equal relevance and every word has mystical power. If we're not careful, we end up distorting and manipulating the sacred text for our own ends. I've seen people read passages such as 'none will miscarry or be barren' (Exod. 23:26) and take it as a blanket guarantee for fertility. Or a verse is taken from the 'blessing' passages of the Old Covenant in Deuteronomy 28 as a promise for personal prosperity, rather than Jesus' teaching on blessing from the Sermon on the Mount in Matthew 5. Such practices have been observed particularly among Pentecostals, sometimes with dire consequences.[30] This misuse of Scripture is more likely to happen when we don't understand the 'word of God' first and foremost to be Jesus.

On the other hand, when we label the Scriptures the 'word of God', the practice of hearing the Spirit as understood in first-century use becomes associated with *only* reading the Bible and we find ourselves back at the cessationist position again. If we are to emulate the theology and practice of Spirit experience of the first-century church, we must use *their* language. We must retain the understanding of the word of God as the living person of Jesus and his ongoing voice through the Spirit.[31]

If not the 'word of God', how then is Scripture best described? A more appropriate term has been coined by British theologian Tom Wright.[32] He calls Scripture the inspired 'story of God'. This phrase reorients us to the true source of authority, which lies in a living deity. Thus, the Bible is 'authoritative' because it gives witness to One who has *all* authority, as Jesus himself said (John 5:39). This authority wasn't diminished when the canon was completed. So, when God speaks to us today, it is as authoritative for us as it was for David, Peter or John. But this does not mean that the Bible is being *added to*, as Joseph Smith, the founder of Mormonism, claimed. As we've seen, the foundation of our faith has already been laid by Jesus' life, death and resurrection and its expression in the apostles' teaching.

This framework also situates our personal Spirit-inspired experiences in their proper perspective. We may have a legitimate Spirit encounter that is phenomenologically equivalent to the experiences of Paul, Peter and John, but this does not put it on a par with theirs in terms of importance or relevance. As we've seen, the Scriptures are unique in content and have universal application. The substance of our personal experience can only *build* on the foundation that has already been laid; it can never add to or detract from it.

Of course, the way for us to know that foundation today is through the New Testament writings. We can trust them because of the extensive testing that was undertaken to ensure they contain a reliable report of first-century events. The process of canonisation meant that only authentic testimony relating to Jesus' time was included. The church asked the same kind of questions we ask: Is this experience inspired? Can we trust its source? Today, the Gospels and the wider New Testament documents have historical, critical weight as a true witness to the story of God culminating in Jesus.[33]

However, we also need to remember that the church was not unclear about the basic core of Christianity *prior* to the canonisation of Scripture in the fourth century. Jesus' life, death and resurrection as expressed in apostolic teaching was the measure and standard for all Christian theology long before the Bible was ever complete. Known as the 'Rule of Faith',[34] this body of truth was passed on orally at first, but as society became increasingly textualised, written documents became necessary. Here, the Rule of Faith was used as the standard for the limits of the gospel, and for the ultimate inclusion of documents in the canon. The reason why *The Shepherd of Hermas* and other later inspired documents were not included was because there was already sufficient content to constitute the foundation. This content has universal relevance and can never be supplemented by an individual's revelatory experience. The Scriptures – as per *Sola Scriptura* – provide us with everything we need to know about God's way of salvation. As Paul reiterates, 'no one can lay any foundation other than the one already laid, which is Jesus Christ' (1 Cor. 3:11).

The New Testament as model

The Bible is unique not only in its content but also in its role in providing a *model* for ongoing Spirit-speaking experiences. It is *because* we believe the Scriptures are reliable that we can fully embrace God's continuing voice. All of Scripture testifies to the reality and potency of God's spoken word. To be true to the Bible is to be true to its teaching on the New Covenant Spirit. Hence, the experiences of the early church in Scripture become the example for our God-speaking experiences today. The God-conversations of the early church demonstrate *how* the Spirit spoke to outwork Jesus' mission in the first-century Greco-Roman world and so become models for our own, as the same Spirit outworks Jesus' mission in our era and society. The context may be different, but the mission is the same.

Specifically, the book of Acts provides us with over twenty accounts of hearing God in the lives of people such as Peter, Philip, Stephen, Paul, Barnabas and Agabus. The patterns and principles embedded in these stories provide us with plentiful examples for how the Spirit speaks, how to recognise it and how to respond to it. From there, the epistles – particularly Paul's first letter to the Corinthian church – provide us with guidelines for further reflection. In 1 Corinthians, we learn about how the gift of prophecy is exercised in the public service and its role in edifying the church; in 2 Corinthians we receive insight into Paul's Spirit encounters as he shares about the thorn in his flesh and his visions of 'paradise'. Finally, the book of Revelation gives us the most complete post-Jesus God-conversation in Scripture and provides us with rich examples of symbolic language that shed light on our own visionary experiences. The stories of the New Testament are echoed in our own.

***

We are privileged to have the Scriptures today. The Bible is still the world's bestselling book. But it was never meant to compete with the ongoing voice of the Spirit. Because we have the book, we must not lose the reality of the One who continues to reveal himself by the

Spirit. The Scriptures bring the proven and reliable story of God to us. They are the foundation of our faith and can never be added to. God continues to speak through them by his Spirit, reminding us of the truths Jesus taught and transforming our hearts.

But when we say that the Scriptures are the only way God speaks to us, we are reinforcing the mistaken idea that the Spirit doesn't speak directly and personally any more. Instead, we must value all that God has said, as well as all that God is saying. Let not the precious gift of the Bible become an obstacle to the precious gift of the Spirit. We need both the Spirit's voice *and* the Bible. But in this, we must always remember that our faith is not founded on the Scriptures per se. Our foundation and cornerstone is, and will always be, Jesus (1 Cor. 3:11; Eph. 2:20). He alone is the true and living 'Word of God'.[35]

17

Resolving the Theological Problem (2): The Spirit on Contemporary Issues

The penny-farthing bicycle

When God called me to plant a church as a 30-year-old single woman, I was indignant. It didn't seem fair that I should be asked to do something so challenging on my own, so I bucked and bargained with God. My arguments were well developed, I thought. I knew of no leadership model for church planting other than a married couple. Every senior pastor I had met in my denomination was married. Each time church planters were profiled on the platform of our National Leadership Conference, there was a pastor *and* his wife. Even the manual at my Bible college on church planting included a chapter on 'Essentials' with 'pastor and his wife' at the top of the list.

When God made it clear that marriage would have to wait (his exact words were 'not yet'), I insisted on an explanation. It just didn't seem fair. Why did I have to do this on my own when others didn't?

The answer came in the form of a vision. I was driving to work one morning when I saw an image of a penny-farthing bicycle in my mind's eye. It had an enormous wheel at the front and a tiny wheel at the back. With the vision came the words: 'That's the old-fashioned way.'

The vision instantly silenced my protests. I *knew* it was from God. I also knew what it meant. God was calling me to pioneer a church as a single woman because he wanted me to grow into the fullness of my giftings in my own right. He wanted me to be a *pastor*, not a *pastor's wife*. I wasn't going to be riding into ministry on the coat-tails of a husband.

My penny-farthing experience was part of a larger transition into understanding God's heart for women in general. Growing up in a religiously conservative home, I had been thoroughly socialised into the idea of myself as the 'small wheel' behind the larger wheel of a husband. While I knew God had called me into some form of church ministry, the only pathway I could conceive was marriage to a pastor. I had also read the parts of Scripture that seemed to affirm women's place as a small wheel and was fully committed to abiding by it. It wasn't until God spoke to me that I was forced to revisit my position and learn about the context of those passages.

Since then, I have shared my story with men and women at leadership conferences around the world. I've exhorted the women to find their identity in their own calling, and the men to partner with them as co-image-bearers of God (Gen. 1:26–28). I have used the image of the penny-farthing to illustrate God's heart for men and women in general and advocate for Spirit-led rather than gender-based leadership.

Yet the question may be asked: is my use of personal experience for wider application appropriate? I believe it is, but most Protestant theologians would not. In this tradition, there is a long-standing belief that contemporary Spirit-encounters do not contain 'doctrinal teaching'. Private experiences are understood to *never* have public implications. Catholic theologians, however, would be more likely to concur with what I was doing; if what I heard from God is authentic, it *could* have ramifications for all male–female relationships in the church. After all, if it is God's intention for one woman, it may be God's intention for another.

My testimony illustrates a second aspect of the theological problem in hearing God's voice. What bearing does one person's revelatory experience have on wider theological teaching? We know that the foundations of our faith are set in Jesus. As the full and complete revelation of the invisible God, there is nothing more to be said about the conditions of our salvation. But now that Jesus has finished his mission and sent us the Spirit, does God have anything else to say to the church?

In this chapter, we explore the relationship of private revelations to public understandings and how they relate to contemporary matters in the church. We see that the Spirit *is* still speaking about issues of concern, but this revelation must be subject to a broader and more rigorous testing process.

'God released me from my marriage'

We know that 'all Scripture' is 'useful for teaching, rebuking, correcting and training in righteousness' (2 Tim. 3:16). Scripture bears a permanent and reliable witness to the truth of the gospel. It provides us with principles for how to live with wisdom. But the Scriptures don't tell us everything we need to know. This is why we need the Spirit.

Let me illustrate from the story of a woman I'll call Natalie. Natalie had been married for nine years when God spoke to 'release her' from her marriage. It was a tragic story. For the entirety of her relationship, Natalie had endured a barrage of emotional and physical abuse. Yet, through it all, she had remained faithful, determined to keep her wedding vows. 'Those promises were made before God,' she told me. 'They were for better or worse – till death do us part.' But then, the Spirit spoke. Natalie was free to go. Her relief was palpable as she experienced a wave of peace and calm.

However, when Natalie shared the experience with her pastor, his response was not so enthusiastic. 'God hates divorce,' he quoted from Malachi 2:16. 'What you heard *cannot be* from God.' His advice to Natalie was to go home and endure the abuse in submission to God's will.

Troubling as his advice was, Natalie's pastor was not trying to be unkind. Neither was he was condoning domestic violence. He was trying to be faithful *to the Bible*. The Scriptures only sanction two grounds for divorce: one, when a partner commits adultery (Matt. 19:9), and two, when an unbelieving partner deserts (1 Cor. 7:15). Neither scenario specifically references a case of abuse. As a result, the pastor had no reference point for Natalie's experience other than to reject it.

The pastor's response reflects the stance of the Protestant tradition, which has historically only offered two grounds for divorce. On the one hand, as we've seen, this tradition allows no place for Spirit experiences in the development of doctrinal teaching. Scripture is held to be all-sufficient, not only as the basis for faith but also for everything in life. Thus, the only way to know God's will for any situation is to study the Bible. The problem is that in Scripture, we only find teaching on first-century concerns. While this provides us with general principles to start from (Scripture is 'useful for training in righteousness' [2 Tim. 3:16]) and grounds our judgements in God's character, it does not always speak directly to situations such as Natalie's.

On the other hand, the Catholic perspective on contemporary revelatory experience allows for the Spirit to speak into new situations and bring light to old understandings (at least in theory). This perspective recognises that what God has said to an individual on a particular matter may have wider application in the church. This is because every member of the body of Christ is connected by the Holy Spirit.[1] So, if God spoke to Natalie about her marriage, what he said may be relevant to others facing domestic violence. Or, to draw on my example, if God was calling me to 'grow my wheel' so that I could partner equally with a man, he may be asking others to do the same.

Indeed, this is the approach we see in the Bible itself. When God reveals an aspect of truth, he usually does it in the context of individual lives.[2] Rarely do we see God making proclamations to large crowds of people. Rather, his revelation is *particularistic* and *situational*. In corporate speak, it is 'just-in-time' learning. Divine insights are made all the more effective *because* they are given on a needs-driven basis. For example, we first learn that God is Jehovah Jireh – the 'God who provides' – because God made provision for Abraham on Mount Moriah with the ram in the thicket (Gen. 22:13–14). We first learn that God is Jehovah Roi – the 'God who sees' – because God attended to Hagar after she had been rejected by her husband Jacob (Gen. 16:1–13). And we know that there will be no suffering in heaven because God spoke to John in exile on Patmos (Rev. 21:4).

Each time, we see that God's revelation to one person may have implications for others. This should not be surprising, given Jesus' description of the function of the New Covenant Spirit. As Jesus said, the Spirit would both 'remind' us of the truths he had established (John 14:26) *and* speak about 'things to come' (John 16:13). There would be situations beyond the immediate lives of the disciples that would require the Spirit's wisdom. Natalie's plight is one of them. The Spirit spoke to apply the wisdom of the living Word to the complexities of her broken marriage.

Indeed, the Scriptures were never designed to tell us everything we need to know. When Jesus spoke about divorce, it was in response to someone who was picking an argument about divorce and adultery (Matt. 19:1–10). Similarly, Paul's writings about unbeliever desertion concerned a particular incident in Corinth (1 Cor. 7:1–16). These writings provide insights that we can still draw from, but neither Jesus' nor Paul's words were intended to speak to every troubled marriage. That is why we were given the Spirit. The Spirit continues to speak the truth of Jesus in new contexts, applying divine insight to issues (such as divorce and women in leadership) that are not covered by the foundations of the gospel.

Slavery, the Bible and the Spirit

This understanding of the Spirit's role in bringing wisdom to contemporary concerns would have helped enormously in the nineteenth-century debates on slavery in North America. More than one million lives were lost as the southern and northern states clashed over the issue in the American civil war. The battle lines had been clear. Southerners argued that God permitted slavery and even ordained that it be so. Northerners argued that slavery was in flagrant opposition to the will of God. Today it is difficult for us to imagine that a nation would go to war partly over an issue that seems so pertinently obvious. We see slavery as a clear aberration of Scripture's teaching that all humanity is created in God's image. We hold 'life, liberty and the pursuit of happiness' to be a God-given right. But a century and a half ago, this right to freedom was not so apparent, and Christians were deadlocked in theological debate. Part of the problem was that the argument went deeper than the question of slavery. It concerned the theological relationship of Spirit to Scripture.

Evangelical writer Mark Noll shows that the crux of the issue was the role of the Bible and how it was used. Hence, the civil war was a theological crisis as much as a civil one.[3] On one side, pro-slavery theologians and preachers based their arguments on direct quotations from the biblical text. They had a strong case. At face value, both the Old and New Testaments appear to affirm the institution of slavery.[4] If you were to compile all the biblical verses on slavery, you would have overwhelming textual evidence for the pro-slavery case. As one preacher put it: 'When the Abolitionist tells me that slaveholding is sin, in the simplicity of my faith in the Holy Scriptures, I point him to this sacred record, and tell him, in all candor, as my text does, that his teaching blasphemes the name of God and His doctrine.'[5] For most nineteenth-century Americans, the 'plain meaning' of Scripture was undisputed. Anyone who argued differently did not respect the integrity and authority of the Bible.

On the other side of the debate were those who believed that slavery directly contravened God's will. They took a different approach to the Bible. With fewer direct references to turn to, their argument was based on the *spirit* of the Scriptures, rather than its letter.[6] Abolitionists highlighted the message of Jesus who came to set the captives free (Luke 4:18) and taught us to treat others as we would ourselves (Matt. 7:12). In effect, they were relying on the *Spirit* of Jesus to guide their ethics.

The question was: what was the Spirit saying about slavery in 1850s America? It may be no coincidence that some of the earliest abolitionists were Quakers, a group of people who regularly practised listening to the voice of the Spirit.[7] The tragedy of the American situation is that more were not doing the same. Too many represented the proof-texting approach of the pro-slavery lobby, and a million men lost their lives for it.

In seeking God's heart on issues such as slavery and others, we must never forget that the Scriptures are *contextualised*. The writers of the Old and New Testament had very different audiences when their thoughts on slavery were first penned. Even though the Scriptures will never stop being relevant for the gospel they present, they were not designed to address *every* situation. The Friday Apostolics of Zimbabwe are correct in saying the Bible is unable to speak to many contemporary concerns. But the Spirit can!

Today, we face issues that the early church could never have dreamed of. While our starting point is always the gospel principles as recorded in the Scriptures, we need to hear from the Spirit afresh. God has something to say about issues such as in vitro fertilisation, social media, gender dysphoria and even space travel! The same Spirit who spoke to the early church continues to apply the truth of Jesus to every situation. This is what positions Christianity at the cutting edge of society. Because the Spirit speaks, we can be true leaders of social progress in bringing God's kingdom from heaven to every situation on earth.

Situational ethics

This perspective also makes room for the Spirit to speak variously on the same matter in different situations. While there usually remains an ideal to strive for, hearing from the Spirit allows God's wisdom to be applied in different ways according to the demands of the situation and our levels of spiritual maturity.

This may well have been what was happening during one of the most contentious ethical debates of the first century: the issue of food offered to idols. In the Greco-Roman world, worship of pagan gods was a regular part of civil activities. Food offerings occurred daily in the temples, and afterwards the meat was sold in the marketplace.

This posed a problem for the first Christians: was it acceptable to eat meat from an animal that had been sacrificed to a foreign god? Or should you stay away from it, since it had already been received by the pagan priest?

In the Scriptures, there appears to be no single answer. Paul told the Corinthians that if their faith was 'strong' enough, then all food was sanctified and they could eat it freely, while still being considerate of those whose faith was 'weak' (1 Cor. 8). John, the author of the book of Revelation, told the Pergamum and Thyatira churches that eating such food was idolatrous and they should stop it immediately (Rev. 2:12–29). The Jerusalem Council said that the church would 'do well' to avoid it (Acts 15:29).

The range of perspectives we see in the early church over this issue may offer us some guidance in resolving the issues of our time. Being Spirit-led may involve being willing to accommodate a variety of perspectives (while remaining uncompromising on core matters). The Spirit may lead one person where another is not free to go. One individual may hear God telling them to abstain from alcohol, while another hears God telling them they're free to drink in moderation. One person hears God saying they should fight for their marriage when there's been adultery, while another is advised to leave. Access to the Spirit's wisdom allows for a diversity of individual situations. It also means that Spirit-leading is driven by relationship rather than rules.

Knowing a person versus knowing a text

We began this chapter by asking how Spirit-speaking experiences impact our theological understandings of contemporary issues (such as women in leadership, divorce and slavery). Different answers to this question lead us to two different ways of relating Spirit to Scripture. The first approach, which doesn't allow for Spirit revelation to revise our thinking, relies largely on the knowledge of a *text*. The second approach, which allows for Spirit revelation to revise our thinking, relies largely on the knowledge of a *person*.

To better delineate these approaches, let's return to the matter of divorce in the case of domestic abuse. In the first approach, our go-to option is consultation with theologians and biblical scholars. Here we apply the skills of historical-critical exegesis to the text. A Bible survey is made where every mention of the topic is taken into account. We examine the words of Scripture in their original Greek and Hebrew languages, investigate any textual variants, and cross-check meanings in different passages to arrive at a solution.

Baptist theologian Wayne Grudem has recently adopted this process in examining the issue of divorce and domestic abuse, and has changed his position as a result. Having always believed that the only biblical grounds for divorce was adultery and unbeliever desertion, he now allows for a third reason: that of emotional and physical abuse. This shift was based on the discovery of a new meaning for a Greek phrase: 'in such a case' (*en tois toioutois*) in 1 Corinthians 7:15 (NRSV). Drawing on other first-century documents in addition to the biblical text, he argues that the phrase should be understood to include *any* case (such as desertion) that can destroy a marriage.[8]

Grudem's discovery brought untold relief to women from his tradition who found themselves in abusive marriages but still wanted to honour God in their situations.[9] Thankfully, they no longer feel the need to choose between God and protecting their lives and those of their children. The problem of course is that up until then, any person in this tradition suffering domestic abuse was beholden by God to stay in their marriage. Access to divine wisdom was only possible for those who could engage in historical-critical exegesis. Grudem's conclusion relied on decades of theological training, an intimate knowledge of *koine* Greek, access to a university database in California, and knowledge of a phrase no one had heard of since the first century. This immediately disqualifies the vast majority of the world's population, especially those who do not have access to education or well-stocked libraries.

Is this the scenario envisaged by Jesus when he poured out his Spirit? Apart from the fact that the New Covenant emphasis is that *all* have access to the wisdom of God via the Spirit, the underlying problem with this approach is that it places more emphasis on relationship to a text than relationship to a person. Here, we need to be reminded of what qualifies us to discern God's voice. Discernment doesn't come via cerebral knowledge or theological training. It comes from experiential knowledge that stems from a living relationship with God. Our ability to hear God's voice develops to the degree to which we follow Jesus.

I do not know Wayne Grudem personally, but his commitment to faith and personal integrity is undoubtable. In outlining his theory, he tells of how hearing the heartbreaking stories of battered women motivated him to revisit the topic in more depth. It was godly compassion that led him to study the Bible in pursuit of a different position. At the same time, he is careful to point out that his conclusions were not *based* on godly compassion. This is not because he doesn't know the heart of God or feel the pain of victims; rather, it is his *theological paradigm* that won't allow him to prefer knowledge of God's person over knowledge of Greek adverbs.

The second approach takes our contemporary God-conversations seriously. Natalie's experience of the Spirit enabled her to receive divine wisdom for her situation. This approach emphasises knowledge of a *person*. It allows for the Spirit to speak into contexts that are not covered by the New Testament text. Hence, discernment is not based on our biblical knowledge but on our knowledge of Jesus.

Of course, this perspective does not displace the value of scholarship, academia and thinking in general. Loving God does *not* mean that our minds are switched off (Matt. 22:37). But it does mean that our human intelligence and theological study become the tools of a greater hermeneutic that starts with Jesus. Our expertise is based on our walk with the Spirit and the degree to which we love God, as demonstrated by our faith and obedience.

Jerusalem Councils in our day

We've seen that the Spirit was given to speak to the issues of our day. Because the Spirit was disseminated to all people regardless of age, culture and gender, God can speak to any individual to bring the truth of Jesus to their situation. These experiences may have ramifications for the wider church because of our connectedness by the Spirit. But the question then arises: how does this work in practice? Our ethics could appear decidedly unstable if there was a church-wide free-for-all. Clearly, the process of discernment again becomes critical. For individual revelations to have wider application, they must be tested by the wider church.

Here again, the issue of the Gentiles in the early church provides the model. We see that God had spoken privately in the lives of two individuals – Peter and Cornelius – regarding a matter that initially had jurisdiction only over their lives and those of the people in their immediate circle (Acts 10). But if the revelation meant that God didn't exclude Cornelius and his household from the gospel, would it apply to other Gentiles? In other words, did the private Spirit-experiences of Peter and Cornelius have public application in the church of Jerusalem, Antioch and even worldwide (Acts 15:1)?

This was one of the drivers behind the meeting of the Jerusalem Council. When people outside Jerusalem challenged the position, the Jerusalem leaders took time to reflect on its potential for wider application (Acts 15:1–2). If Peter and Cornelius's experiences were to have relevance, they would need to be tested by the greater church. During the process, arguments were made from the Hebrew Scriptures by the Pharisees, and testimonies were submitted by Peter, Paul and Barnabas. Finally, a conclusion was arrived at: yes, the message of Peter and Cornelius's visionary experiences represented God's heart for all Gentiles. Private revelation had public application. Thus, the news was disseminated among the churches of the Diaspora (Acts 15:13–31).

If we believe God is still speaking about the issues of our day, we need to conduct our own 'Jerusalem councils'.[10] This would require churches of different denominations and traditions to come together and reflect on what the Spirit is saying. Experiences and testimonies from every culture, tradition and background should be included. Of course, this process also requires a significant level of humility and openness. It will probably involve robust conversations and the kind of healthy conflict we read about at the Jerusalem Council. But if we truly hold to the reality of the revelatory Spirit among us, we would expect the Spirit to be speaking the same message to multiple parties. The Spirit will always be leading us into truth (John 16:13). By definition, hearing from the Spirit will bring us into unity as the body of Christ.

In the case of divorce and domestic abuse, a 'Jerusalem Council' that took revelatory experiences seriously would have helped the church's teaching on the matter. As it turns out, Natalie participated in her own council process. After having her testimony rejected by her pastor, she shared it with a minister from a different tradition. He listened to her story, reflected on the different scriptural interpretations and worked through the discernment process with her. Afterwards, she was able to walk away from her violent husband and has since enjoyed healing and restoration.

Two witnesses to revelation

There are clear answers to the theological tension between Scripture and Spirit. As we've seen, the conflict is resolved when we first recognise the source of authority in the living Word of God. As divine speaker, God continues to express his authority, power and truth in his words so that his mission can continue.

From this revelation, we must recognise the place of two equally important 'witnesses'. The first is the *Scriptures*, which tell us how the early church heard, recognised and responded to God's voice as the Spirit spoke to apply the gospel in the first century. The second is the *church* who, in building on the foundation of the living Word, continues the pattern modelled in the Scriptures and receives the ongoing voice of the Spirit in new and different contexts. Thus, both the Scriptures and the church bear witness to the authority, power and truth of Jesus. The Scriptures bear witness to what the Spirit said in the past (John 14:26) and the church bears witness to what the Spirit is saying in the present (John 16:13). Both Scripture and the church are subordinated to the authority of the living Word of God. Their testimony is consistent because their origin is the same. No competition exists between them since the living Word of God is over and above both.

***

It is significant that in recent times, church entities across the denominational spectrum have been conducting their own 'councils' on the matter of divine revelation. Before this, the divide had been too wide to cross; Protestants emphasised the Scriptures as the primary source of authority and the Catholics emphasised the church ('tradition'). As we've seen, this conundrum lay at the heart of the debates during the Reformation.

But more recently, discussions among leaders of the Orthodox, Anglican and Catholic churches have led to resounding agreement. All are now recognising the concept of *two* witnesses to *one* revelation.[11] When it comes to God's voice, the church and Scripture both act as witnesses to the ultimate authority. As the early church discerned the word of the Spirit, so the contemporary church is able to do the same. In both situations, the word of God continues to speak by the Spirit, and the church together discerns it. This is part of what makes Christianity unique among the world religions. The Spirit has been given to us in our day and age to provide the wisdom of God on every issue of concern! The word of God is not frozen in time, because the living Word Jesus has been and always will be the source. There can be no other.

18

Theological Solutions to Our Ministry Problems

'God told me my wife was going to die'

Robert was a pastor of a thriving church in an inner suburb of a large city. He had four young daughters and a talented wife, who supported him wholeheartedly. Their church was on the cutting edge of ministry, combining Robert's musical giftings with innovative strategies for reaching the bohemian crowd. Story after story told of lives radically turned around. His ministry had garnered a dedicated and passionate leadership team, as well as a high level of respect among the leaders of his denomination.

After twelve years in ministry and many more walking with God, Robert knew how to hear God's voice. He had heard it on several significant occasions before – when he had first planted the church, when he had started his outreach into the music industry and when he heard God speak for those in his church. But now it seemed the voice was telling him something more foreboding – his wife was *going to die*. Afterwards, he would marry the worship leader.

The worship leader was young, pure-hearted and a little insecure. Robert had been spending time encouraging her when she came into the office to volunteer every week.

One Sunday morning, an older woman in the church came up to talk with Robert. She was a faithful attendee and part of the intercessors team, but the conversation was a little awkward. 'Pastor Robert, I feel like God spoke to me about you this week,' she said. 'He wants you to know that your wife is *not* going to die.'

The next day Robert made a booking at a local hotel. There he slept with the worship leader. Afterwards, his marriage broke up and the church fell apart.

Robert's story strikes fear in the hearts of many of us. How could he have got it so wrong?

When we hear stories like these, our gut instinct is to immediately shut the revelatory experience down. We discourage people from hearing from God directly, or we insist that God can only remind them of what has already been said in Scripture. After all, hearing from the Spirit seems to invite a truckload of ministry problems.

But our knee-jerk reaction misses the point. The problem has *never* been the revelatory experience itself. The problem lies in how we manage it in the context of flawed human hearts and our very human churches. In this chapter, we return to the ministry problems of hearing God's voice that were described in Chapter 3. The first problem of theological orthodoxy has been covered in the previous chapter. Here, we look at the remaining two concerns – pastoral fallout and institutional instability – and how they can be resolved. The solutions are both theological and practical. They are found when we remind ourselves of the role of hearing the Spirit in facilitating discipleship and mission.

Discernment as discipleship

The idea of hearing God's voice is an attractive one, but it is also a dangerous one. When you allow for the possibility that God can speak, you unleash the potential for divine power. Ministry problems come *because* the experience is so potent. Happily, people can get it right, but sadly, they can also get it wrong.

Hence, the first way to minimise pastoral fallout is to teach our congregations how to discern their spiritual experiences. When we don't intentionally train people to recognise God's voice, it is a bit like giving a toddler a loaded gun. Problems happen when you place a powerful tool into the hands of a novice. The process of discernment needs to be taught just like any other spiritual discipline (we cover strategies for this in the church in Chapter 19).

However, ignorance is only one of the reasons for poor discernment and it's a relatively minor one. Most of our ministry problems arise because of the *state of our hearts*. Robert's story illustrates this vividly. Robert was deceived into thinking God had told him his wife was going to die. But, when faced with the truth, his immediate reaction was to book a room. His actions showed that he had already made up his mind. There had been options; on hearing from the elderly parishioner, Robert could have tested the experience with his peers, who could have brought correction. Instead, he chose to keep it to himself. The problem was not that he *couldn't* recognise God's voice; it's that he didn't *want* to. He had already chosen *not to follow*. This is what made him vulnerable to deception.

When we look beneath the problem of pastoral fallout, we see that the issue is not with hearing God or even discernment; it is *discipleship*. We become subject to deception when we make a decision to stop following Jesus. Hearing and recognising God's voice is an issue of 'followship', and it needs to be approached that way.

Robert's story is not all bad news. In its own way, it is a heartening reminder of God's ability to speak. Even in our deceived states, God is able to communicate with startling precision. When we set our ears to hear from God, we must also set our hearts to do what God says. This position is one of obedience: 'Whatever you say, God, I will do.' The willingness to obey God's voice becomes our safeguard. We do not need to fear getting it wrong because the Spirit is well able to get his message through.

Of course, people still have the option to say no. The most powerful revelatory experience in the world is useless when the human heart defies it. 'God told me' can become a tool of self-justification and manipulation just like any other experience. But again, the problem is not with God or his manner of speaking. People are always free to resist the process of becoming a disciple.

In our desire to protect people from pastoral damage, we must not shut off the very thing that has the ability to bring truth and conviction

(John 16:8). The elderly woman's prophecy was an act of mercy, giving Robert one last chance to repent. Tragically, he chose not to. Our answer lies not in shutting down the experience, but in doing everything we can to perpetuate a culture of discipleship. The one thing we can do as pastors is to actively encourage people to say yes.

Helicopter parenting or raising adults?

We've seen the problems that arise when people say no to the Spirit's voice. But problems can also come when they're willing to follow. In these cases, hearing from God can actually lead to institutional instability. We saw this in Loren Cunningham's story back in Chapter 3. Loren's visionary experience called him to empower youth for mission, but it also led him to break with his denomination. He was forced to choose between God's will and the human institution. This choice forces us to reconsider our role as pastors and leaders. It calls us back to the goal of discipleship.

Here, it becomes helpful to revisit Glock and Stark's sociological research. We saw in Chapter 3 how revelatory experience is directly linked to institutional stability. The further along the taxonomy, the greater the possibility for disruption. The 'Type 4' experiences that contain higher levels of future-oriented or previously unknown information are most likely to challenge existing leadership goals and institutional structures. Consequentially, churches tend to actively shut down the high-level experiences and promote the low-level ones. 'Hearing God' experiences become restricted to the Bible or to those in leadership. After all, no pastor wants to hear a congregation member tell them that he or she feels called to leave a position or start another ministry elsewhere.

The problem is that Glock and Stark's taxonomy is also a measure of *relational development*. As people heard from God, they became more intimate with him.[1] That is, when the potency of revelatory content increased, people moved from being an 'acquaintance' of God to being a 'friend', and ultimately a 'partner'. While people at the friendship stage heard that they were loved and valued, at the partnership stage they were being asked to change jobs, move locations, start ministries and plant churches. In other words, the higher-level experiences that were most institutionally unstable were also those that actively engaged people with divine plans.

Glock and Stark are sociologists and therefore make no judgement about how their findings should be applied. But for church leaders, the problem must be resolved in ways that are theological. Here, the biblical testimony becomes our standard. We see that the experiences of people like Abraham, Moses, Peter and Paul would all fall into the highest category on Glock and Stark's taxonomy. Their 'hearing God' experiences motivated and empowered them to work with God in his divine plans (1 Cor. 3:9). Like the Bible characters of old, we are called to hear from God and partner with him. We are all called to be God's hands and feet on the earth. This is the ultimate goal of discipleship.

As pastors and leaders, then, we are faced with a choice. Either we encourage people to hear from God and risk disruption, or we shut the experience down and allow our churches to run 'smoothly'. Both options have consequences. When we opt for the low-level, stable experiences, our people will remain 'acquaintances' and spiritual infants who are dependent on the pastor. When we allow for the higher-level experiences, people have the opportunity to grow into maturity and become full partners with God. Our mandate is clear: we are to 'go and *make disciples*' (Matt. 28:19).

Our willingness to allow the Spirit to speak freely also shapes our role. It recognises that when we disciple others, we are helping them to follow Jesus and not ourselves. We acknowledge that the Spirit is responsible for leading a person's spiritual growth. This makes us *facilitators,* rather than directors. It orients people away from us as human leaders to God, the divine leader. Our role is to help others follow the voice of God, rather than trying to *be* the voice of God. We are to model the process of followship: as we follow Christ, we help others to do the same (1 Cor. 11:1; 4:16). As in parenting, this growth trajectory begins with dependency and moves towards interdependency.

The goal is for congregation members to take responsibility for their own walk (Rom. 14:4,12) – to learn to follow Christ first, not us.

As any parent knows, the process of maturation is not easy. It involves constant relinquishment. It also means that one day our 'children' may make decisions we don't like. The temptation to become like 'helicopter parents' who control their child's decision-making is very real. Here we must be reminded of *who* is in charge. When faced with the choice between heeding the voice of humanity and heeding the voice of God, the answer is clear. Jesus called his disciples to leave behind their nets (Matt. 4:19–20) and to prioritise God over their parents, children and possessions (Luke 14:25–27; Matt. 6:33). The call to discipleship is a call to unequivocal surrender.

Such a posture in no way diminishes the importance of church leadership. Church members are still called to submit to their God-appointed authorities (Heb. 13:17a), so that the community can thrive and be maintained. However, leaders are also called to 'keep watch over' their members for whom 'they must give account' (Heb. 13:17b). Keeping watch over a person requires monitoring their spiritual growth and facilitating the work of the Spirit in their life. It involves building a culture that allows for the Spirit's voice to enter the mix. It also means we must defer to the work of God in others' lives – even at our own cost.

When we allow the Spirit to speak, we *will* see more instability in our churches. But this instability is an indicator of divine–human intimacy. People are being led by the One who speaks to bring the kingdom from heaven to earth. As pastors, we must recognise that God is always in charge, not only of our own lives but also the lives of our church members.

God-shifts and divinely inspired instability

Ultimately, the above approach changes our attitude towards social disruption. Instead of despising it, we *welcome* it as a sign of the Spirit at work. The testimony of a couple I'll call Rod and Amy illustrates this perspective powerfully.

Rod and Amy had been ministering together for over ten years. Most of that time, Rod was the senior pastor and Amy was his assistant. But as time wore on, their giftings began to emerge and their roles began to shift. Rod was clearly the pastoral one. An accomplished teacher, he loved to spend time caring for and nurturing people. Just as clearly, his wife thrived in the apostolic giftings, and her strategic thinking and visionary capacity consistently gave the church direction and focus. Eventually, Amy officially became the senior pastor and Rod became the associate. Both were secure with this evolving dynamic in their relationship.

However, the denomination that Rod and Amy belonged to held a different perspective. Their tradition forbade women to be senior pastors, and Rod and Amy found it increasingly difficult to stay. The denomination's institutional structures were inhibiting both their development as individuals and the life of their church.

When Rod and Amy took it to prayer, the Spirit spoke to Amy in a dream. In the scene, she saw herself and Rod dining at a restaurant. During the meal, the waiter came over to serve the drinks. But when he poured the wine, it overflowed the glasses and spilled onto the table. Try as he might, he could not get the glasses to contain the wine. Rod and Amy knew they had to move seats. So they stood up and found another table. This time, when the waiter came over to pour the wine, there was no spillage. The glasses captured the wine perfectly.

The vision led Rod and Amy to make a decision. They met with their denominational heads and explained that God was repositioning them in a different network. The leaders listened graciously and accepted their decision. In the end, there was no fallout. Rod and Amy were honoured in the transition and continue to minister today in churches of their former denomination. Because both parties understood that God can and does reposition people for his purpose, the pain of separation was minimised.

Humanly speaking, growth and change is painful. But it is also a sign of the Spirit's work. This is precisely what we see in the early church. Whenever God spoke, there was disruption. But this disruption led to *growth*. As missiologist Craig Van Gelder observes: 'The actual growth and development of the church under the leading of the Spirit was often introduced as a result of conflict, disruption, interruption and surprise.'[2] He shows that in the book of Acts, the voice of the Spirit agitated, challenged and redirected, rather than merely confirmed, with the immediate consequences bringing undesirable results at first. In other words, the Spirit of God created instability! This dynamic was supported in my own research. Wherever the Spirit spoke, there was movement and change. New initiatives formed. Comfort zones were broken out of and mindsets were challenged. These shifts were not always easy – growing pains never are – but they were evidence of the Spirit at work.

This is why the Spirit-talking experience is so powerful. Disruption occurs, but the disruption is for the good of the kingdom. Fresh ministries are created, old wineskins are thrown off and new opportunities are created. At a big-picture level, the social barriers of gender, race and status are often broken down. This has been the case throughout history. We see it in the early church, when women were released into leadership at a time when they were considered to be second-class citizens. We see it in the American revivals of the nineteenth century with the abolition movement under Charles Finney. We see it in the twentieth century with radical unity among the African Americans and Caucasians in North America, and in the early days of the Australian Assemblies of God, where 50% of church planters were women.[3] These shifts are all evidence of the Spirit's revelatory work. Social barriers were broken down and new cultures were birthed. It is a taste of God's kingdom on earth.

The solution to our ministry problem, then, is to understand that wherever we allow the Spirit to speak, there will be disruption and conflict. Tensions will arise when the Spirit challenges the status quo and begins to reposition relationships for greater fruitfulness. But there's no reason for these shifts to be more painful than they need to be. Once we understand the ways of the Spirit, we can welcome disruption as a sign of the Spirit's work. We will be able to cooperate with it and even celebrate it.

This view also requires us to adopt a kingdom perspective that extends beyond our local spheres and structures. The institutions we work so hard to build must never be an end in themselves. When they have served their purpose, they must always give way to the Spirit's greater good. This understanding helps us to navigate the changes that will inevitably occur wherever the Spirit moves.

Of course, the easy path is to opt for the low-level experiences, so that people still feel loved and valued but are not necessarily challenged to change. The price of this silencing of the Spirit is stagnation and ultimately a rejection of kingdom purpose. When we approach the sociological problem theologically, we see that institutional stability can never be the goal. The Spirit must always be allowed to lead the way.

***

How do we avoid stories like Rob's repeating themselves in our churches? In some ways, we can't. Sociologists remind us that hearing from God is an act of power, a power that can be used for both positive and negative ends. When we encourage people to hear God's voice for themselves, it will always produce ministry 'problems' because of the state of humanity and its propensity for disobedience. People make their own choices and we cannot control them.

At the same time, we can do all that is possible to build a discipleship culture where people are trained to discern their experiences and respond appropriately to them. We can call people to a vision of a transformed life and partnership with God's divine plans. We can inspire them to always say yes to Jesus.

This approach reorients our role as pastors. We are calling people to follow Jesus and not ourselves. We are allowing the Spirit to lead the way. There may be disruption. It may get messy, but this is where we see the kingdom coming from heaven to earth.

Part III

Strategies for Building the Church Who Hears God's Voice

'We can neither make God speak nor make people listen, but we can create environments where people are encouraged to believe that God will speak and know what to do when he does.'

19

A Church Who Hears God's Voice

Eat more vegetables

Roslyn was having problems hearing God's voice. So she came forward for prayer after my sermon one Sunday morning. Her request was familiar: 'Could you please pray that God will speak to me?'

'I'd be happy to,' I answered, 'but before I do, can you think of anything that God may already be speaking to you about?'

Roslyn paused and then told me about a dream she had had a few months earlier: 'I heard a voice and the voice said, "Eat more vegetables."'

I admit I rolled my eyes on the inside, but then came a flash of inspiration: 'How is your health at the moment?'

'Oh, it's dreadful!' she groaned and began to list off a litany of ailments.

'Do you think the voice was from God?'

'Well, yes. I do.'

'So . . . have you been eating more vegetables?'

'Oh, you know, it's really hard. Carrots and broccoli and all that.'

'Yes, I know,' I said gently. 'Changing your diet is tough. But I'm not praying for you to hear God's voice – you *already have*. Now, go and eat more vegetables!'

With that, Roslyn returned to her seat. There was no need for prayer. God had already spoken.

Roslyn's problem was not that she wasn't *hearing* God's voice; it was that she hadn't *recognised* it. The question is: why? Quite likely it was because she hadn't taken the time to reflect on it. Roslyn only shared her dream with me because I asked. Our conversation meant she was able to discern her experience and work on the appropriate response.

I hope that since our conversation, Roslyn has been eating more vegetables. Of course, I don't know if she has. As a visiting minister, I can't follow her up. The truth is that this conversation didn't belong with a stranger passing through Roslyn's church. It belonged with those in her community who loved her and were familiar with her story. These people could help her discern her experience and then her accountable for what God had said. They would be the ones who could say, 'How are you going with eating those vegetables?' and 'Here are some recipes that might help.' Yet none of this was possible because Roslyn hadn't talked about her experience with her friends.

The Spirit's message about vegetables had the potential to change Roslyn's life. As 'bread' to her body and life to her spirit (John 6:63; Matt. 4:4), it would help address her health problems and draw her closer to God. Eating vegetables was the next step in Roslyn's path of discipleship, but she hadn't taken it. The opportunity for spiritual growth and health was almost lost.

This scenario happens repeatedly in our churches. God is speaking and people are 'hearing', but they're not recognising. And because they're not recognising, they're not following. Roslyn's story emphasises the role of the church in helping people to hear God's voice for themselves. We've seen that we don't need the church for the Spirit to speak, but we do need the church to help us recognise and respond when he does. This is where church leaders have a crucial role to play. The revelatory experience is designed to operate *in community*. We need to build churches where hearing from God is welcomed and expected: where mechanisms for discernment are accessible and where people are encouraged to respond to God's voice appropriately.

In this chapter, we investigate the features of a church that enables everyone to hear God's voice for themselves. Then, in the following chapter, we look at strategies for how to build them.

Introducing churches A, B and C

What does a church who hears God's voice look like? This was one of the questions I investigated in my PhD research. I studied three different Pentecostal churches in Sydney, Australia (we'll call them Church A, Church B and Church C), in order to learn about revelatory experiences in the context of each community. All three churches believed that the Spirit spoke in the same way today as in biblical times. My question was: how did they facilitate and manage the experience in their congregations?

The study involved extensive interviews with between fifteen and twenty members in each congregation, as well as a period of two months spent in each church. This research method, known as *participant observation*, involved immersing myself in the life of the church to observe the ways of a community first-hand. So, for six months, I visited Sunday services, prayer meetings and small groups. I listened to conversations from the pulpit and the pews, read websites and printed material, reviewed training courses and programmes, and examined any church practice that involved hearing from God.

My findings showed that people in all three churches reported 'hearing God' experiences, but there were differences in their frequency and intensity. In Church A, there was a large number of revelatory experiences across the breadth of the church. Many of these experiences were in the highest category of Glock and Stark's taxonomy, containing previously unknown or future-oriented information. Members spoke freely and easily of their experiences and shared common theological understandings about them.

In Church B, a good number of people also reported hearing from God. However, there was a significant difference between the generations. On the one hand, the older age groups reported hearing God's voice regularly. While their experiences weren't quite as high on the taxonomy as those in Church A, there was a general ease to them. The younger generations, on the other hand, struggled with the 'hearing God' experience. Many of them could not identify a time when they had ever heard from the Spirit for themselves. There was a lot of interest, as well as a lot of frustration. For this younger group, hearing God's voice came largely through the vehicle of Scripture.

Church C was different again. People reported revelatory experiences, but the phenomenon wasn't uniform across the congregation. Experiences appeared to occur in 'pockets'; they were common in some small groups but absent in others. The number and intensity of experiences seemed to depend on which group you attended and whether the group leader was experienced in hearing God themselves. There was also a significant level of confusion among the youth. Everyone was curious, but also uncertain.

Overall, Church A experienced a significantly higher level of experiences throughout the congregation than Churches B and C. In Church A, people were hearing regularly and powerfully from God. Of course, there were mistakes, but these were managed with minimal fallout. It was clear that the Spirit was at work speaking, healing, growing, sending and saving. Church A had successfully created a community where a large proportion of the congregation was hearing from God in ways that were both theologically orthodox and pastorally safe.

The question is: what was Church A doing that Churches B and C were not? Although the small sample size in my study meant that I was unable to make conclusive judgements about the frequency of experiences and their relationship to different variables in the community, it was possible to detect a number of key themes and patterns. I describe four of them in this chapter.

Features of a church who hears God's voice

When we look at the features of a church who hears God's voice, it is important to note from the outset that these findings are primarily *sociological*, not theological. We are not making an assessment about who had 'more' of the Spirit and why. Instead, we are looking at the sociological factors that influence the experience. Sociologists cannot give us good theology, but they can provide insight into how communities work. We can identify the human processes involved in building and maintaining a community that facilitates revelatory experiences. While we can neither make God speak nor make people listen, we *can* create environments where people are encouraged to believe that God will speak and know what to do when he does.

In order to analyse how Church A facilitated Spirit-speaking experiences so effectively, I drew on the work of a well-known North American sociologist called Peter Berger. Berger is considered a legend in his field, having articulated a theory of religion in the 1960s that has stood the test of time. He taught that communities are like social 'worlds' that act as a 'sacred canopy' under which people can flourish.[1] These social worlds carry the customs, beliefs, values and patterns of a certain group; another way to describe this is *culture*. Culture is that invisible element in your church that says, 'This is how things work around here.' It is the collection of invisible drivers that shape and define our communities. We notice these features of culture most when we first meet them as an outsider. They are often subtle and intangible, but they pervade everything we are and everything we do.

Berger showed that these social worlds are constructed and maintained by a variety of tools and processes. Language is one of the most important of these. Rituals and practices further act to reinforce the values and beliefs of a group, and regulatory controls sanction unacceptable behaviours. These processes protect the social worlds from falling apart and allow the group's beliefs to be passed on to the next generation.

In the case of a church who hears God's voice, the goal is to build a 'social world' that replicates the early church. This is a world where the supernatural is ever present and hearing the Spirit is a normal part of life. But, as we can see in my study, this world doesn't just happen because we want it to. The leaders of Churches A, B and C all had faith in a God who speaks, but they were not equally successful in seeing it manifest in their congregations. Sociologists tell us how important the social setting is for facilitating spiritual experiences.

They say that a world organised towards spiritual experience is more likely to experience it.[2] This means that we can be actively involved in creating and sustaining a community that hears from God.

My research highlighted a number of factors in Church A that were not present in Churches B and C. These features have also been observed in churches I've visited throughout my ministry. The 'church who hears God's voice' has four common features: 1) a leader who hears God's voice; 2) intentional teaching and training; 3) a shared language for spiritual conversations; and 4) relational openness and vulnerability.

1. A leader who hears God's voice

The first feature of a church who hears God's voice is a leader who hears God's voice. On this, the research is clear. Margaret Poloma found that the key predictor for the degree of Spirit phenomena in a congregation was the pastor's own experience.[3] Students of leadership should not be surprised by this correlation. As leaders, we reproduce after ourselves. In the same way that our children reflect our DNA, so do our churches.

Therefore, the starting point in building a church who hears God's voice is to be *the person who hears God's voice*. We need to experience how the Spirit is heard and responded to in our own lives if it is to be replicated in others. It is difficult, if not impossible, to lead others where we ourselves have not been.

The process begins with our personal devotional lives. It involves listening to the Spirit as part of our regular practice. It also means that we need to be willing to do whatever God says. We need to be asking what the Spirit is saying to us, using the process of discernment with our own personal communities, and then responding to it with faith and action. We need to be meditating on what the Spirit has already said in our lives and fighting in faith to see it manifest. Ultimately, we need to live out our conviction that after having our lives established in the truths of the gospel, hearing from the Spirit is the primary New Covenant vehicle for knowing God and partnering with his plans on earth.

2. Intentional teaching and training

The second feature of a church who hears God's voice involves intentional theological teaching and training for every phase of the Spirit-speaking experience. As detailed in Part II, Scripture provides us with the foundational understandings about what God says and why he says it. It also provides us with a demonstration of how the Spirit's voice was heard, recognised and responded to in the early church. These truths must be communicated clearly and regularly in our churches. We need to allow our theology to permeate every aspect of church life.

In my study, this was one of the most prominent differences between Church A, and Churches B and C. In Church A, the reality of Spirit-speech was consistently referenced in gatherings through songs, sermons, public prophecy and testimonies. When testimonies were shared, they were used as an opportunity for theological reflection and backed up with scriptural teaching. The leadership modelled *how* God's voice was heard, recognised and responded to in testimonies, teaching and prayer ministry. These are the practices sociologist Peter Berger calls 'legitimations'. Each time they occurred, the world of the Spirit was reinforced and developed. The result was that people came to see hearing God as a legitimate part of the Christian life and learned to anticipate it in their own lives. The world of the early church was being built in the contemporary setting.

While Churches B and C both believed in the reality of the Spirit's voice, references to the experience in the public space were noticeably rare. While there was plenty of emphasis on the truth that God has spoken (as recorded in Scripture), there was very little on the truth that God is still speaking. The experience of hearing from the Spirit was hardly ever mentioned and never in detail.

The culture of Church A didn't just happen. As with any ministry goal, we need to be intentional about implementing strategies that build a church who hears God's voice. We need to actively *train* people to hear from God and implement the tools that keep the experience within safe boundaries. Many of the problems that arise in our churches come because we've assumed God is speaking but we haven't trained people to recognise and respond to his words. As I've said earlier, encouraging people to hear from God without training them is like giving a toddler a loaded gun. We are setting ourselves up for a barrage of pastoral problems. Spiritual experiences will go underground and surface later in the pastor's office as the dreaded 'God told me'. God may still be speaking, but the full potential of the experience will not be harnessed.

This process requires an honest appraisal of our existing church training. We need to ask the questions: Where are people learning how to hear God's voice? Are we preaching about it in our sermons? Do we incorporate it into our New Christian courses, our regular small groups or the leadership training at our colleges? I still find it astounding that in many of our Bible colleges and seminaries, students can study for years without a single class on the subject of hearing the Spirit. We need to be proactive in equipping people to know God's voice for themselves. After grounding people in the truth of Jesus (Matt. 28:20), it is our primary role.

3. A shared language for spiritual conversations: three questions of discipleship

The third feature of a church who hears God's voice is a shared language for spiritual conversations. Our words are carriers of belief and experience. The goal is to provide a language that supports conversations about revelatory experiences as well as the framework for how to respond to them. Again, this feature was notably present in Church A. The language of revelatory experience was modelled in public life and reflected in private.

Without a way to talk about their experiences, people risk losing the power of them. We've seen this in Roslyn's story. As someone who visits a myriad of churches every year, I meet people like Roslyn all the time. They are eager to share their experiences and often preface them with, 'I've never told anyone this, but . . .' While I feel honoured to be taken into their confidence, I also find the conversations disturbing – for I am *not* the one who should be hearing this. As we've seen, the testing and interpretation of revelatory experiences needs to happen within our inner circles of relationships. Only these can provide a perspective that exposes deceptions and allows proper discernment to occur.

Not only do we need to encourage people to share their experiences but we also need to give them the vocabulary to do it. Three simple questions can be used:

1. What do you think the Spirit is saying?
2. How do you know it's God?
3. How can I help you follow?

These questions are carefully worded to highlight the Spirit's role in discipleship and to facilitate a healthy discernment process.

The first question, 'What do you think the Spirit is saying?' gives opportunity for people to open up about their experiences. People won't always share unless they're asked. Further, in asking what they *think* God is saying, we're allowing for learning and mistakes. It takes time before we know it's the Spirit we're sensing. People do not need to be definitive about their initial claims to revelation. We need to train them to say 'I think' or 'I feel' until the experience has been fully tested.

The second question, 'How do you know it's God?' reinforces the importance of testing. This works to prevent the 'God told me' scenario so abhorrent to us as leaders. Too often I hear pastors remark: 'When people say "God told me", there's nothing I can say. After all, who am I to argue with God?' But this is just not true. There *is* something we can say – and must say. The follow-up to 'God told me' is always, 'How do you know God told you?' 'God told me' is never the end of the conversation, since we need to be able to substantiate the source. As we've seen, this process should follow the testing pattern of the early church: Would Jesus say this? Is someone else saying this? Are spiritual signs following this?

The third question, 'How can I help you follow?' actively enlists the church community in responding to the Spirit. It invites encouragement and practical assistance in the process of discipleship – our key role as disciplers.

These private conversations about revelatory experiences are more likely to happen when the process has been modelled in public. As leaders, we need to *demonstrate* how to hear, recognise and respond to God's voice for all to see. This is where Church A excelled. The experience of hearing the Spirit was front and centre at public events. In every service, it was clear that the Spirit had spoken and continued to speak. Public prophecy, in particular, represented a unique opportunity to demonstrate how God's voice was heard, recognised and responded to.

4. Relational openness and vulnerability

Related to having a shared language for hearing God's voice is a culture that actively encourages it. As we've seen, the testing and interpretation of our revelatory experiences requires spiritual conversations. This in turn requires relational openness and vulnerability.

The importance of this was highlighted in a British church I visited recently. After I had taught the leadership team about the role of shared language, we took time to practise the three discipleship questions together. One by one, each staff member was invited to share what God had been speaking to them about. As we went around the group, faces reddened and awkward silences filled the room. Several team members struggled to say anything at all. Clearly, this activity was not a common one for the group. I realised that if we were going to train people to hear God's voice here in this church, there was work to be done with the leadership team first.

It may just be the British culture that struggles with relational openness, but as Brené Brown has so effectively reminded us, vulnerability is never easy.[4] Spiritual conversations do not always come naturally and there is evidence to suggest that they are on the decline in contemporary Western culture.[5] At the same time, it's encouraging to remember that the Spirit is on our side. It is the very nature of God to draw us closer to him and one another. As the writer of Hebrews says, the word of God acts like a sword – penetrating our hearts and dividing our soul and spirit (Heb. 4:12). Spirit-talking experiences expose the parts of ourselves that separate us from God and others. Only when our wounds, insecurities and sins are uncovered can healing and restoration occur. Allowing the Spirit to speak freely opens up our hearts to God and invites others on the journey with us. This is the beauty of the church and the Spirit working together.

I've seen this dynamic often in church life. A leader from a church in New Zealand once shared his feedback with me after participating in the seven-week God Conversations course with his small group. He told me how the first week or two had been awkward, but as the study progressed and people began to hear from the Spirit, conversation flowed. Then, as the study continued, the group began to open up about other areas of their lives. Suddenly they were talking about their marriages and relationships. Tears flowed and burdens were lifted. This was a group who had never related at this level of intimacy before. The voice of the Spirit opened up hearts and relationships so that healing and freedom came. Through it all, disciples were being formed and the church was being built.

***

To build the church who hears God's voice, we must reorient our churches to the work of the Spirit. The Spirit's voice must be at the centre of our teaching, training and conversations. It starts with our own lives as we attend daily to the voice of the Spirit. Then we need to actively implement strategies that will facilitate the 'hearing God' experience in our churches. We lead by sharing about our own experiences, using a language that reflects good theology and facilitates vulnerability before God and one another. It all starts with a simple but profound question that we should first ask ourselves and then put to others: 'What is God speaking to you about?'

If we truly believe that humanity cannot live without every word that proceeds from the mouth of God, we will honour what the Spirit is doing in the church by supporting and cooperating in it. The outcome will be a powerful New Covenant church that forms disciples and enables God's mission to be fulfilled.

20

A Strategy That Lasts

More than an event

I started the ministry of God Conversations in early 2008. The first twelve years were largely spent conducting seminars in local churches and ministry organisations around the world. Our seminars lasted for about half a day and included three one-hour teaching sessions and a variety of small-group activities. As a weekend event, they were usually attended by 20%–35% of the church. The feedback was always positive. People left inspired and equipped, feeling that God's voice was accessible to them. Many of them experienced the voice of the Spirit during the seminar. But, after finishing at the church and moving on to the next, I always wondered what I would find if I visited again a year later. Would people have continued to hear from God on a regular basis?

My growing hunch was that the answer would be 'no'. Unless there was a significant shift in the culture, people would probably forget the message and move on. My PhD research confirmed it. A weekend seminar and a couple of sermons – no matter how inspiring or well presented – are simply not enough to build a community that sustains 'hearing God' experiences. It certainly didn't help those who couldn't make it to the seminar. Hosting a conference or service with a guest prophetic ministry is simply not enough. In sociological terms, a one-off event doesn't create a social world where experiencing God's voice is the norm. It definitely isn't sufficient to implement the various legitimations needed to sustain a discernment process in the everyday conversations of people.

When we consider how to build the church who hears God's voice, we must stand back and consider the bigger picture. How do we saturate our community with theological understandings about hearing God and equip people with the skills needed to recognise the Spirit's voice in the context of genuine relationships?

It was these questions that led to a change in our ministry strategy. Instead of a special event, we repurposed the God Conversations teaching into a package called '50 Days of God Conversations' that can be implemented via a church's small groups. Our goal was to see mature disciples following Jesus and partnering with his mission long after God Conversations was forgotten. But whether you employ the '50 Days' package in your church or not, the strategy underlying it remains.

This chapter describes the approach needed to build a culture that allows for ongoing God-conversations in your church. The principles outlined will embed the Spirit-speaking experience in relationships, allow for the development of language essential to spiritual conversations, and cultivate hunger through the testimonies of those who have heard from God and followed. We start with your leadership team, then your Sunday service, your prophetically gifted people, your small groups and weekly activities, and finally your wider community.

Your leadership team

As we saw in the previous chapter, building a church who hears God's voice begins with leadership. Shared understandings about the theology of revelatory experience and how it is discerned and responded to are especially crucial. As church leaders, we also need to be actively encouraged to hear God's voice for ourselves. This includes *all* leaders – pastors and board members, administration staff and department heads. The aim is to get everyone on the same page.

We begin by creating an atmosphere of openness within our leadership teams so that experiences can be shared and tested together. The best way to start is with the three questions of discipleship introduced in the previous chapter: 1) What do you think the Spirit is saying? 2) How do you know it's God? and 3) How can I help you follow? These conversations will not only facilitate discipleship among your leaders but will also build a culture of transparency that can then be reproduced in the life of the church. Of course, the testimonies themselves will act as a source of inspiration and encouragement. They will also provide opportunity to work through the theological questions that will inevitably arise.

It is also in this context that you will be able to develop pastoral protocols for the wider church community, explore the problems that may be distinctive for your church, and design policies that will enable the team to navigate any pitfalls. For example, you may want to discuss what to do when individuals claim 'God told them' to do something precarious or unsafe. (We discuss this more fully in the next chapter.)

Your Sunday service

The Sunday service is not only a window to our churches but also a window to our spiritual lives. Our services provide a snapshot of the different components of Christian living and set the expectation for their everyday expression. The elements in our services and the amount of time we give to them reflect our priorities. We worship, pray, give, learn and commune together. These public activities model our private ones. Thus, our services become the template for how to build relationship with God.

This public–private template is also true of our God-conversations. If we are to bring the truth of the New Covenant Spirit into everyone's reality, we need to model the experience of hearing God in the public forum. Sermons and communion often place emphasis on the past, reminding us of the truths Jesus has established (John 14:26). But we also need to give attention to the truth that the Spirit is speaking about things to come (John 16:13). Throughout the service, we need to reinforce the fact that God *is speaking* as much as God *has spoken*. Talking about our God-conversations on Sundays will give people the language and confidence they need to talk about them during the week.

In practical terms, there are three ways we can do this: 1) worship and reflection, 2) sermons, and 3) a dedicated God Conversations segment.

1. Worship and reflection

Worship is a powerful way to reinforce the truth of God-speech. It also provides an opportunity for active listening. We can use all the elements of worship to reflect the truth that the Spirit is speaking. Here, it is a good idea to regularly select songs, drama, poetry, art and reflective liturgies that echo God's heart to communicate. Then, as people sing, invite them to listen to the voice of the Spirit. Allow the worship time to stir spiritual hunger, maintain expectancy and reinforce the message that God wants to speak to everyone.

2. Sermons

Just as the Spirit experience can be incorporated into worship, so it can be included in the sermon. You can devote entire messages to the topic or simply incorporate anecdotal mentions. It is also helpful to encourage your entire teaching team in the process to add strength to the common voice.

Not only do sermons reinforce the truth of the revelatory Spirit but they also provide the opportunity to demonstrate the *process* of hearing from God. We need to show people *how* hearing God works in the context of twenty-first-century living. This was the strategy

God gave to me when I first started God Conversations. Like Aaron in the wilderness, I was to show people the 'manna' God gave me to eat (Exod. 16:32; Matt. 4:4 compared with Deut. 8:3). This involved describing *how* God spoke in my life and what went on behind the scenes. Too often, we say 'God said' in our preaching and then move on to the next point, even while our congregations are wondering about the details. For me, 'showing them' involved providing examples of how God's voice was heard, what was said, how it was tested and what happened as a result. The fruit of this approach has been seen in the most common form of feedback I receive: 'I didn't think I could hear from God, but now I realise I always have.'

As part of the process of 'showing', it is important to be honest about the doubts and fears that occur along the way. It may even be appropriate to share stories of when we got it wrong and why. This is where the biblical accounts of people like Gideon and Jeremiah are so helpful. Both Gideon and Jeremiah wrestled with their experiences and showed uncertainty about what God was saying. When we are open about our own stories, we reinforce our shared humanity and enable our congregations to be open about theirs. This removes the distance between the experience of the preacher and the experience of those in the pews, as well as the distance between the biblical characters and ourselves. It provides a clear pathway to overcome the problems we all face.

As for sermon content, Scripture gives us a plethora of ideas based on the God-conversations of the biblical characters.[1] There are at least thirty God-conversations in the books of Luke and Acts, as well as several experiences that are alluded to in the epistles (e.g. 2 Cor. 12:1–10). And of course, the book of Revelation is entirely a revelatory experience. Accounts post-Jesus are particularly helpful in showing how New Covenant experiences are connected to Jesus' ministry and mission. When you teach from the God-conversations of the Old Covenant, be sure to reference Jesus as the 'filter' through which they should applied. For example, the revelatory experiences of Joshua, Hosea and Ezra should all be filtered by a Christocentric hermeneutic.

3. God Conversations segment: testimonies and prophecy

If Scripture is the most effective way to model the truth that God *has spoken*, testimonies and prophecy are the most effective ways to model the fact that God *is still speaking*. These can both be incorporated into the regular Sunday service via a five-minute God Conversations segment that alternates between a testimony and a public prophecy.

When testimonies are thoughtfully selected and prepared, they become powerful models for hearing God's voice. They are particularly effective because they illustrate the experience of ordinary congregation members and reinforce the truth that hearing God is not just for the 'spiritually elite'. Testimonies also provide an ideal opportunity for the pastor to reflect theologically on the experience in the light of the biblical pattern.

The best way to incorporate testimonies into your service is to gather testimonies from your small-group leaders on behalf of their group (with people's permission). Testimonies do not need to be dramatic. Some of the simplest stories can be the most powerful (e.g. 'God told me to buy my wife a bunch of flowers this week'). Indeed, these kinds of testimonies model the normal Christian life, since we don't typically have life-changing visions every week.

After selecting a testimony for the service, it is important to coach the individual through the process. Three to five minutes should be sufficient time for this. Use the three discipleship questions as a framework: 1) What do you think the Spirit is saying? 2) How do you know it's God? 3) How can I help you follow?

Public prophecy is another powerful tool for modelling the *what* and *how* of God conversations. Many churches already incorporate prophecy into the life of their services with the use of an 'open mike'. This set-up is well intended, since it emphasises the possibility that anyone can hear from God, but it is also difficult to regulate. The open mike can become an opportunity for the loudest voice in the room, and its spontaneous nature means that there is little time for discernment. The better option is to empower those in the congregation who are prophetically gifted. They can receive a message from

God for the church beforehand, submit it for testing by the leadership and then present it in the service.

Your prophets and prophetically gifted individuals

As we've seen, God has appointed prophets and those with gifts of prophecy in the local church (Eph. 4:11–12; 1 Cor. 12:1–11). These specialist giftings are given to equip the church to hear God's voice for themselves. By faith, we believe that there are prophetically gifted people in *every* church. Unfortunately, we don't always know who they are, so their giftings often lie dormant. Hence, it is essential that we identify, train and mobilise them. They will stand out as people who can hear from God for themselves and others with ease.

Once you have identified the prophetically gifted in your congregation, train them to lead prophetically in the church. Training occurs best in a group setting. In the same way that worship leaders gather to rehearse for services, prophetic types should meet regularly to listen to what the Spirit is saying with the aim of presenting it on Sundays. This process allows for both testing and preparation. It also models much of the prophetic activity of the Scriptures. As we've seen, Bible writers often took time to craft their prophetic words (e.g. John's Revelation[2] and Isaiah's poetic oracles). In the same way, prophetic words can be carefully prepared to ensure that the tone and content of the message will build up and encourage the congregation (1 Cor. 14:3).

This set-up also allows for adequate testing. Once the group has heard from God, prophecies can be submitted for discernment by the senior leadership in keeping with the model of the Jerusalem Council. Feedback can then be given to the group. Once the group is trained, they can then be released to share spontaneously in the service.

The delivery of prophecy in the God Conversations segment of the Sunday service can further be used to model the process of hearing from God. Theological reflection can be built into the segment to show how the message was first received and then tested.

Your small groups and weekly activities

The small group is the optimal place for discipleship and development of the Spirit-speaking experience. Here, genuine relationships can form, allowing for mutual discernment and encouragement in hearing God's voice. It is important, then, to train your small-group leaders to employ the three questions of discipleship regularly. This will facilitate a shared language for hearing God that promotes safety and accountability.

Your wider church

Consider how you can reinforce the message of God Conversations beyond the small groups into every facet of your church community. We need to hear the message *more than once* in order for it to become part of our regular experience. Worship pastors can invite their team to share what the Spirit is saying at rehearsals. Youth and children's pastors can practise hearing from God in their gatherings. Prayer teams can be encouraged to use a common language around the experience. The aim is to saturate the congregation with faith and expectation, as well as provide the language needed to support the 'hearing God' experience.

Remember too that building a church who hears God's voice takes time. Habits and language need to develop, truths need to be processed, hearts require preparation, and relational openness needs to form. But, as we continue to believe in the power of the New Covenant Spirit and actively prioritise it in our churches, we will begin to see the fruit of the New Covenant church.

***

As with our personal walk with God, building the church who hears God's voice is a lesson in divine–human partnership. We do all we can, humanly, to set our hearts and create the culture that will facilitate openness to the Spirit's voice. We stimulate spiritual hunger, train people in discernment and teach them how to respond to the ongoing mission of Jesus. We can teach and model the ways of the Spirit as seen in the New Testament church.

Then we look to God in faith, expecting that the Spirit will speak in response to our heart cry. As we preach, train and disciple, we trust that God will remind us of the truths Jesus established and then speak about things to come. While we do everything in the natural realm to orient our churches towards hearing from God, we trust the supernatural Spirit to speak to hungry hearts and lead us in the ways of Jesus. Like Samuel of old, together we pray, 'Speak, for your servant is listening' (1 Sam. 3:10).

21

Pastoring the Church Who Hears God's Voice

A tale of two visions

After a difficult divorce, Richard reaffirmed his commitment to God and was happily single when he experienced a surprising vision. He saw himself with a blonde-haired, blue-eyed woman and her two young sons. They met in a coastal town a few hours' drive from his home.

Three months later, Richard was visiting the coastal town from his vision. On the first day of his trip, he stopped by a supermarket. There in the car park was the blonde-haired, blue-eyed woman! Excited, he approached her and introduced himself. But the conversation didn't go well. He walked away disappointed, consoling himself with the fact that she had no young children accompanying her, so probably wasn't the one.

The next day Richard was having lunch with his friend Jane. 'I hope you don't mind,' she said with a smile, 'but I've invited a friend of mine to join us. I have a really good feeling about this.'

It wasn't long before Jane's friend arrived. To Richard's astonishment, it was the woman from the vision. This time she was trailed by two young boys. As they were introduced, one of the boys looked up at Richard and called him 'Dad'. The conversation flowed. An easy courtship followed. Ten years later, they are happily married and the two boys are like Richard's own sons. To this day, he is amazed by their first meeting when one of them called him Dad.

Like Richard, Cecilia had committed herself fully to God when she received a surprising vision. She saw herself with a dark-haired man named Scott. In the vision, they were being introduced as husband and wife at a church in Los Angeles.

A year later, Cecilia was visiting the church from the vision when she met a dark-haired man named Scott. Soon afterwards, they began dating. Cecilia was excited; the vision was coming to pass! But as time went on, their relationship became increasingly troubled. Cecilia persevered, believing Scott was the man for her. But Scott was unwilling to work through their problems. They even tried counselling, but the issues wouldn't go away. Eventually they broke up.

As far as we can tell, both Richard and Cecilia heard from the Spirit. Both visionary experiences were born out of a lively, committed relationship with God. Both were consistent with God's nature and accompanied by supernatural manifestations. Yet one spectacularly came to pass and the other failed dismally.

These stories remind us of the complexities we face when we hear God's voice. Even when we get it right, things can still go wrong. The dynamic interaction between God's revelation and our fallen humanity means that there are few hard and fast rules. This can make pastoring people through the Spirit-speaking process a challenge. In this chapter, we look at five of the most common issues we face and how to pastor people through them. We discuss: 1) the struggle to hear God's voice; 2) the overuse of the claim 'God told me'; 3) the problem of 'experience junkies'; 4) how to protect the vulnerable; and 5) what to do when God's words fail.

1. The struggle to hear God's voice

We've seen earlier that there are often two groups of people in churches. The first group finds it easy to hear God's voice. They seem to hear from God every day: 'God said this; God said that; God told me where to go shopping and where to park my car.' They are the group that says, 'God has *always* got something to say.'

Then there's the second group. This group hasn't heard from God in months, or even years. It pains them to hear the stories of those who hear from God regularly. They may have experienced God's voice five years ago, but nothing has been heard since.

While we know that God *is* speaking, he seems to be engaging a lot more with some people than others. The question is: why? And then: how often should we expect the Spirit to speak? The issue is important because it sets our expectations. It also points to the struggle many have to hear God's voice. I've seen this in churches regularly. A person discovers that God can speak. They get excited and set out to hear his voice. Then nothing happens. They end up frustrated and disillusioned. Sometimes, they become cessationists.

The struggle to hear from God is not an uncommon one. It has occurred throughout biblical history. The ancient narrator of Job, for example, writes about the complaint: 'Why do you complain to him that he responds to no one's words?' (Job 33:13). David too had experienced God's silence, even though he had heard God's voice many times before. Psalm 22 describes his sense of loss and frustration: 'My God, I cry out by day, but you do not answer, by night, but I find no rest' (v. 2). His words express how we've all felt at times.

Part of the answer lies in how we *label* our experiences. This may have more to do with our personality than anything else. Some people are simply more likely than others to attribute their inspirational experiences to God. I came to this conclusion after an 'experiment' with a friend. Pete is a member of our leadership team at God Conversations and a prophetically gifted leader. We had been talking about the role of personality in hearing God and decided to test our theory. So we stopped to listen to the Spirit about a particular ministry strategy. When I prayed, I saw an image of rough hessian cloth. My immediate thought was: 'You may prefer to have an elaborately embroidered piece of fabric, but just start with what you have.' When Pete prayed, he heard the words: 'Start with what's in your hand.'

Our little experiment taught us an important lesson. While Pete and I were both hearing from God, we would have labelled our experiences differently. I was far less likely to attribute my experience to God and, without Pete's confirmation, I would have said the idea was my own. Pete, however, would have naturally assumed that his word came from God. Our different conclusions reflect our different personalities. As a sceptic who does not easily trust her spiritual senses, I need a more dramatic experience before I call it 'God'. This means I am likely to be hearing from the Spirit more than I realise, but wouldn't necessarily describe it as such. By contrast, Pete, as an intuitive type, is quicker to attribute a moment of inspiration to God.

What we see here is that what one personality attributes to God, another attributes to human inspiration or 'intuition'. Perhaps the only truly objective way to know if something is from God is if it includes information that is unobtainable by human means. But it is also true that God speaks about the small things that don't require larger-than-life manifestations. In many ways, these insights are more difficult to discern.

The added challenge in the mix is that as we become more mature in our walk, it may be harder to tell the difference between what *God's Spirit* is saying and what *our spirit* is saying. The process of sanctification means that as we grow in faith, our thinking becomes more in line with that of Jesus. In the words of the apostle Paul, we have the 'mind of the Lord' (1 Cor. 2:16).

All this means that the struggle to hear God's voice is not always clear cut. There are a number of reasons why a person may not be hearing from God.

So how do we pastor the person for whom God is silent?

The problem takes on one of two angles. Either God *isn't* speaking, or God *is* speaking and we haven't recognised it. For the first, God may have chosen to be silent – as is his prerogative. God's wisdom lies not only in knowing *what* to say but also *when* to say it. In such cases, we should exhort people to trust God's character, hold on to what God has spoken in the past and keep going. This was David's response in his season of silence. When he couldn't hear God, he reminded himself of God's faithfulness and their shared history (Ps. 22:3–10).

However, we should not be too quick to arrive at this conclusion. As we saw in Chapter 5, we have a knowable God; his heart is that we may know his higher ways (Isa. 55:9). In the midst of our darkness, we're invited to 'give ear' and 'listen' so that we may live (Isa. 55:2–3). As we've seen, Spirit-speech is the primary vehicle through which God reveals himself and the means through which we know God personally. We must remember too that as central to biblical history as King David was, he did not share the benefits of the New Covenant Spirit that are available to us. We must not become like those in the wilderness whose wanderings didn't prompt them to enquire of the Lord (Jer. 2:6–8). God's silence is the exception, not the rule.

In these cases, then, the problem is more likely to be with us. Our default should be that God *is* speaking; either we haven't recognised it or God is waiting for us to heed the last thing he said.

In the first instance, the problem is largely due to a lack of awareness. People do not always know how God speaks and therefore don't recognise it when he does. This was the case with Roslyn and her vegetables, and the woman with the money bags. It was also the writer's conclusion in the book of Job. God had been speaking 'now one way or another, in a dream or a vision of the night', but people didn't 'perceive it' (Job 33:14–15). So, we should first use the question I asked of Roslyn: 'Is there anything that God may already be speaking to you about?'

Another possible reason why people don't recognise God's voice is because of their misplaced expectations. They may have read a story from the Bible or heard a story from the pulpit and compared it to their own. A message about eating vegetables pales in the light of Abraham's revelation of a new nation or a preacher's promise for a future spouse. People come to God expecting some grand vision of their future and instead hear God telling them to eat vegetables. It's no wonder they miss it.

As pastors, the solution to misguided expectations lies in reinforcing the role of revelatory experience in relation to Jesus' ministry and mission. The Spirit will speak to the greater matters of life as well as the smaller. When we see Roslyn's experience in the light of discipleship, we understand its significance. Following Jesus for Roslyn meant submitting herself to the next step on the Spirit's path. In our Spirit-led journeys, there will be high points of breathtaking promise, but there are also the low points of humble self-denial. This is a long road of obedience. Discipleship takes time and requires active change. Like any relational development, there will be no instant fixes. We need to remind our congregations that hearing from God is not primarily about *our* agenda. God speaks to continue the mission of *Jesus*. While this may include immediate concerns, God always has the wider purpose of sanctification and mission at heart.

The other factor in the struggle to hear God's voice may be our lack of response to past revelation. God may be silent because he's waiting for us to act on the last thing he said. The Spirit may have spoken to us about forgiving our brother, while we're waiting for him to speak about a new promotion. The Spirit may be speaking about reaching out to our neighbour, while we're waiting for him to speak about our finances. It's unlikely that God will change the topic of conversation. Again, this calls us back to the main function of Spirit-speech. God knows what we need to hear. Responding to *his* priorities, whatever they may be, will set us free. We'll find that after forgiving our brother, we'll know which job to take. God is still the one in charge. When God appears silent, we should encourage people to look back to the last thing he said, and ask them, 'Have you done it?'

In returning to our original question of how often God speaks, there can be no standard answer. This is because every person's relationship with God is unique. Each of us grows at our own pace. In this process, God's words are usually more like steak than candyfloss. They take time to digest. As God told Ezekiel, we need to 'eat' his words, meditate on them and allow them to become a part of us (Ezek. 3:1–3).

The danger comes when we start comparing our experiences with those of others. The sceptic is at risk of feeling condemned when hearing about someone who hears from God every day. The one hearing God speak about vegetables feels inadequate when hearing of another's revelation of an angel. Our comparisons can lead to discouragement on the one hand and pride on the other.

In the struggle to hear God's voice, our job as pastors is to remind our congregations that God speaks to everyone by his Spirit and does not discriminate. There is *no condemnation* for those who may not be hearing from God frequently or who are experiencing 'less sensational' encounters. This truth needs to be reinforced repeatedly. Everyone's walk with God is unique and our journeys are tailor-made. Spiritual maturity is not measured by the number of our experiences but by our response to them. What's more, a truly intimate relationship does not always require a constant flow of chatter. As in our human connections, we can simply enjoy God's presence without speaking.

Let's not forget, however, that God's intention is for everyone to know him personally through Spirit revelation. There is always more to receive! By faith we know that God is speaking, and by faith we know that we *can* hear it. We need to allow the experiences of others to inspire us to a closer walk with the Spirit, not to push us away.

2. Overuse of 'God told me'

The second pastoral issue we face in our churches is the overuse of the claim 'God told me'. While we cannot definitively know how often God speaks, some people are too quick to attribute all their insights to God. 'God told me' becomes the label for any prompting, thought or idea.

There is a real tension between promoting open access to the Spirit and encouraging a healthy scepticism towards the experience. We want to reinforce the fact that the Spirit is speaking, but we must not be too quick to call every inspirational thought 'God'. As pastors, we need to gently remind those who overuse the phrase 'God told me' that the claim to hearing God is a serious one. Once we call something 'God', we are declaring the weight of heaven behind it. This is a claim to divine authority. It places onus on the human hearer *and* the divine speaker. If God has *not* spoken, we have effectively put words into God's mouth! The overuse of 'God told me' is most common in Pentecostal circles. Instead, the Catholic tradition has a natural scepticism towards revelatory experience, which is healthy. Wisdom adopts a cautious reverence and avoids easy claims to divine inspiration. We do well not to make such claims lightly.

The overuse of 'God told me' may also point to a deeper psychological issue – the inability to take responsibility for our lives. When we attribute every inspirational experience to God, we run the risk of diminishing our sense of self and, in doing so, inadvertently quash the potential God has placed within each one of us. The use of 'God told me' becomes a compensation for our insecurity. This dynamic has even been investigated in academic circles. American psychologist-theologian Stephen Parker examined experiences of Spirit-leading in a Pentecostal church and found that *diminished ego control* was linked to an overemphasis on Spirit-leading.[1] That is, an overreliance on Spirit-experiences marked a tendency towards childlike behaviour, such that the weight of responsibility for decision-making was shifted *away* from the person.

I have also seen this tendency among students at Bible college. Often, they would arrive on the doorstep claiming God had 'told them' to come. But as soon as the pressure on them mounted, God suddenly 'changed his mind' and they packed their bags. 'God told me' became a way of compensating for a lack of resilience and commitment. This attitude renders God the controlling parent, and the Christian the child who never grows up.

Our solution to this scenario is to reorient our congregations to the partnership dynamic in the divine–human relationship. As we've seen (Chapter 14), when we listen to God's voice and cooperate with it, we become 'co-workers' and 'friends' with God's plans (1 Cor. 3:9; John 15:9–15). The role of partner validates our human input. Hence, Spirit-leading should provoke our creativity and ingenuity, rather than quash it. As Paul writes, we are 'God's handiwork' created for 'good works, which God prepared in advance for us to do' (Eph. 2:10). Our giftings, talents and efforts are all required in the fulfilment of God's purpose.

This also means that we do not *need* to hear from God for every decision we make. If God is not speaking, we can assume we have the resources to make our own decision. God's words empower us to live freely. They are not a restriction to a smaller life, but an invitation to a fuller one. Hence, there are times when God will say, 'This is the way you should go.' Other times, God will say, 'Which way would you like to go?'

These situations remind us again of the uniqueness of our Spirit-led journeys. Our revelatory experiences are as individual as our circumstances and personalities. One person is hearing God speak about their future spouse; another is hearing about their anger problem. One person is given clear and specific directives about their career; another relies entirely on their own research and common sense.

As pastors, we need to remind our congregations that each of us has our own spiritual walk. There is a relational dynamic involved in following the Spirit's voice that is tailor-made for every individual. God does not use a cookie-cutter approach. Why does one receive a certain kind of vision, while another does not? Why does God speak about one area for one person and ignore it in another? We don't know. But we do know that the Spirit knows each of us well enough to determine what will bring us closer to God. There will be common patterns, but the content, type and pace of our experiences will be as different as one person is from another. We are responsible for what God is saying to *us*, not to the person in the next pew. As Paul writes, each of us will give our own account (Rom. 14:12). The more pressing question is: what is God saying right now and are we acting on it?

Finally, the claim 'God told me' can be used in more sinister ways. People can use it to manipulate others in pursuit of their own agenda, often prefacing it with: 'God told me that you should . . .' Such claims are difficult to rebut if the person is already in a position of power. This makes church leaders particularly prone. Margaret Poloma investigated the devastating consequences of this scenario in a North American church.[2] She noted the lack of accountability in the life of the senior leader and no proper process of discernment in the church.

Those who questioned the pastor's assertions were threatened with God's wrath in opposing 'God's anointed one'.[3]

Our antidote to this problem is to apply the model of the Jerusalem Council consistently. The revelatory experiences of leaders must be subject to the same level of accountability as congregation members. As leaders, we are just as vulnerable to error and deception as those we lead. While we may be more mature in our spiritual walk, submitting our revelatory claims to a proper process of discernment is a form of protection and acts to ward off any temptation to the abuse of power. If our Spirit experiences are authentic, they will always stand up to scrutiny.

3. Experience junkies

There is nothing quite as spectacular as hearing the voice of the Spirit. When we receive previously unknown information that is later validated, or the future is unveiled before our eyes, we experience a taste of God's love and sovereignty. This is the thrill of hearing God for yourself. However, it also leaves us with another problem. People start to love a revelatory experience for its own sake. They become 'experience junkies' – lovers of encounters rather than lovers of God. Pride creeps in as people exult in what they've seen and heard. In the same way that a church leader can take pride in the number of people in their pews and a businessperson can take pride in the number of dollars in their account, the prophetic person can take pride in how many experiences they've had or how many angels they've seen. No matter how well intended a Spirit-message is, the heart that receives it can sour its beauty.

This problem, like all the others, is not new. Spiritual pride was an issue in the Corinthian church (1 Cor. 4:6,18; 5:2,6) and obsession with experience was the reason for the rebuke to the church of Colossae (Col. 2:18). Even the apostle Paul struggled with temptations to pride after his visits to the 'third heaven' (2 Cor. 12). When our sinful hearts mingle with God's good gifts, the outcomes can become distorted.

The solution to our problem is not to discourage people away from revelatory experiences but to encourage them to continue seeking legitimate ones. Authentic Spirit-experiences will ultimately lead us down the path of humility as God crucifies the old self in sanctification. God will speak to curtail religious pride, as he did for Paul with his 'thorn in the flesh' (2 Cor. 12:7).

As pastors, we can aid the process by reminding people of the function of revelatory experiences. As Paul wrote to the Colossians, who went 'into great detail about what they had seen' and were 'puffed up with idle notions', Spirit experience must stay connected 'with the head', who is Jesus (Col. 2:18,19). Our 'hearing God' encounters must always serve their God-given purpose as an extension of Christ's ministry, ultimately producing the fruits of humility and grace. In this way we can guard against the 'cult of experience'. The joy is always in the outcome.

4. Protecting the vulnerable

Early on in my ministry, I visited a church in a regional town of Australia to do a dreams seminar. This seminar focuses on hearing God specifically in dreams and visions. But after teaching the first session on the Friday evening, I became increasingly concerned about Saturday's events. The church had a heart for the needy in their community and was full of recovering addicts, people with suicidal tendencies and the mentally ill. Story after story told of God's grace in individual lives, but recovery was a work in progress and there were few established leaders to guide them through. Increasingly, I realised that teaching the church to hear from the Spirit in visions and dreams at that time was pastorally dangerous. There was just not enough wisdom and maturity in the church to sustain a healthy environment for discernment and follow-up. The scenario is a stark reminder of our duty of care as pastors and leaders. When it comes to helping people hear from the Spirit, we need to remain mindful of the vulnerable in our communities and particularly those with mental illness.

So where do we draw the line? While Christians have always believed in a God who speaks, the claim to 'hearing voices' has often attracted accusations of mental instability. As the comedian Lily Tomlin once quipped, prayer to God is acceptable, but if you claim to 'hear back, you're schizophrenic'. As leaders who believe in the New Covenant promises, our foremost concern is not that 'we're crazy', but that promoting Spirit experience in our congregations presents a risk to the mentally unstable.

From the outset, it's important to recognise that the claim to hearing voices is not held to be a symptom of mental illness by experts in the field. In other words, we are *not* crazy. Psychological anthropologist Tanya Luhrmann investigated the relationship between revelatory experience and mental stability in her study.[4] She noted that 'hearing God' (or experiencing 'sensory overrides' in her terms) is a common experience in the United States; between 15% and 50% of Americans have reported such an event.[5] Similar statistics can be found in other nations of the world.[6] If we are crazy, there's a lot of us!

Luhrmann goes on to explain that hearing the Spirit has a different pattern and quality from psychosis. Unlike the experiences of 'voices' among the mentally ill, the experience of hearing from God among the mentally stable is comparatively rare. She also noted a cautiousness towards the experience that was not evident among the mentally ill; when people claimed to hear from God, the voice was neither pushy nor grandiose. Further, such experiences generally led to health and happiness – not madness.[7]

At the same time, Luhrmann observed that there are some prayer practices and beliefs that may lead to psychological distress among the vulnerable. As pastors, we need to be aware of these. Two key measures are crucial to creating a place of safety: first, a solid grounding in teaching about the nature of God as revealed in Jesus, and second, a network of supportive and trusted relationships.

These two elements are what prevented tragedy in the life of a woman I met in my research. Joyce had a heart to know God, but also suffered from severe schizophrenia. Even though she had immersed herself in church life, the voices didn't stop. At one point, she became confused over a sermon where it was taught that God wanted her to 'die to herself'. The 'voice' said that the best way to do that was to lie down on the railway tracks.

Thankfully, Joyce didn't follow the voice in her head. When I asked what kept her back, she told me about an older woman from her church. This woman was always looking out for Joyce and reminding her of who God was. As a result, Joyce was familiar with the character of God in Jesus. When she couldn't work out the voices in her head, she was able to compare them to the one she knew from the Bible. It was clear that it was *not* God telling her to lie on the railway tracks.

While Joyce's story is not the experience of the majority, we do not always know who is in our congregations or what they may have suffered that week. When we encourage people to hear from God, we must also help them carefully discern it. Safety comes when they are grounded in the revelation of Jesus and a network of godly relationships. In this way we can protect the vulnerable.

5. When God's word fails

A middle-aged woman once approached me on the arm of her husband after a God Conversations seminar at a Bible college in Germany. Tears spilled from her eyes as she shared her story. Eight years earlier, she had heard God speak about giving birth to a child. Since then, the promise had been confirmed by two reputable prophets. And yet here she was, infertile and fast approaching menopause. The cycle of raised hopes and disappointment had been relentless and she was overwrought with grief.

How do we respond when God's words seem to fail?

This is a heartbreaking situation. Most often, our reaction is to protect people from this kind of pain by discouraging them from hearing from God in areas such as marriage and children. When it comes to the issues of the heart, discernment can be particularly difficult.

Yet at the same time, it makes no sense to close off the possibility that God would speak about the areas in our lives that are most dear to us. If God is the one who is intimately acquainted with the hairs on our head, would he not be intimately concerned with the desires of our heart? After all, he has demonstrated this type of concern many times, with people like Abraham, Hannah and Elizabeth (Gen. 18:1–15; 1 Sam. 1:9–28; Luke 1:13–14).

When God's words appear to have failed, our first stop is to consider the possibility of error in discernment. We hear what we want to hear. Prophets say what people long for them to say. When it comes to matters of the heart, we must double down on our level of caution. This is particularly the case among those who are still learning to know the Spirit's voice or among young people who tend to be idealistic and overzealous. But even mature Christians can get it wrong. Our desires run so deeply; they easily override our ability to get it right.

But what if, to all intents and purposes, we discern our experiences to be from God? This was the case in Cecilia's story at the opening of the chapter. Cecilia's testimony bore all the components of Richard's testimony, yet it had the opposite outcome. The answer probably lies in the dynamic of human free will. Cecilia's story reveals the painful outcome of a word from God intersecting with the will of a person. Even if God's plan was for Cecilia and Scott to marry, it could never happen without Scott's participation. There is nothing one party can do if the other isn't willing. The problem is not the faithfulness of God and his word; the problem is the unfaithfulness of humanity to that word.

So, where does that leave Cecilia? Here we turn to the pattern of the biblical narratives. As we've seen, when a person fails to carry God's words in faith, God passes it on to someone who will (Chapter 14). As Samuel declared at the transfer of the promise from Saul to David, God is 'not a human' who speaks and does not act. He does *not* promise and then not fulfil (1 Sam. 15:29). There is hope for Cecilia as she continues to carry the word of the Lord in her heart – even as fulfilment comes through another man.

That still leaves us with our childless friend in Germany. In her case, the problem cannot be due to the interference of human will. Of course, she may have got it wrong; it is not hard to do. But what if she heard correctly? And what does it mean as she approaches her mid-forties? We know that our role, whenever we hear from God, is to have faith in what he has said. God's word is as good as his character. This is a non-negotiable.

Perhaps the best option is to consider the example of Mary as she pondered the death of her own prophetic promise at Lazarus's tomb (John 11:1–44). To all appearances, Jesus had said that Lazarus's sickness would 'not end in death' (v. 4). Yet in the darkness of subsequent events, it literally did. As Mary grieved at her brother's tomb, it was clear to all that Jesus' promise had failed. It is difficult to appreciate the utter despair of the situation because we know the story's ending. Not only had Mary lost her brother, but she had also lost the integrity of God's words. Yet, God had something greater in mind . . . something that no one could have conceived because it had never been seen before. A resurrection (John 11:25–26).

We are reminded that even when the promise dies, God's faithfulness means that greater things are at work. Jesus is still saying, 'I am the resurrection and the life. Your promise will rise again. Do you believe this?' (see vv. 23–26). We may not see it now, but Mary's story teaches us that God can be trusted to work in and through the death of any Spirit promise. The pillar of God's truthfulness and integrity is what we hold on to.

***

The challenges we face when pastoring a church who hears God's voice are real and often complex. This is the nature of discipleship. Helping humanity to grow in the ways of God will always be messy. But if God's words are truly a vehicle of his divine power and love, we need them more than ever. The pastoral problems we face must never be a reason to dismiss Spirit-speech. When God seems to be silent, when people overuse the claim 'God told me', become experience junkies, suffer from mental illness or experience the 'failure' of God's words, we must be there to reassure them of God's character in Jesus and guide them through the process with wisdom. We must remain steadfast to the truth of God's words even as we wait in faith and patience. God's words are a reflection of his character. They do not return empty. They can always be counted upon.

Epilogue: A Call to Hear and See

Sarah was waiting for life-threatening brain surgery outside the hospital emergency department when the Holy Spirit spoke: 'Your X-rays have been read wrongly. Go and tell the doctor.'

Sarah was flummoxed by the thought, but she knew the Spirit's voice well enough to take it seriously. So she went inside, found a doctor and asked to see her X-rays. Unsure of what to say, she explained that she was far from her home and 'just wanted to be sure'. The doctor was sympathetic and, even though it broke protocol, retrieved the X-rays for her. Of course, Sarah had no idea what she was looking for. She had been told that the shunt in her brain had snapped and needed immediate attention (it had been placed there many years earlier because of a problem with excess fluid). So she cast her eyes over the X-rays, then sheepishly gave them back, thanking the doctor.

Half an hour later, the doctor reappeared. He apologised to Sarah and explained that they had taken a second look at the X-rays and realised the shunt in her brain hadn't snapped after all. The original doctor was not a brain specialist and had misinterpreted what he had seen.

Sarah didn't have brain surgery that night. God had spoken to prevent an unnecessary and risky operation. His deep love and protection for Sarah was evident to all.

Here's a question to ponder: would God have still been watching over Sarah that night if she hadn't heard the words of the Spirit? Of course, the answer is yes. The truths of God's love and care are ones that we all hold on to when we're fearful and alone in our own hospital rooms. No Spirit experience can take away from God's character and nature most fully expressed in Jesus.

But for Sarah the impact of hearing the Spirit for her particular situation was profound. This was *applied faith* as she witnessed first-hand the direct intervention of God. Alone and isolated from her family, Sarah knew that her heavenly Parent was watching over her. The experience left her with a taste of divine reality that cannot be easily shaken. This is the difference that hearing the Spirit makes.

We've seen throughout this book the problems that come when we open ourselves up to the voice of the Spirit. History tells the horror story of strife and atrocities done as a result of our distorted lenses. False religions and sects have been born of 'revelatory' experiences that have damaged and obscured the revelation of God in Jesus. Humanity makes mistakes; we always have and always will.

But we've also seen that the God of heaven knows our frailties and weaknesses and speaks to us in spite of them. When we are open to following Jesus, we *can* hear the Spirit clearly, since God himself participates in the discernment process. The incarnation of Jesus, the witness of the Spirit in community and the reality of signs accompanying God's revelation set the boundaries and create a place of safety. We can walk confidently into the fullness of the New Covenant as we follow the pattern of the early church.

We've also seen the life-giving impact of hearing and obeying God's words; how they work to shape and sanctify us, by first putting to death the sins of the flesh and then resurrecting us into the abundant life Jesus promised; how they lead us to become true disciples of Jesus, equipping us in his mission to bring the kingdom of heaven to earth in whatever sphere we find ourselves.

We are left with the choice to fear or to follow, to walk in cerebral knowledge or experiential knowledge, to live with the direct touch of God or in the shadow of second-hand revelation. We can fearfully revert to the dryness of cessationism or we can faithfully step into Spirit-led living. Our decision will affect not only our own lives but also the lives of every member of our churches. We will either allow the Spirit to lead the process or take on that role ourselves.

As we close, I'm reminded of the story of Elisha and his servant Gehazi (2 Kgs 6:8–23). The king of Aram had suffered the consequences of Elisha's prophetic insights and sent his army to capture him. With Aramean horses and chariots surrounding the city, there was good reason for Gehazi's despair. Instead, Elisha's response was full of conviction: 'Those who are with us are more than those who are with them' (v. 16). Then he prayed for Gehazi's eyes to be opened 'so that he may see' (v. 17). Suddenly Gehazi saw what Elisha had already seen: there was no need to fear because they were surrounded by heaven's army.

Here were two men in an identical situation. One could only see what was happening naturally; the other could see what was happening spiritually. One could only see hopelessness; the other, victory. The truth is that the armies of heaven were *always present*, whether they could be seen or not. The difference was the impact on Elisha and on Gehazi. The one who had eyes to see was full of faith; the one who didn't was full of fear.

My prayer today is the same for us as it was for Gehazi. In the midst of our everyday situations, 'Lord, open our eyes so that we can see. Open our ears that we may hear. Open our hearts that we may determine to follow wherever you lead.'

Let not fear stifle our faith. The promise of the New Covenant stands. Let us understand that the kind of insight we see in biblical characters like Elisha facing an army, and contemporaries like Sarah facing brain surgery, is the type of revelation God has for each one of us. As Jesus said, God's words are 'full of the Spirit and life' (John 6:63); we cannot live without them (Matt. 4:4). When we hear from God, we receive life – spiritually, emotionally and physically. We receive eyes that see from God's perspective and we get to know God personally (Eph. 1:17). The Christian God stands alone – knowable, personal and powerful. He is the One who sees our every thought and situation. The Spirit has been given so that we *know* it to be so. Jesus with us; our New Covenant inheritance and the greatest gift of all.

Notes

Foreword

[1] *The Confessions of St Augustine*, Book 8, Ch. 12. From 'Nicene and Post-Nicene Fathers', First Series, Vol. 1. Trans. J.G. Pilkington, Ed. Philip Schaff. (Buffalo, NY: Christian Literature Publishing Co., 1887.) Revised and edited for New Advent by Kevin Knight. http://www.newadvent.org/fathers/110108.htm (accessed 6 December 2021).

[2] *The Autobiography of Charles H. Spurgeon*, Vol. 2: 1854–1860, p.226–7 (Philadelphia, American Baptist Publication Society, 1899), www.canonglenn.com/2011/10/05/spurgeons-word-of-knowledge/ (accessed 6 December 2021).

Preface

[1] We 'build' the church as God's co-workers (1 Cor. 3:10), while acknowledging that Christ remains the ultimate builder (Matt. 16:18).

1. The Power of Hearing God's Voice

[1] Margaret M. Poloma, *The Assemblies of God at the Crossroads: Charisma and Institutional Dilemmas* (Knoxville, TN: University of Tennessee Press, 1989).

2   Margaret M. Poloma and John C. Green, *The Assemblies of God: Godly Love and the Revitalization of American Pentecostalism* (New York, NY: New York University Press, 2010).

3   Poloma and Green, *Godly Love and Revitalization*, p. 134.

4   William K. Kay, *Pentecostals in Britain* (Carlisle: Paternoster, 2000).

5   William K. Kay, 'Pentecostals and the Bible', *Journal of the European Pentecostal Theological Association* 24 (2004): pp. 71–83.

6   Poloma, *Assemblies of God at the Crossroads*, p. 176.

7   Tania M. Harris, 'Towards a Theology of Pentecostal Revelatory Experience', PhD thesis, Alphacrucis College, Sydney, 2020, pp. 78–82; https://www.ac.edu.au/cms-documents/198/Harris_Tania_-_Hearing_Gods_Voice.pdf.

8   See Roger Stronstad's work in *The Charismatic Theology of Saint Luke* (Peabody, MA: Hendrickson, 1984) and *The Prophethood of All Believers: A Study in Luke's Charismatic Theology*, Journal of Pentecostal Theology Supplement 16 (Sheffield: Sheffield Academic Press, 1999).

9   Craig Van Gelder, *The Ministry of the Missional Church: A Community Led by the Spirit* (Grand Rapids, MI: Baker, 2007), pp. 19, 38–41.

10 Surveys reveal the frequency of this type of experience in Pentecostal and charismatic groups. In a 2006 study of Pentecostal–Charismatics in ten countries around the world (USA; Brazil, Chile and Guatemala in Latin America; Kenya, Nigeria and South Africa in Africa; India, the Philippines and South Korea in Asia), direct revelations from God were reported to have been received two to three times more than the average Christian: Pew Research Center, 'Spirit and Power: A 10-Country Survey of Pentecostals', *Pew Forum* (5 Oct. 2006) https://www.pewforum.org/2006/10/05/spirit-and-power (accessed 21 Apr. 2020). In Poloma and Green's study of a large Pentecostal denomination in North America, 81% of adherents reported such experiences; *Godly Love and Revitalization*, p. 135. These types of revelatory experiences are also seen in the charismatic streams of the Catholic Church. For example, in a survey of Hispanic Catholic charismatics in 2012, nearly half reported experiencing direct revelations from God: Pew Research Center, 'The Shifting Religious Identity of Latinos in the United States', *Pew Forum* (7 May 2014) http://www.pewforum.org/2014/05/07/the-shifting-religious-identity-of-latinos-in-the-united-states (accessed 21 Dec. 2019). Also, prophecy was found to be extensively practised among Pentecostals in Asia: Dennis Lum, *The Practice of Prophecy: An Empirical-Theological Study of Pentecostals in Singapore* (Eugene, OR: Wipf & Stock, 2018), Kindle edition: location 122.

[11] For a comprehensive discussion of Jesus as a prophet, see Ben Witherington III, *Jesus the Seer: The Progress of Prophecy* (Peabody, MA: Hendrickson, 1999).

2. History's Pendulum Swing

[1] *The Passion of Saints Perpetua and Felicity*, in St Gallen, *Stiftsbibliothek*, Cod. Sang. 577 (ninth/tenth centuries).

[2] Jeff Oliver, *Pentecost to the Present, Book 1: Early Prophetic and Spiritual Gifts Movements* (Newberry, FL: Bridge-Logos, 2017), p. 97. See also Books 2 and 3.

[3] Morton T. Kelsey, *God, Dreams and Revelation* (Minneapolis, MN: Augsburg Fortress, 1991), pp. 100–14.

[4] For an excellent description of dreams and visions among the early church fathers, see Kelsey, *God, Dreams and Revelation*, pp. 100–01.

[5] Unknown, *The Martyrdom of Polycarp*.

[6] Oliver, *Pentecost to the Present, Book 1*, p. 95.

[7] Pentecostal historian Cecil M. Robeck Jr identifies a number of contributing factors in 'Canon, Regulae Fidei, and Continuing Revelation in the Early Church', in *Church, Word and Spirit: Historical and Theological Essays in Honor of Geoffrey W. Bromiley* (ed. J.E. Bradley and R.A. Muller; Grand Rapids, MI: Eerdmans, 1987), pp. 72–3.

[8] Niels C. Hvidt, *Christian Prophecy: The Post-Biblical Tradition* (New York, NY: Oxford University Press, 2007), p. 88.

[9] Hvidt, *Christian Prophecy*, p. 80.

[10] Hvidt, *Christian Prophecy*, p. 93.

[11] Oliver, *Pentecost to the Present: Book 1*, p. 161.

[12] Oliver, *Pentecost to the Present: Book 1*, p. 169.

[13] Oliver, *Pentecost to the Present: Book 1*, p. 199.

[14] Martin Luther, 'The Preface to the Complete Edition of Luther's Latin Writings' (1545), in *Luther's Works, vol. 34: Career of the Reformer IV* (ed. Lewis W. Spitz; St Louis, MO: Concordia, 1960), pp. 336–7.

[15] John Calvin, *The Epistles of Paul the Apostle to the Romans and to the Thessalonians*, Calvin's Commentaries (ed. Thomas F. Torrance and David W. Torrance; trans. Ross MacKenzie; Grand Rapids, MI: Eerdmans, 1961), p. 269.

[16] Martin Luther, 'Letter to the Christians at Strasbourg in Opposition to the Fanatic Spirit' (1524), in *Luther's Works, vol. 40: Church and Ministry II* (ed. Jaroslav Pelikan; St Louis, MO: Concordia, 1975), p. 70.

[17] Kelsey, *God, Dreams and Revelation*, p. 146.

[18] For more on this, see Jon Mark Ruthven, *What's Wrong with Protestant Theology? Tradition vs. Biblical Emphasis* (Tulsa, OK: Word and Spirit, 2013).

[19] Ruthven, *What's Wrong with Protestant Theology?*, pp. 26, 193.

[20] Jeff Oliver, *Pentecost to the Present, Book 2: Reformations and Awakenings* (Newberry, FL: Bridge-Logos, 2017), pp. 38–41.

[21] Oliver, *Pentecost to the Present: Book 1*, pp. 161–203; Hvidt, *Christian Prophecy*, p. 80. Read Teresa of Avila's work, *The Interior Castle* or *The Mansions, Christian Classics Ethereal Library* (n.d.) http://www.ccel.org/ccel/teresa/castle2.iv.html.

[22] Colt Anderson, 'Discernment of Spirits in the Theology of John Cassian: A Potential Bridge for Dialogue', *Journal of Ecumenical Studies* 53.2 (2018), pp. 303–11.

[23] Laurent Volken, *Visions, Revelations and the Church* (New York, NY: Kenedy, 1963), p. 95; Hvidt, *Christian Prophecy*, pp. 141–5; John of the Cross, *The Ascent of Mount Carmel*, in *The Collected Works of St. John of the Cross* (trans. Kieran Kavanaugh OCD and Otilio Rodriguez OCD; Washington, DC: ICS Publications, 1991), 2.112–18, ch. 19: 'On the Danger of Visions'.

[24] For more on this see Ruthven, *What's Wrong with Protestant Theology?*, p. 101.

[25] See Norman C. Kraus, *Evangelicalism and Anabaptism* (Scottsdale, PA: Herald, 1979).

[26] For a good overview of this period see Oliver, *From Pentecost to the Present, Book 2*.

[27] Examples of contemporary translations and commentaries that equate contemporary prophecy with inspired preaching include: W.E. Vine and Merrill Unger, *Vine's Complete Expository Dictionary of Old and New Testament Words: With Topical Index* (Nashville, TN: Thomas Nelson, 1996), p. 492; *The Living Bible* (Carol Stream, IL: Tyndale House, 1974), see 1 Cor. 14:4; and J.B. Phillips, *The New Testament in Modern English* (London: Collins, 2009), see 1 Cor. 14:29.

[28] Eugene Peterson, *The Message* (Colorado Springs, CO: NavPress, 2018), see 1 Cor. 14:4–5.

3. The Ministry Problems of Hearing God's Voice

[1] Church of Jesus Christ of Latter-day Saints, 'Teachings of Presidents of the Church: Joseph Smith', ch. 38: The Wentworth Letter, *The Church of Jesus Christ of Latter-day Saints* (2012) https://www.churchofjesuschrist .org/study/manual/teachings-joseph-smith/chapter-38?lang=eng (accessed 7 Oct. 2021).

[2] Church of Jesus Christ of Latter-day Saints, 'Joseph Smith – History' 1.25, *The Church of Jesus Christ of Latter-day Saints* (2013) https://www. churchofjesuschrist.org/study/scriptures/pgp/js-h/1.25?lang=eng#p25 (accessed 3 Nov. 2020).

[3] Charles G. Finney, *Memoirs of Rev. Charles G. Finney: Written by Himself* (New York, NY: A.S. Barnes & Co., 1876), pp. 12–14.

[4] Oliver, *Pentecost to the Present, Book 2*, pp. 161ff.

[5] BBC News, 'Boko Haram "to Sell" Nigeria Girls Abducted from Chibok', *BBC* (5 May 2014) https://www.bbc.com/news/world-africa-27283383 (accessed 27 May 2021).

[6] Office of the Clark County Prosecuting Attorney. 'Paul Jennings Hill.' *Prosecuting Attorney* (1998–2021) http://www.clarkprosecutor.org/html/ death/US/hill873.htm (accessed 28 Feb. 2021).

[7] John Bevere, *Thus Saith the Lord?* (Lake Mary, FL: Creation House, 1999), pp. 15, 59. For an additional Pentecostal perspective on the problems of hearing God experiences, see Michael L. Brown's book, *Playing with Holy Fire* (Lake Mary, FL: Charisma House, 2018).

[8] Ruth A. Tucker, *God Talk: Cautions for Those Who Hear God's Voice* (Downers Grove, IL: IVP, 2005), p. 28.

[9] The story is told in Loren Cunningham's book, *Is That Really You, God? Hearing the Voice of God* (Seattle, WA: YWAM Publishing, 2001).

[10] Read more of the history of YWAM at 'Our Story: His/Story', *YWAM* (2021) https://www.ywam.org/about-us/history (accessed 3 Nov. 2020).

[11] James S. Coleman, 'Social Cleavage and Social Change', *Journal of Social Issues* 12 (1956), p. 56.

[12] Poloma, *Assemblies of God at the Crossroads*, pp. 129–30.

[13] Angelo U. Cettolin, *Spirit, Freedom and Power* (Eugene, OR: Wipf & Stock, 2016), pp. 76, 97–8; Matthew S. Clark, 'An Investigation into the Nature of a Viable Pentecostal Hermeneutic', PhD thesis, University of Pretoria, 1997, p. 218.

[14] Charles Y. Glock and Rodney Stark, *Religion and Society in Tension* (Chicago, IL: Rand McNally, 1965).

[15] Glock and Stark, *Religion and Society*, p. 60.

16 Philip Richter, 'Charismatic Mysticism: A Sociological Analysis of the "Toronto Blessing"', in *The Nature of Religious Language: A Colloquium* (ed. Stanley E. Porter; Sheffield: Sheffield Academic, 1996), pp. 100–30.

17 Margaret M. Poloma, *Main Street Mystics: The Toronto Blessing and Reviving Pentecostalism* (Walnut Creek, CA: AltaMira Press, 2003).

4. The Theological Problem of Spirit versus Scripture

1 James I. Packer, *God's Words* (Downers Grove, IL: IVP, 1981), p. 39.

2 Wayne A. Grudem, *The Gift of Prophecy in the New Testament and Today* (Wheaton, IL: Crossway, 2000), Kindle edition: location 98.

3 Douglas Oss, 'A Pentecostal/Charismatic View', in *Are Miraculous Gifts for Today? Four Views* (ed. Wayne A. Grudem; Grand Rapids, MI: Zondervan, 1996), p. 239.

4 Tucker, *God Talk*, p. 64.

5 John F. MacArthur Jr, *Charismatic Chaos* (Grand Rapids, MI: Zondervan, 1992), p. 64.

6 See Jon Mark Ruthven, '"This Is My Covenant with Them": Isaiah 59.19–21 as the Programmatic Prophecy of the New Covenant in the Acts of the Apostles (Part 2)', *Journal of Pentecostal Theology* 17 (2008): pp. 219–37; and Jon Mark Ruthven, '"This Is My Covenant with Them": Isaiah 59.19–21 as the Programmatic Prophecy of the New Covenant in the Acts of the Apostles (Part 1)', *Journal of Pentecostal Theology* 17 (2008): pp. 32–47.

7 Matthew Engelke, *A Problem of Presence* (Berkeley, CA: University of California Press, 2007), pp. 1–2.

8 Engelke, *Problem of Presence*, p. 5.

9 James K.A. Smith, 'The Closing of the Book: Pentecostals, Evangelicals, and the Sacred Writings', *Journal of Pentecostal Theology* 11 (1997): p. 59; Daniel E. Albrecht, *Rites in the Spirit: A Ritual Approach to Pentecostal/Charismatic Spirituality* (Sheffield: Sheffield Academic Press, 1999), p. 246.

10 As observed by Robert E. Sears in 'Dreams and Christian Conversion: Gleanings from a Pentecostal Church Context in Nepal', *Mission Studies* 35 (2018): pp. 183–203. Recent exceptions include Anna Marie Droll's work on dreams and visions in Africa, '"Piercing the Veil" and African Dreams and Visions: In Quest of the Pneumatological Imagination', *Pneuma: The Journal of the Society for Pentecostal Studies* 40 (2018): pp. 345–65; and John B.F. Miller's work in biblical studies, *Convinced*

That God Had Called Us: Dreams, Visions and the Perception of God's Will in Luke-Acts (Leiden and Boston: Brill, 2007).

[11] Paul explicitly mentions his own Spirit experiences on multiple occasions: 1 Cor. 9:1; 15:8; 2 Cor. 12:1–7; Gal. 1:11–16.

[12] Cecil M. Robeck Jr highlights this disconnect between theory and practice in 'Written Prophecies: A Question of Authority', *Pneuma: The Journal of the Society for Pentecostal Studies* 2 (1980): pp. 26–45.

[13] Pete Ward, *Introducing Practical Theology: Mission, Ministry, and the Life of the Church* (Grand Rapids, MI: Baker Academic, 2017).

[14] For further discussion of this theory, see Jeff Astley, *Ordinary Theology: Looking, Listening and Learning in Theology* (Aldershot: Ashgate, 2002).

5. The 'Knowable' God

[1] Jenny Awford, '"World's Largest Child Sacrifice Site" Discovered in Peru', *News.com.au* (29 Aug. 2019) https://www.news.com.au/travel/travel-updates/worlds-largest-child-sacrifice-site-discovered-in-peru/news-story/09bc-c86bed6d564371780c3b6f5e9746 (accessed 16 Feb. 2021).

[2] John Loren Sandford, *Elijah Among Us* (Grand Rapids, MI: Chosen, 2002), p. 163.

7. How to Hear the Voice of God

[1] Tanya M. Luhrmann, *When God Talks Back* (New York, NY: Vintage, 2012), p. 190.

[2] Luhrmann, *When God Talks Back*, pp. 184, 158–88.

[3] Luhrmann, *When God Talks Back*, p. 195.

[4] Danah Zohar and Ian Marshall, *Spiritual Intelligence: The Ultimate Intelligence* (London: Bloomsbury, 2000), pp. 93–5.

[5] Zohar and Marshall, *Spiritual Intelligence*, pp. 107–11.

[6] Hvidt also suggests this may be due to the fact that women were unable to access formal authority in leadership, so God gave them charismatic authority: *Christian Prophecy*, pp. 98, 128.

8. How God Speaks (1): The Incarnational Spirit

[1] Craig S. Keener, *Spirit Hermeneutics* (Grand Rapids, MI: Eerdmans, 2016), pp. 19, 99.

[2] Gregory A. Boyd, *Seeing Is Believing: Experience Jesus through Imaginative Prayer* (Grand Rapids, MI: Baker, 2004), p. 16.

[3] For a helpful overview of New Testament terminology see Kelsey, *God, Dreams and Revelation*, pp. 82–6. Also, Miller, *Convinced That God Had Called Us*, p. 9.

[4] Miller, *Convinced That God Had Called Us*, p. 10.

[5] Luke 1:11–22,26–38,46–55,67–69.

[6] Miller, *Convinced That God Had Called Us*, p. 244.

[7] As well as being an echo of Leviathan, the great dragon with seven heads of Canaanite imagery is referenced by the psalmist as Yahweh's enemy (Ps. 74:14); see Boyd, *God at War*, p. 94.

[8] According to the Social Science Research Network.

[9] Rachel Gillett, 'Why We're More Likely to Remember Content with Images and Video', *Fast Company* (18 Sept. 2014) https://www.fastcompany.com/3035856/why-were-more-likely-to-remember-content-with-images-and-video-infogr (accessed 12 Nov. 2020).

[10] Miller, *Convinced That God Had Called Us*, pp. 11–13.

[11] The voice at Jesus' baptism (Luke 3:22) and the voice just prior to his death (John 12:28–29) appear to be rare exceptions.

[12] God often uses different figures as messengers to represent his voice. For example, in Stephen's case, God uses an 'angel'; the 'angel' and the 'Spirit' are used interchangeably to represent God's voice (Acts 8:26–40).

[13] Charles H. Kraft's work provides an excellent model for divine–human communication: *Christianity in Culture: A Study in Dynamic Biblical Theologizing in Cross-Cultural Perspective* (Maryknoll, NY: Orbis, 2nd edn, 2005).

9. How God Speaks (2): God's Modus Operandi

[1] It was only during the Enlightenment that the idea of revelation shifted from 'inspired experience' to 'inspired reflection'. Up until this time, hearing God's voice had always been associated with inspired experience: Hvidt, *Christian Prophecy*, p. 153.

[2] Kelsey, *God, Dreams and Revelation*, pp. 99–100.

3 For example, out of the twenty-four *Conferences* of the fifth-century Orthodox writer John Cassian, only twenty-two were translated. The two that were omitted were on dreams and visions.

4 Jerome inserted the word 'dreams' into the text of Lev. 19:26 and Deut. 18:10 and in doing so added it to the list of unauthorised cult activities: Kelsey, *God, Dreams, and Revelation*, pp. 138–9.

5 Kelsey, *God, Dreams and Revelation*, pp. 145–67.

6 Kelsey, *God, Dreams and Revelation*, p. 188.

7 Mircea Eliade, *Myths, Dreams and Mysteries* (New York, NY: Harper & Brothers, 1960). See also Kelsey, *God, Dreams and Revelation*, p. 55.

10. How to Recognise God's Voice (1): Getting It Wrong – and Right

1 Karl Rahner, *Visions and Prophecies* (New York, NY: Herder & Herder, 1963), p. 12, emphasis added.

2 For an excellent discussion on Paul's revelatory experience regarding his trip to Jerusalem, see Craig S. Keener, *Acts: An Exegetical Commentary, vol. 3: 15:1 – 23:25* (Grand Rapids, MI: Baker Academic, 2012).

3 For a detailed overview of the canonisation process, see Craig Allert, *A High View of Scripture? The Authority of the Bible and the Formation of the New Testament Canon* (Grand Rapids, MI: Baker Academic, 2007).

11. How to Recognise God's Voice (2): Would Jesus Say This?

1 The Catholic tradition includes three criteria for discernment, the first two being 'intrinsic' to the person and the third being extrinsic to the person: 1) The content of the revelation (which is in keeping with the revelation of Jesus and the 'Deposit of Faith', i.e. the core teachings of Christianity); 2) The physiology, psychology and spiritual life of the recipient; 3) The effects of the revelation or its fruits, including signs: Hvidt, *Christian Prophecy*, pp. 287–93.

2 For more insights on this, see John Christopher Thomas, 'Women, Pentecostalism and the Bible: An Experiment in Pentecostal Hermeneutics', *Journal of Pentecostal Theology* 5 (1994): pp. 41–56.

3   David Potter, *Constantine the Emperor* (Oxford: Oxford University Press, 2013), p. 148.

4   Potter, *Constantine the Emperor*, p. 142.

5   Old Testament biblical scholar Peter Enns shows that the approach to the role of Israel's God in tribal warfare (specifically the Canaanite genocide) is typical of other Ancient Near Eastern cultures (including the language used): *The Bible Tells Me So* (San Francisco, CA: Harper One, 2014), Kindle edition: location 823.

6   Seventy years after Constantine, Christianity was proclaimed the 'official' religion of the Roman Empire and it became a crime *not* to be a Christian. Not long after, the first instance of Christians killing non-Christians is reported. For more on this, read Gregory A. Boyd, *The Myth of a Christian Nation: How the Quest for Political Power Is Destroying the Church* (Grand Rapids, MI: Zondervan, 2005), p. 76.

7   In his conversation with the disciples, for example, Jesus *corrected* those who suggested that the tower in Siloam fell on and killed eighteen Galileans because of their sin (Luke 13:4).

12. How to Recognise God's Voice (3): The Church and Signs

1   Old Testament scholar Gerald T. Sheppard warns against trying to generalise Old Testament revelatory experience across time, regions and subcultures, due to the widespread variation in nomenclature, testing criteria and prophetic expression in the Scriptures: 'Prophecy: From Ancient Israel to Pentecostals at the End of the Modern Age', *The Spirit and Church* 3.1 (2001): pp. 48, 50, 63.

2   Christopher Forbes, *Prophecy and Inspired Speech in Early Christianity and Its Hellenistic Environment* (Peabody, MA: Hendrickson, 1997), pp. 265–69; Jon K. Newton highlights the additional input of experienced prophets and those recognised as operating in the discernment of spirits in 'Holding Prophets Accountable', *Journal of the European Pentecostal Theological Association* 30.1 (2010): p. 69.

13. After God Speaks (1): The Making of a Disciple

1   See esp. Matthew's account of the gospel events: Matt. 2:16–18 in the light of Jer. 31:15, and Matt. 21:1–5 in the light of Zech. 9:9; Isa. 62:11.

2   Learn more from the work of Jackie David Johns and Cheryl Bridges-Johns in this area: 'Yielding to the Spirit: A Pentecostal Approach to Group Bible Study', *Journal of Pentecostal Theology* 1 (1992): pp. 109–34.
3   Johns and Bridges-Johns, 'Yielding to the Spirit', p. 112.
4   Jonathan Haidt draws on the 2009 and 2011 work of Schwitzgebel and Rust in *The Righteous Mind* (London: Penguin, 2013), p. 89.
5   St Thomas Aquinas, *Summa Theologica* (trans. The Fathers of the English Dominican Province; New York, NY: Benzinger Bros., Inc., various dates).
6   Mortimer J. Adler and the University of Chicago, *Great Books of the Western World, vol. 19: Thomas Aquinas* (Chicago, IL: Encyclopaedia Britannica, 1952), p. vi.

14. After God Speaks (2): Bringing Heaven to Earth

1   In the Greek, *pro-* meaning 'forth' and *phemi* meaning 'to speak': W.E. Vine and Merrill Unger, *Vine's Complete Expository Dictionary of Old and New Testament Words: With Topical Index* (Nashville, TN: Thomas Nelson, 1996), p. 492. The Septuagint translates the Hebrew word for prophet *nabi* as 'seer', meaning 'either one in whom the message from God springs forth' or 'one to whom everything is secretly communicated': Ernest B. Gentile, *Your Sons and Daughters Shall Prophesy* (Grand Rapids, MI: Chosen, 1999), p. 166.
2   Lloyd Lewis, *Myths After Lincoln* (New York, NY: Grosset & Dunlap, 1957), pp. 294–5.
3   Thanks to Morton Kelsey for the testimonies of Lincoln and Newton in *God, Dreams and Revelation*, pp. 81, 160–62.
4   Witherington argues that one of the problems in the Corinthian church was that they were incorporating Greek ideas into their theology: *Jesus the Seer*, pp. 316ff.

15. When the Prophet Comes to Town: The Role of Prophecy and Prophets

1   This scenario has been observed in Zimbabwe, where a number of prophets have become 'mega-church superstars': Masiiwa Ragies Gunda, 'Prediction and Power: Prophets and Prophecy in the Old Testament and

Zimbabwean Christianity', *Exchange* 41 (2012): pp. 335–51. These individuals base their identity on the pre-classical prophets (especially Elijah and Elisha) rather than on Christ. Similar observations have been made in the North American church where prophets are depended upon for personal 'words of the Lord' (often for a fee): Michael L. Brown, *Playing with Holy Fire*, pp. 29–34.

2   Ruthven, *What's Wrong with Protestant Theology?* p. 67.

3   Ruthven, *What's Wrong with Protestant Theology?* p. 138.

4   David E. Aune, *Prophecy in Early Christianity and the Ancient Mediterranean World* (Grand Rapids, MI: Eerdmans, 1983), p. 92; Forbes, *Prophecy and Inspired Speech*, p. 277; Gordon D. Fee, *God's Empowering Presence: The Holy Spirit in the Letters of Paul* (Peabody, MA: Hendrickson, 1994), pp. 890–91; Richard Bauckham, *The Theology of the Book of Revelation* (Cambridge: Cambridge University Press, 1993), p. 4.

5   In the mid-twentieth century, Australian Pentecostal leaders banned prophesying over individuals and only allowed generalised public words of 'edification, comfort and exhortation', and in Canada, personal prophecy was rejected due to the bizarre manifestations that sometimes took place: David Cartledge, *The Apostolic Revolution: The Restoration of Apostles and Prophets in the Assemblies of God in Australia* (Chester Hill, NSW, Australia: Paraclete Institute, 2000), pp. 47–8. In the early twentieth century in the UK, warnings were given repeatedly about prescriptive personal messages: Gavin Wakefield, *Alexander Boddy: Pentecostal Anglican Pioneer* (Milton Keynes: Authentic Media, 2007), pp. 170–71. Similarly, older Pentecostal denominations in the USA rejected prophecy as foretelling and permitted it only as 'exhortation for edification': Walter J. Hollenweger, *The Pentecostals* (Peabody, MA: Hendrickson, 1972), p. 345.

6   Donald Gee, *Concerning Spiritual Gifts* (Springfield, MO: Gospel, 1980), pp. 120–21.

7   See Jon Mark Ruthven, 'The "Foundational Gifts" of Ephesians 2:20', *Journal of Pentecostal Theology* 10.2 (2002): pp. 28–43, for an excellent discussion of the nature of this foundation.

8   The Greek word *apostolos*, meaning 'sent-out one' (*Vines Complete Expository Dictionary of the New Testament*, pp. 30–31), was a secular term used by Greeks and Romans in the first century to describe special envoys who were commissioned to explore new territories and expand the Roman Empire. They were particularly tasked with establishing the culture and laws of the empire in new lands, Lyssichus, *Or.* 19.21; Demosthenes, *Or.* 18.107.

16. Resolving the Theological Problem (1): The Word of God

1 This testimony is retold with permission: Tom Doyle and Greg Webster, *Dreams and Visions: Is Jesus Awakening the Muslim World?* (Nashville, TN: Thomas Nelson, 2012), pp. 63–5.

2 See Tom Doyle's book, *Breakthrough: The Return of Hope to the Middle East* (Downers Grove, IL: IVP, 2009). Since the publication of this book, missionaries estimate the figure to be more like 50%.

3 Eugene Bach, *Jesus in Iran* (Back to Jerusalem Inc., 2015). See also Eugene Bach, 'God is Using Dreams', *The Pneuma Review* (1 June 2019) http://pneumareview.com/god-is-using-dreams/3 (accessed 6 Oct. 2020) and http://morethandreams.org.

4 For example, Reformed pastor John Piper is suspicious of Muslims receiving Christ through visions and dreams: Anugrah Kumar, 'Why John Piper Doubts Muslims Having Jesus Dreams', *The Christian Post* (1 Nov. 2011) https://www.christianpost.com/news/why-john-piper-doubts-muslims-having-jesus-dreams-59988 (accessed 6 Oct. 2020).

5 John Walton and Brent Sandy, *The Lost World of Scripture* (Downers Grove, IL: IVP Academic, 2013), p. 13.

6 Walton and Sandy, *Lost World of Scripture*, p. 13.

7 For example, the apostle Paul only hints at some of his revelatory experiences without going into detail (e.g. 2 Cor. 12:1–10).

8 For an excellent discussion of literacy in the Greco-Roman world, see Paul Rhodes Eddy and Gregory A. Boyd, *The Jesus Legend: A Case for the Historical Reliability of the Synoptic Jesus Tradition* (Grand Rapids, MI: Baker Academic, 2007), pp. 240–52.

9 For example, Eddy and Boyd write about how the audience may correct an oral performer in the middle of a performance when they misrepresent the tradition: *Jesus Legend*, pp. 237–68.

10 Walton and Sandy, *Lost World of Scripture*, p. 103. See also Mathilde Cambron-Goulet, 'The Criticism – and the Practice – of Literacy in the Ancient Philosophical Tradition', in *Orality, Literacy and Performance in the Ancient World* (ed. Elizabeth Minchin; Leiden: Brill, 2012), pp. 201–26; Alexander Loveday, 'The Living Voice: Scepticism towards the Written Word in Early Christian and in Graeco-Roman Texts', in *The Bible in Three Dimensions: Essays in Celebration of Forty Years of Biblical Studies in the University of Sheffield* (ed. David J. A. Clines, Stephen E. Fowl and Stanley E. Porter; London: Sheffield Academic Press, 1990), pp. 221–47, esp. pp. 237–42.

[11] Over time, the Israelite community became increasingly literate, even though debates exist over the process and timing. William M. Schniedewind argues that the roots of greater literacy are evident as early as the seventh century BC: *How the Bible Became a Book* (New York, NY: Cambridge University Press, 2004), p. 2.

[12] Walton and Sandy, *Lost World of Scripture*, pp. 21–3.

[13] Evangelical writer Nicholas Wolterstorff makes a philosophical case for the entire Bible being called the 'Word of God' by emphasising God's intention for the overall message: *Divine Discourse* (Cambridge: Cambridge University Press, 1995).

[14] Colin Brown, ed., *New Testament Theology*, vol. 3 (Exeter: Paternoster, 1978), p. 1087.

[15] Walton and Sandy, *Lost World of Scripture*, p. 218.

[16] Walton and Sandy, *Lost World of Scripture*, p. 219.

[17] Greek lexicons and dictionaries tell us that *logos* is chiefly oral. See W. Bauer, W.F. Arndt and F.W. Gingrich, *A Greek-English Lexicon of the New Testament and Other Early Christian Literature* (rev. and ed. F.W. Danker; Chicago, IL: University of Chicago Press, 3rd edn, 2000), pp. 598–601; Henry George Liddell and Robert Scott, *A Greek-English Lexicon with a Revised Supplement* (rev. and augmented H.S. Jones and R. McKenzie; Oxford: Clarendon, 9th edn, 1996), pp. 1057–9; Johannes P. Louw and Eugene A. Nida, *Greek-English Lexicon of the New Testament Based on Semantic Domains* (New York, NY: United Bible Societies, 1988), §33.98–9; William D. Mounce, ed., *Mounce's Complete Expository Dictionary of Old and New Testament Words* (Grand Rapids, MI: Zondervan, 2006), pp. 801–4. See Walton and Sandy, *Lost World of Scripture*, pp. 121–7, for a full discussion of the meaning of 'word' in the gospels.

[18] Craig S. Keener, *Acts: An Exegetical Commentary, vol. 1: Introduction and 1:1 – 2:47* (Grand Rapids, MI: Baker Academic, 2012), Har/Com edition, p. 523.

[19] Walton and Sandy, *Lost World of Scripture*, p. 123.

[20] Jesus spoke about God's word to honour your parents in reference to the divine word spoken to Moses in Exodus (Matt. 15:4–6, compare with Exod. 20:12). John wrote about God's word through Isaiah that must be fulfilled (John 12:38, compare with Acts 1:16).

[21] Walton and Sandy, *Lost World of Scripture*, p. 124; Max Turner, *The Holy Spirit and Spiritual Gifts: In the New Testament Church and Today* (Grand Rapids, MI: Baker Academic, rev. edn, 2012), p. 313; Mark McLean, 'Toward a Pentecostal Hermeneutic', *Pneuma: The Journal of the Society for Pentecostal Studies* 6.2 (1984): p. 52.

22 My thanks to philosopher James K.A. Smith who so eloquently clarified my thoughts on this issue: 'Closing of the Book', pp. 49–71.

23 Schniedewind, *How the Bible Became a Book*, pp. 114–17.

24 Smith, 'Closing of the Book', pp. 49–71.

25 Craig Allert shows that the early church fathers, including Ignatius, Clement and Polycarp, recognised divine authority in the words of Jesus and apostolic preaching, and not necessarily in any written document. The important thing was that Jesus said it, not where it was found: *A High View of Scripture? The Authority of the Bible and the Formation of the New Testament Canon* (Grand Rapids, MI: Baker Academic, 2007), pp. 109–12.

26 Private correspondence, member, SIL International.

27 Allert, *A High View*, pp. 59–60.

28 Allert, *A High View*, pp. 44–6.

29 John Goldingay, *Models for Scripture* (Toronto: Clements, 2004), p. 5.

30 See Keener, *Spirit Hermeneutics*; Jacqueline Grey, *Three's a Crowd: Pentecostalism, Hermeneutics, and the Old Testament* (Eugene, OR: Pickwick, 2014).

31 Significantly, this reflects the tradition of the Eastern Orthodox Church.

32 N.T. Wright, *The New Testament and the People of God* (London: SPCK, 1992), p. 1537; see also N.T. Wright, 'How Can the Bible Be Authoritative?' *Vox Evangelica* 21 (1991): pp. 7–32.

33 An excellent reference for the historical and critical reliability of the New Testament documents is *The Jesus Legend* by Boyd and Eddy.

34 The Rule of Faith is also variously described as 'the word of truth', 'apostolic teaching', 'tradition', 'apostolic deposit', 'sound doctrine' and 'the faith': Allert, *A High View*, p. 55. See also I. Howard Marshall, *Beyond the Bible: Moving from Scripture to Theology* (Grand Rapids, MI: Baker Academic, 2004), p. 55.

35 It is significant that Bishop Irenaeus (*c.* AD 130–200), perhaps the chief theologian of the second century, insisted that the 'gospel' to be preached to the world was nothing other than the content of the four gospels. This was a basic insight of the early church (Irenaeus, *Against Heresies* 3.1.1).

17. Resolving the Theological Problem (2): The Spirit on Contemporary Issues

1 Hvidt, *Christian Prophecy*, pp. 11, 304.

2 Thanks to Charles Kraft for this insight: *Christianity in Culture*, pp. 135–6, 153.

³ Mark A. Noll, *The Civil War as a Theological Crisis* (Chapel Hill, NC: University of North Carolina Press, 2006), Kindle edition.

⁴ In Deuteronomy, God sanctions the enslavement of Israel's enemies (Deut. 20:10–11), and in Leviticus, divine permission is given to buy and sell foreigners (Lev. 25:45–46a). In Genesis, slavery was pronounced by God as a result of Noah's curse on his son Ham (Gen. 9:25–27); indeed, it was this scripture that gave birth to the idea that since the descendants of Ham's son Canaan were seen to be Africans, they were destined by God to be slaves. In Ephesians, it was *right* for slaves to honour their masters (Eph. 6:5; also Col. 3:22; 4:1; 1 Tim. 6:1–2). In Corinthians, Christian slaves are to be content with their station (1 Cor. 7:20–21), and in Philemon Paul sends an escaped slave *back* to his master.

⁵ Noll, *Civil War as Theological Crisis*, location 270.

⁶ Noll, *Civil War as Theological Crisis*, location 528–93.

⁷ You can read more about the Quakers and their relationship to Protestant movements in Bradley P. Holt, *Thirsty for God: A Brief History of Christian Spirituality* (Minneapolis, MN: Fortress, 3rd. edn, 2017).

⁸ Wayne A. Grudem, 'Grounds for Divorce: Why I Now Believe There Are More Than Two', *Wayne Grudem* (2019) http://www.waynegrudem.com/grounds-for-divorce-why-i-now-believe-there-are-more-than-two (accessed 15 Oct. 2020).

⁹ Their testimonies can be found in a *Christianity Today* article by Morgan Lee, 'Wayne Grudem Tells Us Why He Changed His Divorce Position' (4 Dec. 2019) https://www.christianitytoday.com/ct/2019/december-web-only/wayne-grudem-divorce-abuse-complementarianism.html (accessed 15 Oct. 2020).

¹⁰ Significantly, the Catholic tradition has a long-standing formal process for this that is modelled on the Jerusalem Council: Hvidt, *Christian Prophecy*, pp. 294, 299.

¹¹ Anglican–Orthodox Joint Doctrinal Commission, 'Moscow Statement 1976 #9', in *Growth in Agreement: Reports and Agreed Statements of Ecumenical Conversations on a World Level* (ed. Harding Meyer and Lukas Vischer; New York, NY: Paulist Press / World Council of Churches, 1984), p. 42.

18. Theological Solutions to Our Ministry Problems

¹ Glock and Stark, *Religion and Society*, pp. 43, 60.

² Van Gelder, *Ministry of the Missional Church*, p. 158.

3 For a description of egalitarian leadership and opportunities for women in early American Pentecostalism, see Harvey Cox, *Fire from Heaven: The Rise of Pentecostal Spirituality and the Reshaping of Religion in the 21st Century* (London: Cassell, 1996), pp. 123–36.

19. A Church Who Hears God's Voice

1 Peter L. Berger, *The Sacred Canopy: Elements of a Sociological Theory of Religion* (New York, NY: Doubleday, 1967) (later reprinted as *The Social Reality of Religion* [Harmondsworth: Penguin, 1973]).

2 Ralph W. Hood Jr, 'Normative and Motivational Determinants of Reported Religious Experience in Two Baptist Samples', *Review of Religious Research* 13.3 (1972): p. 193; Rodney Stark, 'A Theory of Revelations', *Journal for the Scientific Study of Religions* 38.2 (1999): p. 289.

3 Poloma, *Assemblies of God at the Crossroads*, p. 86.

4 Brené Brown, *Daring Greatly: How the Courage to Be Vulnerable Transforms the Way We Live, Love, Parent and Lead* (London: Penguin, 2016).

5 Jonathan Merritt shares his research findings of the frequency of spiritual conversations in the American culture in his recent book, *Learning to Speak God from Scratch* (New York, NY: Convergent, 2018). His work shows that only 7% of Americans (out of a population in which 70% of people claim to be Christian) talk about spiritual matters on a once-a-week basis (Kindle edition, location 316).

20. A Strategy That Lasts

1 Further inspiration can be found at the God Conversations blog and podcasts at www.godconversations.com.

2 Bauckham, *Theology of Revelation*, p. 3.

21. Pastoring the Church Who Hears God's Voice

1 Stephen E. Parker, *Led by the Spirit: Toward a Practical Theology of Pentecostal Discernment and Decision-Making* (Sheffield: Sheffield Academic Press, 1996).

2   Margaret Poloma and Ralph. W. Hood Jr, *Blood and Fire: Godly Love in a Pentecostal Emerging Church* (New York, NY: New York University Press, 2008).
3   Poloma and Hood, *Blood and Fire*, p. 186.
4   Luhrmann, *When God Talks Back*, pp. 227–48.
5   Luhrmann draws on research from the late 1980s in her study, *When God Talks Back*, p. 236.
6   See ch. 1, n. 10.
7   Similar conclusions were made in Michael Jackson's work, 'A Study of the Relationship between Spiritual and Psychotic Experience', unpublished DPhil thesis, Oxford University, 1991. He shows that 'in general, the descriptions offered by the clinical group [the psychotic patients] were more disturbing, negative and bizarre both in the way they were expressed, and in their content' (p. 236).

Bibliography

Adler, Mortimer J. and the University of Chicago. *Great Books of the Western World, vol. 19: Thomas Aquinas* (Chicago, IL: Encyclopaedia Britannica, 1952).

Albrecht, Daniel E. *Rites in the Spirit: A Ritual Approach to Pentecostal/Charismatic Spirituality* (Sheffield: Sheffield Academic Press, 1999).

Allert, Craig. *A High View of Scripture? The Authority of the Bible and the Formation of the New Testament Canon* (Grand Rapids, MI: Baker Academic, 2007).

Anderson, Colt. 'Discernment of Spirits in the Theology of John Cassian: A Potential Bridge for Dialogue'. *Journal of Ecumenical Studies* 53.2 (2018): pp. 303–11.

Anglican–Orthodox Joint Doctrinal Commission. 'Moscow Statement 1976 #9.' In *Growth in Agreement: Reports and Agreed Statements of Ecumenical Conversations on a World Level* (ed. Harding Meyer and Lukas Vischer; New York, NY: Paulist Press; Geneva: World Council of Churches, 1984).

Astley, Jeff. *Ordinary Theology: Looking, Listening and Learning in Theology* (Aldershot: Ashgate, 2002).

Aune, David E. *Prophecy in Early Christianity and the Ancient Mediterranean World* (Grand Rapids, MI: Eerdmans, 1983).

The Autobiography of Charles H. Spurgeon, Vol. 2: 1854–1860, p.226–7 (Philadelphia, American Baptist Publication Society, 1899), www.canonglenn.com/2011/10/05/spurgeons-word-of-knowledge/ (accessed 6 December 2021).

Awford, Jenny. '"World's Largest Child Sacrifice Site" Discovered in Peru.' *News.com.au* (29 August 2019) https://www.news.com.au/travel/travel-updates/worlds-largest-child-sacrifice-site-discovered-in-peru/news-story/09bcc86bed6d564371780c3b6f5e9746 (accessed 16 February 2021).

Bach, Eugene. 'God Is Using Dreams', *The Pneuma Review* (1 June 2019) http://pneumareview.com/god-is-using-dreams/3 (accessed 6 October 2020).

———. *Jesus in Iran* (Back to Jerusalem Inc., 2015).

Bauckham, Richard. *The Theology of the Book of Revelation* (Cambridge: Cambridge University Press, 1993).

Bauer, W., W.F. Arndt and F.W. Gingrich. *A Greek-English Lexicon of the New Testament and Other Early Christian Literature* (rev. and ed. F.W. Danker; Chicago, IL: University of Chicago Press, 3rd edn, 2000).

BBC News. 'Boko Haram "to Sell" Nigeria Girls Abducted from Chibok.' *BBC* (5 May 2014) https://www.bbc.com/news/world-africa-27283383 (accessed 27 May 2021).

Berger, Peter L. *The Sacred Canopy: Elements of a Sociological Theory of Religion* (New York, NY: Doubleday, 1967).

Bevere, John. *Thus Saith the Lord?* (Lake Mary, FL: Creation House, 1999).

Boyd, Gregory A. *God at War: The Bible and Spiritual Conflict* (Downers Grove, IL: IVP Academic, 1997).

———. *The Myth of a Christian Nation: How the Quest for Political Power Is Destroying the Church* (Grand Rapids, MI: Zondervan, 2005).

———. *Seeing Is Believing: Experience Jesus through Imaginative Prayer* (Grand Rapids, MI: Baker, 2004).

Brown, Brené. *Daring Greatly: How the Courage to Be Vulnerable Transforms the Way We Live, Love, Parent and Lead* (London: Penguin, 2016).

Brown, Colin, ed. *New Testament Theology*, vol. 3 (Exeter: Paternoster, 1978).

Brown, Michael, L. *Playing with Holy Fire* (Lake Mary, FL: Charisma House, 2018).

Calvin, John. *The Epistles of Paul the Apostle to the Romans and to the Thessalonians*, Calvin's Commentaries (ed. Thomas F. Torrance and David W. Torrance; trans. Ross MacKenzie; Grand Rapids, MI: Eerdmans, 1961).

Cambron-Goulet, Mathilde. 'The Criticism – and the Practice – of Literacy in the Ancient Philosophical Tradition.' Pages 201–26 in *Orality, Literacy and Performance in the Ancient World* (ed. Elizabeth Minchin; Leiden: Brill 2012).

Cartledge, David. *The Apostolic Revolution: The Restoration of Apostles and Prophets in the Assemblies of God in Australia* (Chester Hill, NSW, Australia: Paraclete Institute, 2000).

Cettolin, Angelo U. *Spirit, Freedom and Power* (Eugene, OR: Wipf & Stock, 2016).

Church of Jesus Christ of Latter-day Saints. 'Joseph Smith – History' 1.25, *The Church of Jesus Christ of Latter-day Saints* (2013) https://www.church ofjesuschrist.org/study/scriptures/pgp/js-h/1.25?lang=eng#p25 (accessed 3 November 2020).

———. 'Teachings of Presidents of the Church: Joseph Smith', ch. 38: The Wentworth Letter, *The Church of Jesus Christ of Latter-day Saints* (2012) https://www.churchofjesuschrist.org/study/manual/teachings-joseph-smith/chapter-38?lang=eng (accessed 7 Oct. 2021).

Clark, Matthew S. 'An Investigation into the Nature of a Viable Pentecostal Hermeneutic.' PhD thesis, University of Pretoria, 1997.

Coleman, James S. 'Social Cleavage and Social Change'. *Journal of Social Issues* 12 (1956): pp. 49–60.

Cox, Harvey. *Fire from Heaven: The Rise of Pentecostal Spirituality and the Reshaping of Religion in the 21st Century* (London: Cassell, 1996).

Cunningham, Loren. *Is That Really You, God? Hearing the Voice of God* (Seattle, WA: YWAM Publishing, 2001).

Doyle, Tom. *Breakthrough: The Return of Hope to the Middle East* (Downers Grove, IL: InterVarsity Press, 2009).

———, and Greg Webster. *Dreams and Visions: Is Jesus Awakening the Muslim World?* (Nashville, TN: Thomas Nelson, 2012).

Droll, Anna Marie. '"Piercing the Veil" and African Dreams and Visions: In Quest of the Pneumatological Imagination'. *Pneuma: The Journal of the Society for Pentecostal Studies* 40 (2018): pp. 345–65.

Eddy, Paul Rhodes, and Gregory A. Boyd. *The Jesus Legend: A Case for the Historical Reliability of the Synoptic Jesus Tradition* (Grand Rapids, MI: Baker Academic, 2007).

Eliade, Mircea. *Myths, Dreams and Mysteries* (New York, NY: Harper & Brothers, 1960).

Engelke, Matthew. *A Problem of Presence* (Berkeley, CA: University of California Press, 2007).

Enns, Peter. *The Bible Tells Me So: Why Defending Scripture Has Made Us Unable to Read It* (San Francisco, CA: Harper One, repr., 2014). Kindle edition.

Fee, Gordon D. *God's Empowering Presence: The Holy Spirit in the Letters of Paul* (Peabody, MA: Hendrickson, 1994).

Finney, Charles G. *Memoirs of Rev. Charles G. Finney: Written by Himself* (New York, NY: A.S. Barnes & Co., 1876).

Forbes, Christopher. *Prophecy and Inspired Speech in Early Christianity and Its Hellenistic Environment* (Peabody, MA: Hendrickson, 1997).

Gee, Donald. *Concerning Spiritual Gifts* (Springfield, MO: Gospel, 1980).

Gentile, Ernest B. *Your Sons and Daughters Shall Prophesy* (Grand Rapids, MI: Chosen, 1999).

Gillett, Rachel. 'Why We're More Likely to Remember Content with Images and Video.' *Fast Company* (18 Sept. 2014) https://www.fastcompany .com/3035856/why-were-more-likely-to-remember-content-with-images-and-video-infogr (accessed 12 November 2020).

Glock, Charles Y., and Rodney Stark. *Religion and Society in Tension* (Chicago, IL: Rand McNally, 1965).

Goldingay, John. *Models for Scripture* (Toronto: Clements, 2004).

Grey, Jacqueline, *Three's a Crowd: Pentecostalism, Hermeneutics, and the Old Testament* (Eugene, OR: Pickwick, 2014).

Grudem, Wayne A. *The Gift of Prophecy in the New Testament and Today* (Wheaton, IL: Crossway, 2000). Kindle edition.

——. 'Grounds for Divorce: Why I Now Believe There Are More Than Two.' *Wayne Grudem* (2019) http://www.waynegrudem.com/grounds-for-divorce-why-i-now-believe-there-are-more-than-two (accessed 15 October 2020).

Gunda, Masiiwa Ragies. 'Prediction and Power: Prophets and Prophecy in the Old Testament and Zimbabwean Christianity'. *Exchange* 41 (2012): pp. 335–51.

Haidt, Jonathan. *The Righteous Mind* (London: Penguin, 2013).

Harris, Tania M. 'Towards a Theology of Pentecostal Revelatory Experience.' PhD thesis, Alphacrucis College, 2020 https://www.ac.edu.au/cms-documents/198/Harris_Tania_-_Hearing_Gods_Voice.pdf (accessed 14 October 2021).

Hollenweger, Walter J. *The Pentecostals* (Peabody, MA: Hendrickson, 1972).

Holt, Bradley P. *Thirsty for God: A Brief History of Christian Spirituality* (Minneapolis, MN: Fortress, 3rd edn, 2017).

Hood, Ralph W., Jr. 'Normative and Motivational Determinants of Reported Religious Experience in Two Baptist Samples'. *Review of Religious Research* 13.3 (1972): pp. 192–96.

Hvidt, Niels C. *Christian Prophecy: The Post-Biblical Tradition* (New York, NY: Oxford University Press, 2007).

Jackson, Michael. 'A Study of the Relationship between Spiritual and Psychotic Experience.' DPhil thesis, Oxford University, 1991.

John of the Cross. *The Ascent of Mount Carmel.* In *The Collected Works of St. John of the Cross* (trans. Kieran Kavanaugh OCD and Otilio Rodriguez; Washington, DC: ICS Publications, 1991).

Johns, Jackie David, and Cheryl Bridges-Johns. 'Yielding to the Spirit: A Pentecostal Approach to Group Bible Study'. *Journal of Pentecostal Theology* 1 (1992): pp. 109–34.

Kay, William K. 'Pentecostals and the Bible'. *Journal of the European Pentecostal Theological Association* 24 (2004): pp. 71–83.

———. *Pentecostals in Britain* (Carlisle: Paternoster, 2000).

Keener, Craig S. *Acts: An Exegetical Commentary, vol. 1: Introduction and 1:1 – 2:47* (Grand Rapids, MI: Baker Academic, 2012). Har/Com edition.

———. *Acts: An Exegetical Commentary, vol. 3: 15:1 – 23:25* (Grand Rapids, MI: Baker Academic, 2012).

———. *Spirit Hermeneutics* (Grand Rapids, MI: Eerdmans, 2016).

Kelsey, Morton T. *God, Dreams and Revelation* (Minneapolis, MN: Augsburg Fortress, 1991).

Kraft, Charles H. *Christianity in Culture: A Study in Dynamic Biblical Theologizing in Cross-Cultural Perspective* (Maryknoll, NY: Orbis, 2nd edn, 2005).

Kraus, Norman C. *Evangelicalism and Anabaptism* (Scottsdale, PA: Herald, 1979).

Lee, Morgan. 'Wayne Grudem Tells Us Why He Changed His Divorce Position.' *Christianity Today* (4 December 2019) https://www.christianity today.com/ct/2019/december-web-only/wayne-grudem-divorce-abuse-complementarianism.html (accessed 15 October 2020).

Lewis, Lloyd. *Myths After Lincoln* (New York, NY: Grosset & Dunlap, 1957).

Liddell, Henry George, and Robert Scott. *A Greek-English Lexicon with a Revised Supplement* (rev. and augmented H.S. Jones and R. McKenzie; Oxford: Clarendon, 9th edn, 1996).

The Living Bible (Carol Stream, IL: Tyndale House, 1974).

Louw, Johannes P. and Eugene A. Nida. *Greek-English Lexicon of the New Testament Based on Semantic Domains* (New York, NY: United Bible Societies, 1988).

Loveday, Alexander, 'The Living Voice: Scepticism towards the Written Word in Early Christian and in Graeco-Roman Texts.' Pages 221–47 in *The Bible in Three Dimensions: Essays in Celebration of Forty Years of Biblical Studies in the University of Sheffield* (ed. David J. A. Clines, Stephen E. Fowl and Stanley E. Porter; London: Sheffield Academic Press, 1990).

Luhrmann, Tanya M. *When God Talks Back* (New York, NY: Vintage, 2012).

Lum, Dennis. *The Practice of Prophecy: An Empirical-Theological Study of Pentecostals in Singapore* (Eugene, OR: Wipf & Stock, 2018), Kindle edition.

Luther, Martin. 'Letter to the Christians at Strasbourg in Opposition to the Fanatic Spirit' (1524). In *Luther's Works, vol. 40: Church and Ministry II* (ed. Jaroslav Pelikan; St Louis, MO: Concordia, 1975).

———. 'The Preface to the Complete Edition of Luther's Latin Writings' (1545). In *Luther's Works, vol. 34: Career of the Reformer IV* (ed. Lewis W. Spitz; St Louis, MO: Concordia, 1960).

MacArthur, John F., Jr. *Charismatic Chaos* (Grand Rapids, MI: Zondervan, 1992).

Marshall, I. Howard. *Beyond the Bible: Moving from Scripture to Theology* (Grand Rapids, MI: Baker Academic, 2004).

McLean, Mark. 'Toward a Pentecostal Hermeneutic'. *Pneuma: The Journal of the Society for Pentecostal Studies* 6.2 (1984): pp. 35–56.

Merritt, Jonathan. *Learning to Speak God from Scratch* (New York, NY: Convergent, 2018). Kindle edition.

Miller, John B.F. *Convinced That God Had Called Us: Dreams, Visions and the Perception of God's Will in Luke-Acts* (Leiden and Boston: Brill, 2007).

Mounce, William, D. *The Analytical Lexicon to the Greek New Testament* (Grand Rapids, MI: Zondervan, 1993).

Newton, Jon K. 'Holding Prophets Accountable'. *Journal of the European Pentecostal Theological Association* 30.1 (2010): pp. 63–79.

Noll, Mark, A. *The Civil War as a Theological Crisis* (Chapel Hill, NC: University of North Carolina Press, 2006). Kindle edition.

Office of the Clark County Prosecuting Attorney. 'Paul Jennings Hill.' *Prosecuting Attorney* (1998–2021) http://www.clarkprosecutor.org/html/death/US/hill873.htm (accessed 28 February 2021).

Oliver, Jeff. *Pentecost to the Present, Book 1: Early Prophetic and Spiritual Gifts Movements* (Newberry, FL: Bridge-Logos, 2017).

———. *Pentecost to the Present, Book 2: Reformations and Awakenings* (Newberry, FL: Bridge-Logos, 2017).

Oss, Douglas. 'A Pentecostal/Charismatic View.' Pages 238–83 in *Are Miraculous Gifts for Today? Four Views* (ed. Wayne Grudem; Grand Rapids, MI: Zondervan, 1996).

Packer, James I. *God's Words* (Downers Grove, IL: InterVarsity Press, 1981).

Parker, Stephen E. *Led by the Spirit: Toward a Practical Theology of Pentecostal Discernment and Decision-Making* (Sheffield: Sheffield Academic Press, 1996).

The Passion of Saints Perpetua and Felicity. In St Gallen, *Stiftsbibliothek*, Cod. Sang. 577 (ninth/tenth centuries).

Peterson, Eugene. *The Message: The Bible in Contemporary Language* (Colorado Springs, CO: NavPress, 2014).

Pew Research Center. 'The Shifting Religious Identity of Latinos in the United States.' *Pew Forum* (7 May 2014) http://www.pewforum. org/2014/05/07/the-shifting-religious-identity-of-latinos-in-the-united-states (accessed 21 December 2019).

———. 'Spirit and Power: A 10-Country Survey of Pentecostals.' *Pew Forum* (5 October 2006) https://www.pewforum.org/2006/10/05/spirit-and-power (accessed 21 April 2020).

Phillips, J.B. *The New Testament in Modern English* (London: Collins, 2009).

Poloma, Margaret M. *The Assemblies of God at the Crossroads: Charisma and Institutional Dilemmas* (Knoxville, TN: University of Tennessee Press, 1989).

———. *Main Street Mystics: The Toronto Blessing and Reviving Pentecostalism* (Walnut Creek, CA: AltaMira Press, 2003).

———, and John C. Green. *The Assemblies of God: Godly Love and the Revitalization of American Pentecostalism* (New York, NY: New York University Press, 2010).

———, and Ralph W. Hood, Jr. *Blood and Fire: Godly Love in a Pentecostal Emerging Church* (New York, NY: New York University Press, 2008).

Rahner, Karl. *Visions and Prophecies* (New York, NY: Herder & Herder, 1963).

Richter, Philip. 'Charismatic Mysticism: A Sociological Analysis of the "Toronto Blessing"'. Pages 100–30 in *The Nature of Religious Language: A Colloquium* (ed. Stanley E. Porter; Sheffield: Sheffield Academic Press, 1996).

Robeck, Cecil M., Jr. 'Canon, Regulae Fidei, and Continuing Revelation in the Early Church.' Pages 65–92 in *Church, Word and Spirit: Historical and Theological Essays in Honor of Geoffrey W. Bromiley* (ed. J.E. Bradley and R.A. Muller; Grand Rapids, MI: Eerdmans, 1987).

——. 'Written Prophecies: A Question of Authority'. *Pneuma: The Journal of the Society for Pentecostal Studies* 2 (1980): pp. 26–45.

Potter, David. *Constantine the Emperor* (Oxford: Oxford University Press, 2013).

Ruthven, Jon Mark. 'The "Foundational Gifts" of Ephesians 2:20'. *Journal of Pentecostal Theology* 10.2 (2002): pp. 28–43.

——. '"This Is My Covenant with Them": Isaiah 59.19–21 as the Programmatic Prophecy of the New Covenant in the Acts of the Apostles (Part 1)'. *Journal of Pentecostal Theology* 17 (2008): pp. 32–47.

——. '"This Is My Covenant with Them": Isaiah 59.19–21 as the Programmatic Prophecy of the New Covenant in the Acts of the Apostles (Part 2)'. *Journal of Pentecostal Theology* 17 (2008): pp. 219–37.

——. *What's Wrong with Protestant Theology? Tradition vs. Biblical Emphasis* (Tulsa, OK: Word and Spirit, 2013).

Sandford, John Loren. *Elijah Among Us* (Grand Rapids, MI: Chosen, 2002).

Schniedewind, William M. *How the Bible Became a Book* (New York, NY: Cambridge University Press, 2004).

Sears, Robert E. 'Dreams and Christian Conversion: Gleanings from a Pentecostal Church Context in Nepal'. *Mission Studies* 35 (2018): pp. 183–203.

Sheppard, Gerald T. 'Prophecy: From Ancient Israel to Pentecostals at the End of the Modern Age'. *The Spirit and Church* 3.1 (2001): pp. 47–70.

Smith, James K.A. 'The Closing of the Book: Pentecostals, Evangelicals, and the Sacred Writings'. *Journal of Pentecostal Theology* 11 (1997): pp. 49–71.

St Augustine. *The Confessions of St Augustine*, Book 8, Ch. 12. From 'Nicene and Post-Nicene Fathers', First Series, Vol. 1. Trans. J.G. Pilkington, Ed. Philip Schaff. (Buffalo, NY: Christian Literature Publishing Co., 1887.) Revised and edited for New Advent by Kevin Knight. http://www.newadvent.org/fathers/110108.htm (accessed 6 December 2021).

St Teresa of Avila. *The Interior Castle* or *The Mansions, Christian Classics Ethereal Library* (n.d.) http://www.ccel.org/ccel/teresa/castle2.iv.html.

St Thomas Aquinas. *Summa Theologica* (trans. The Fathers of the English Dominican Province; New York, NY: Benzinger Bros., various dates).

Stark, Rodney. 'A Theory of Revelations'. *Journal for the Scientific Study of Religions* 38.2 (1999): pp. 287–308.

Stronstad, Roger. *The Charismatic Theology of Saint Luke* (Peabody, MA: Hendrickson, 1984).

——. *The Prophethood of All Believers: A Study in Luke's Charismatic Theology*. Journal of Pentecostal Theology Supplement 16 (Sheffield: Sheffield Academic Press, 1999).

Thomas, John Christopher. 'Women, Pentecostalism and the Bible: An Experiment in Pentecostal Hermeneutics'. *Journal of Pentecostal Theology* 5 (1994): pp. 41–56.

Tucker, Ruth A. *God Talk: Cautions for Those Who Hear God's Voice* (Downers Grove, IL: InterVarsity Press, 2005).

Turner, Max. *The Holy Spirit and Spiritual Gifts: In the New Testament Church and Today* (Grand Rapids, MI: Baker Academic, rev. edn, 2012).

Unknown. *The Martyrdom of Polycarp*.

Van Gelder, Craig. *The Ministry of the Missional Church: A Community Led by the Spirit* (Grand Rapids, MI: Baker, 2007).

Vine, W.E., and Merrill Unger. *Vine's Complete Expository Dictionary of Old and New Testament Words: With Topical Index* (Nashville, TN: Thomas Nelson, 1996).

Volken, Laurent. *Visions, Revelations and the Church* (New York, NY: Kenedy, 1963).

Wakefield, Gavin. *Alexander Boddy: Pentecostal Anglican Pioneer* (Milton Keynes: Authentic Media, 2007).

Walton, John, and Brent Sandy. *The Lost World of Scripture* (Downers Grove, IL: IVP Academic, 2013).

Ward, Pete. *Introducing Practical Theology: Mission, Ministry, and the Life of the Church* (Grand Rapids, MI: Baker Academic, 2017).

Witherington, Ben, III. *Jesus the Seer: The Progress of Prophecy* (Peabody, MA: Hendrickson, 1999).

Wolterstorff, Nicholas. *Divine Discourse* (Cambridge: Cambridge University Press, 1995).

Wright, N.T. 'How Can the Bible Be Authoritative?' *Vox Evangelica* 21 (1991): pp. 7–32.

——. *The New Testament and the People of God* (London: SPCK, 1992).

Youth With a Mission. 'Our Story: His/Story.' *YWAM* (2021) https://www.ywam.org/about-us/history (accessed 3 November 2020).

Zohar, Danah, and Ian Marshall. *Spiritual Intelligence: The Ultimate Intelligence* (London: Bloomsbury, 2000).

God Conversations

*Stories of how God speaks and
what happens when we listen*

Tania Harris

Stories of God talking to his people abound throughout the
Bible, but we usually only get the highlights. We read: 'God
said "Go to Egypt,"' and then, 'Mary and Joseph left for
Egypt.' We're not told how God spoke, how they knew it was
him, or how they decided to act on what they'd heard.

In *God Conversations*, international speaker and pastor Tania
Harris shares insights from her own story of learning to hear
God's voice. You'll get to eavesdrop on some contemporary
conversations with God in the light of his communication
with the ancients. Part memoir, part teaching, this unique and
creative collection will help you to recognise God's voice when
he speaks and what happens when you do.

978-1-78078-188-4

Paternoster:
thinking faith

We trust you enjoyed reading this book
from Paternoster. If you want to be informed
of any new titles from this author and other
releases you can sign up to the Paternoster
newsletter by scanning below:

Online:
authenticmedia.co.uk

Follow us: